教材项目规划小组
Teaching Material Project Planning Group

严美华   姜明宝   王立峰
田小刚   崔邦焱   俞晓敏
赵国成   宋永波   郭 鹏

加拿大方咨询小组
Canadian Consulting Group

Dr. Robert Shanmu Chen
Mr. Zheng Zhining
University of British Columbia

Dr. Helen Wu
University of Toronto

Mr. Wang Renzhong
McGill University

中国国家汉办规划教材

NEW PRACTICAL CHINESE READER

(2nd Edition)

1

新实用汉语课本

刘珣 主编

课 本
TEXTBOOK

英文注释
Annotated in English

编 者：张 凯　刘社会　陈 曦
　　　　左珊丹　施家炜　刘 珣
英译审订：Jerry Schmidt　余心乐

（第2版）

北京语言大学出版社
BEIJING LANGUAGE AND CULTURE
UNIVERSITY PRESS

图书在版编目（CIP）数据

新实用汉语课本：英文注释本.1 /刘珣主编.
—2版.—北京：北京语言大学出版社，2010.1（2022.1重印）
ISBN 978-7-5619-2623-9

Ⅰ.新… Ⅱ.刘… Ⅲ.汉语—对外汉语教学—教材
Ⅳ.H195.4

中国版本图书馆CIP数据核字（2010）第007438号

书　　　名：新实用汉语课本（第2版 英文注释）课本 1
责任编辑：付彦白
英文编辑：侯晓娟
责任印制：邝　天

出版发行：北京语言大学出版社

社　　址：北京市海淀区学院路 15 号　　邮政编码：100083
网　　址：www.blcup.com
电　　话：国内发行 8610-82303650/3591/3651
　　　　　海外发行 8610-82300309/0361/3080/3365
　　　　　编辑部 8610-82303647/3592/3395
　　　　　北语书店 8610-82303653
　　　　　网上订购电话 8610-82303908
　　　　　客户服务信箱 service@blcup.com
印　　刷：北京联兴盛业印刷股份有限公司
经　　销：全国新华书店

版　　次：2010 年 1 月第 2 版　2022 年 1 月第 18 次印刷
开　　本：889毫米×1194毫米　1/16　印张：19.25　插表 1　彩表 1
字　　数：369千字
书　　号：ISBN 978-7-5619-2623-9 /H.09313
　　　　　06800

CONTENTS 目　录

1　你　好
How do you do?　　　　　　　　3

一、课文　Text

二、练习　Exercises

三、语音　Phonetics

　1. 声母和韵母　Initials and finals

　2. 发音要领(1) Key points of pronunciation (1)

　3. 声调　Tones

　4. 三声变调(1)　Third-tone sandhi (1)

　5. 拼写规则(1)　Spelling rules (1)

四、语法　Grammar

汉语的语序　Word order in Chinese

五、汉字　Chinese Characters

汉字基本笔画

Basic strokes of Chinese characters

文化知识　Cultural Note

The Chinese Language (*Hanyu*) and

"Common Speech" (*Putonghua*)

2　你　忙　吗
Are you busy?　　　　　　　　15

一、课文　Text

二、练习　Exercises

三、语音　Phonetics

　1. 轻声　Neutral tone

　2. 发音要领(2) Key points of pronunciation (2)

　3. 拼写规则(2) Spelling rules (2)

四、语法　Grammar

　1. 形容词谓语句

Sentences with an adjectival predicate

　2. 用"吗"的是非问句

"Yes-no" question with "吗"

五、汉字　Chinese Characters

文化知识　Cultural Note

Chinese Characters and Simplified Characters

3　她是哪国人
Which country does she come from?　　27

一、课文　Text

二、练习　Exercises

三、语音　Phonetics

　1. 三声变调(2)　Third-tone sandhi (2)

　2. "不"的变调　Tone sandhi of "不"

　3. 发音要领(3)　Key points of pronunciation (3)

四、汉字　Chinese Characters

文化知识　Cultural Note

Scheme for the Chinese Phonetic Alphabet

　　《新实用汉语课本》系列教材自2002年陆续问世以来，受到世界各地汉语学习者和汉语教师的欢迎与关注。几年来，包括配套制作的音像产品在内，总发行量已达百万册；一些国家还购买了该教材的版权，他们自行出版、发行的数量尚未统计在内。在很多地区的汉语教学研讨会或中文教师年会上，这套教材也经常成为讨论的题目。这些都表明《新实用汉语课本》正和它的上一代教材《实用汉语课本》一样，已成为世界上使用最广泛的基础汉语教材之一；同时也表明《新实用汉语课本》系列所坚持的以语言结构为纲，结构与功能、文化相结合的教学理念和教材编写路子，符合汉语的教学实际。在语言点和句型结构的安排上多下功夫，尽量做到循序渐进、不断重现，有助于减轻汉语学习的难度；课文内容紧密结合中国文化，特别是多介绍中国的习俗和行为文化，有助于提高学习者的兴趣和运用汉语进行跨文化交际的能力。

　　汉语教学界同行们的关爱，使得我们感受到作为教材编者责任的重大。这期间我们曾多次进行调查研究，以了解《新实用汉语课本》在各地的使用情况，并通过自己进行的反思性教学发现教材中存在的问题。海内外很多热心的同行和学生，在使用这套书的同时给我们提出了很多宝贵的意见和建议。所有这些促成了这一修订版的面世。

　　考虑到使用者的方便，此次修订主要针对教材中一些已发现的不当之处加以修改，教材的整体框架特别是课文和主要语言点未作大的修改。繁体字课文等参考资料，我们将放在网上供使用者免费下载(www.blcup.com)。

　　为了更方便学习者使用，第二版各册的配套录音均采用MP3形式，随书附赠。

　　期望本教材的使用者继续对我们提出意见和建议，使《新实用汉语课本》系列不断得到改进和拓展。

刘珣

2010年1月

修订说明

Foreword of the Revised Edition

Since *New Practical Chinese Reader* was published in 2002, it has been well received by learners and teachers of Chinese around the world and aroused a lot of concern among them. In the past few years, the total volume of the books and the accompanying audio-visual products has hit 1 million, not including those published and issued in the countries that have imported its copyright. In the seminars and annual meetings on Chinese language teaching held in many regions, this textbook often became a topic for discussion. It shows, just like *Practical Chinese Reader*, its previous edition, *New Practical Chinese Reader* has become one of the basic Chinese learning resources that are most widely used. It also shows that the teaching concepts *New Practical Chinese Reader* adheres to and the methods adopted in the compilation of the book correspond to the reality of Chinese teaching. The teaching concepts *New Practical Chinese Reader* upholds are taking language structure as the guideline and combining the teaching of language structure with the teachings of language functions and culture. Due to the compilers' utmost efforts, the language points and sentence structures are carefully arranged, gradually taught and constantly recurred, which have made it easier for students to learn Chinese. The content of the texts is closely related to Chinese culture, with an emphasis on introducing Chinese customs and Chinese behavioral culture, which have effectively aroused learners' interest and improved their ability to communicate in Chinese.

The attention given by our colleagues in the field of Chinese teaching to *New Practical Chinese Reader* has helped us see the heavy responsibility we are carrying as the textbook compilers. During the past years we conducted a lot of investigations and research to learn how *New Practical Chinese Reader* was used in various regions. And we found there is room for improvement in the textbook through our reflective teaching. Many warm-hearted colleagues and students home and abroad have put forward lots of valuable opinions and suggestions on *New Practical Chinese Reader*. All this has contributed to the publication of this revised edition.

For users' convenience, in this new edition we have revised those we found improper, but have not revised the framework, the texts and the main language points of the textbook. Users can visit www.blcup.com to learn the traditional Chinese version of the texts.

To facilitate students, in the second edition of this series, the recording is in the MP3 attached to each book.

We look forward to more opinions and suggestions from our users and will continue to improve and develop *New Practical Chinese Reader*.

Liu Xun

January 2010

　　《新实用汉语课本》是新世纪之初，我们为以英语为母语或媒介语的学习者学习汉语而编写的一套新教材。本教材的目的是通过语言结构、语言功能与相关文化知识的学习和听说读写技能训练，逐步培养学习者运用汉语进行交际的能力。全书共六册70课，前四册为初级和中级以前阶段，共50课；后两册为中级阶段，共20课。海外专修或选修中文的学习者可用作一至三年级听说读写综合教学的汉语教材，基本上每周学一课，每学期用一册书；也可以作为学习者的自学教材。前四册每册均配有《综合练习册》、《教师手册》、录音磁带、CD及教学DVD光盘，后两册只配有《教师手册》。

为什么叫《新实用汉语课本》

　　本书之所以起名为《新实用汉语课本》，是因为我们希望能继承原《实用汉语课本》深受使用者欢迎并经过时间考验的一些主要特点，但它又是一套全新的教材。《实用汉语课本》是从1981年开始陆续出版的。20年来，这套教材一直得到世界各地的汉语教师和汉语学习者的支持与关爱。书中的主人公古波、帕兰卡和丁云等，伴随了一届又一届的各国汉语学习者度过了他们的汉语启蒙阶段。现在，古波、帕兰卡、丁云已经人到中年，该他们的孩子辈——《新实用汉语课本》的主人公丁力波（丁云与古波所生的孩子，加拿大学生）、马大为（美国学生）和林娜（英国学生）等学习汉语了。今天，汉语作为第二语言学习的环境、条件和基础比起20年前已有了很大的变化，不论在中国还是在海外都积累了更丰富的教学经验，取得了更多的研究成果。新的时代、新的形势，对汉语教材也提出了新的要求。我们希望《新实用汉语课本》在很多方面将有所创新和突破。

第一版前言

新教材，新理念

　　正如愈来愈多的汉语教学领域的同行们所主张的那样，语言教学的根本目的在于培养学习者用目的语进行交际的能力。为达到这一目的，语言教材的编写首先要体现"以学习者为中心"的原则：即教学内容要适合学习者的需要，有利于学习者创造性地学习，使学习者不断增强学习动力并获得成就感。在教学方法上，需要汲取从语法翻译法到交际法的各种教学法流派的长处：既重视学习语言的交际功能，又要牢固地掌握语言结构；既要让学习者通过大量操练和练习培养四种基本技能，又要让学习者懂得必要的语法知识和组词造句的规则。语音、词汇、句型、语法和话语等语言结构的学习是语言交际的基础，要特别注意体现由简单到复杂、由易到难、循序渐进、不断重现的原则，才能使学习过程更为容易，更为顺利。语言教材还应该有助于学习者了解目的语的文化和社会，从而更好地运用目的语进行交际。这就是我们编写《新实用汉语课本》所主张的主要理念。

《新实用汉语课本》的新特色

1.改变以往汉语教材线式编排的做法，本教材不论是语言结构、语言功能还是文化因素的教学均采取圆周式的编排，多次循环重现，螺旋式上升。以语言结构教学为例，六册中共进行四次大的循环。第一册前6课，在集中学习语音的同时，通过掌握简易的口语会话让学习者先接触多种基本句式，但暂不作系统的语法讲解；第一册的后8课及第二册全册12课共20课，是语言结构教学的第二次循环，逐个介绍并练习主要句型结构。这样，学习者在学习汉语的第一年内就能初步掌握汉语基本句型。第三、四册共24课，为第三次循环，进一步巩固、扩大并深化语法句型教学和词语教学；第五、六册共20课，除了词语和语法教学外，更把重点放在以往教材不太强调的复句和语段教学方面。这种四次大循环以及课与课之间又有小循环和单元复习、环环相扣的安排，不仅可以通过多次重现加深学习者对语言结构和功能的掌握，更重要的是让学习者在学习的每一个阶段——第一个月、第一学期、第一年都能在一定的水平上运用汉语进行交际，时时有成就感。

2.改变以往教材重结构、轻功能的做法，本教材加强功能项目的教学。从第一课学习语音开始，就把功能放在突出的地位，结合各课的音素教学，练习学生急需的功能项目（如问候、介绍等）。前四册强调基本功能和话题的教学，着重培养学习者运用语言结构进行交际的能力。第五、六册强调培养理解和表达高一级的功能和话题的能力，特别是成段交际的能力。功能项目的教学贯穿全书，以保证学习者听说读写交际能力不断提高。书中附有一定的实物图片及原文材料，如火车时刻表、菜单、广告、启事、报刊、经典作品片段等。

3.改变以往绝大多数汉语教材未突出汉字教学的缺陷。本教材考虑到非汉字文化圈学生的难点，第一、二册特别强调按汉字的规律由易到难，从基本笔画、部件和独体字学起。为此，第一册前六课采用语、文适当分开的做法：先选学六十个常用、易学、组合能力强的基本汉字和一些部件，让学习者在先掌握汉字部件的情况下，再组合成合体字。

4.改变基础阶段大多数教材内容局限于学校生活的做法，本教材扩大题材范围，加强教材的趣味性。本书前四册情节主线索围绕上述三个外国学生在中国的生活及与中国学生宋华、王小云、记者陆雨平、导游小燕子和几位中国教师的友情、恋情、师生情而展开一些风趣的故事。第一、二册结合校园及日常生活，介绍与汉语表达和理解有关的习俗文化；第三、四册围绕青年学生感兴趣的话题进行中西文化对比；第五、六册着重介绍中国社会的方方面面，体现中国传统文化和当代文化。

5.克服以往教材的教学模式过于机械、单一、弹性不够的缺点，加强教材对不同起点和不同需求的学习者的适应性。本教材一方面适当加大输入的内容、词汇量和练习量，同时通过板块式的安排注意处理好核心内容和补充内容的关系。在保证学好核心内容的基础上，增加补充内容，有利于学习者根据自己的需要自由习得；也有利于教师根据本班学生的水平因材施教。

此外，为有助于学习者更好地掌握汉语的规律，培养交际能力，本教材在突出词语结构的教学、加强语素和话语的教学以及书面语教学等方面，也力图作一些新的尝试。

《新实用汉语课本》一～四册体例

《课本》

课文部分为各课提供一定的话题与情境，第一、二册课文基本上用对话体（每课两段），以利于基础阶段在听说读写全面要求的基础上，加强听说的训练。第一册1～6课语音阶段突出拼音课文，第7～14课转入以汉字课文为主，下注拼音；第二册课文不再注拼音，只留调号；从第三册起，不再有调号。由利用拼音到逐步摆脱对拼音的依赖。生词部分对组成生词的语素（汉字）进行分析，便于学习者理解和记忆，同时强调通过连词组的练习掌握生词的用法。补充生词由学习者量力吸取。

注释部分主要内容为：解释词语的用法，补充已学过的语法点，介绍必要的文化背景知识。对课文中已出现但先不讲解语法点的句子，通过翻译让学习者弄懂意思。

"练习与运用"和"会话练习"（除前六课）中的"核心句"体现了本课所介绍的主要语言结构及主要功能，希望学习者熟练掌握。通过操练词组、句型替换、会话练习、交际练习等步骤，完成由机械操练到交际运用的过程。

"阅读与复述"重现已学过的句型与词汇，着重培养口头与书面连贯表达的能力。从第二册开始，扩展阅读短文的内容，加强阅读能力的训练。

语音部分和"语音练习"（前六课）针对汉语语音的特点和以英语为母语学习者的难点，有重点地介绍汉语语音规律和发音、拼写的方法，并通过拼音、四声、辨音、辨调、变调、声调组合、双音节或多音节连读以及朗读课堂用语等步骤，逐步练好语音。

语法部分针对汉语的特点和难点，对本课出现的主要语言结构进行必要的说明。着重介绍句子组装的规律，不求语法知识的全面系统。每册有两课复习课，帮助学习者对已学过的语法点进行小结。

汉字部分先介绍部件，后组合成汉字，并适当介绍汉字的结构规律和书写规律，帮助学习者认写汉字。

文化知识开始都用英文介绍，便于学习者了解与汉语有关的必要的文化知识。随着汉语水平的提高，文化知识将逐渐融合到课文中去。

《综合练习册》

主要供学习者课下练习使用。除了汉字练习外，还有语音、句型、词汇的练习以及听说读写全面的技能训练。

《教师手册》

《教师手册》就每课的教学目的、教学步骤和方法等提出建议，并对教材内容进行说明。对语音、语法、词汇的有关知识作较详细的介绍，供教师参考。前四册每册书有两套单元测试题，供教师选用。书中还附有测试题与《综合练习册》中部分练习的参考答案。

VI

鸣谢

本教材为中国国家对外汉语教学领导小组办公室（简称"国家汉办"）所主持的一项重点科研项目的一部分，委托北京语言大学承担编写。原国家汉办主任严美华、姜明宝教授、李桂苓女士进行了整个项目的策划与组织工作。北京语言大学前任校长曲德林教授、校务委员会主任王路江研究员对北语所承担的此项教材编写工作一直给予关注和大力支持，保证了我们编写工作的顺利进行。为了解海外汉语教学的现状，我们在开始编写教材前对加拿大六所大学的中文教学情况进行了考察。特别感谢我国驻温哥华总领馆许琳教育领事，她为我们与加拿大不列颠·哥伦比亚大学亚洲学系建立有关本教材的协作关系及实施协作计划提供了极其宝贵的帮助。国家汉办教学业务处宋永波先生在我们完成此项目的整个过程中给了我们很多具体的帮助，特此一并致谢。

感谢加拿大麦吉尔大学、蒙特利尔大学、多伦多大学、不列颠·哥伦比亚大学、西蒙菲莎大学及维多利亚大学在我们的考察访问中对我们的热情接待和各校中文教学同行们所提供的宝贵建议。感谢皇后大学、西安大略大学休伦学院、约克大学、兰格拉学院、道格拉斯学院、卡莫森学院等校的同行热心参加有关汉语教材的座谈讨论。要特别感谢不列颠·哥伦比亚大学陈山木博士、郑志宁先生，多伦多大学吴小燕博士和麦吉尔大学王仁忠先生同意担任我们教材的加方咨询委员。

作为我们这次编教工作的加拿大协作方的负责人，不列颠·哥伦比亚大学亚洲学系中国语文主任陈山木博士和郑志宁先生全程参与了协作活动的组织和协调工作，并进行了全书的中英文总校读，提出了很多宝贵的建议。陈山木博士、程茂荣博士、何冬晖博士、李天明博士、郑志宁先生和夏蔚女士承担了本书的英文翻译工作。郑志宁先生、吕鸣珠女士和夏蔚女士参加了第一、二册中文稿的校读，牟怀川博士、何冬晖博士、李天明博士参加了第三、四册中文稿的校读，程茂荣博士、林惠敏女士、杨丽琼女士参加了第五、六册中文稿的校读。Mr. Allen Haaheim 和 Mr. Paul Crowe 编校了英文译文的初稿，施吉瑞教授进行了全书英文译文的总校读。郑志宁先生和夏蔚女士进行了本教材第一、二册的样课试教；何冬晖博士、杨丽琼女士进行了本教材第三、四册的样课试教；程茂荣博士、林惠敏女士进行了本教材第五、六册的样课试教。对他们为本书所作的努力，我们表示衷心的谢意。

我们还要特别感谢北京语言文化大学出版社社长兼总编辑王建勤教授、王弘宇编辑和王飙编辑，感谢画家杨可千先生，他们为本书的出版做了大量工作。

本书主编为刘珣教授，编者为张凯副教授、刘社会副教授、陈曦副教授、左珊丹女士、施家炜女士和刘珣教授。第一、二册执笔为施家炜、刘珣，第三、四册执笔为刘社会、陈曦，第五、六册执笔为张凯、左珊丹。

我们期待使用本教材的教师和学习者提出宝贵的意见，以便我们对本教材作进一步的修改。

编者
2002年1月
于北京语言文化大学

Preface

New Practical Chinese Reader is a series of Chinese textbooks compiled at the beginning of the new millennium for the purpose of teaching Chinese to native English speakers or those who use English as their principal second language. It aims to develop the learner's communicative ability in Chinese by learning language structures, functions and related cultural knowledge as well as by training their listening, speaking, reading and writing skills. The series consists of 70 lessons in six volumes. The first four volumes, consisting of 50 lessons, are for beginners and pre-intermediate level learners. The last two volumes contain 20 lessons for learners at an intermediate level. This set of textbooks is designed for overseas students who either take Chinese as an elective or major in the language for a period of three years, studying about one lesson a week, or one volume a semester. It can also be used by self-study learners. The first four volumes come along with Workbooks, Instructor's Manuals, tapes, CDs and DVDs. The last two volumes are only accompanied by Instructor's Manuals.

Why have we named our teaching materials *New Practical Chinese Reader*?

We have given our textbooks this name, because it follows in the footsteps of the highly acclaimed and time-tested *Practical Chinese Reader* (hereinafter referred to as *PCR*). However, in the meantime, it is an entirely new set of textbooks. *PCR* has been published in numerous editions since 1981 and has been adopted as a textbook by Chinese language educators and learners worldwide during the last two decades. The characters in the lessons of *PCR* (Gu Bo, Palanca and Ding Yun etc.), have accompanied two generations of students of different nationalities during their study of beginning Chinese. Now these characters have finally reached middle age, and it is time for their children's generation to learn Chinese and become the principal characters in *New Practical Chinese Reader*. These include Ding Libo, a Canadian student, who is the son of Gu Bo and Ding Yun; Ma Dawei, an American student; and Lin Na, a British student. The teaching of Chinese as a second language has changed greatly during the last twenty years as a result of the experience accumulated by many Chinese language teachers, both at home and abroad. The new age in which we live requires that we improve our approaches and teaching materials. We hope that this new teaching material will be able to make a breakthrough to the teaching of Chinese language in a number of areas.

New Teaching Materials, New Concepts

More and more Chinese language teachers advocate the idea that the fundamental goal of language teaching is to cultivate the learner's communicative ability in the target language. We believe new teaching materials should be learner-centered. What is taught must be determined by students' needs and must enable them to learn creatively, gradually strengthening their motivation and sense of achievement. We must create a synthesis of all pedagogical schools, ranging from the grammar-translation method to the communicative approach. We should emphasize the study of the communicative function of a language and the firm grasp of its structure. We should let students develop the four basic skills through a great deal of practice and exercises while also master the necessary grammatical knowledge and rules for word and sentence formation. The study of phonetics, vocabulary, sentence patterns, grammar, and discourse are the foundation of language communication. The only way that we can make the learning process easier and smoother is by emphasizing the principle of moving from the simple to the complex and from the easy to the difficult, progressing gradually as we constantly review what has come before. Language teaching materials must help students understand the culture and society of the target language so that they can use the target language more effectively. The above are the basic concepts that guided us while writing *New Practical Chinese Reader*.

Features of *New Practical Chinese Reader*

1. *New Practical Chinese Reader* does not follow the linear structure formerly adopted by Chinese teaching materials, instead it adopts a cyclical arrangement with constant review of language structure and function together with important cultural information. The teaching of language structure went through four cycles in the six volumes. In the first six lessons of Volume One, the focus of which is learning phonetics, students are exposed to various basic sentence patterns by engaging in simple dialogues, although grammar is not discussed systematically at this stage. The second cycle is found in the twenty lessons that comprise the last eight lessons of Volume One and all the lessons of Volume Two. In this cycle, students learn and practice fundamental sentence patterns. As a result, by the end of the first year of study, they should have an elementary command of basic Chinese language structure. Volumes Three and Four contain the 24 lessons of the third cycle, which further consolidate, expand and deepen students' understanding of lexical items and sentence patterns. The fourth cycle is found in the 20 lessons of the last two volumes. Besides introducing more new words and grammatical points, these lessons concentrate on the teaching of complex sentences and paragraphs not emphasized in previous Chinese teaching materials. These four large cycles contain smaller ones that closely interact with the unit reviews, not only increasing the students' command of language structures and functions, but also (and more importantly) giving them a sense of accomplishment in communicative abilities at each stage of the learning process.

2. *New Practical Chinese Reader* doesn't only emphasize on structure as the previous teaching materials did. Even in its introduction to phonetics, this new series gives prominence to function, training the students in the most needed functional items, such as greetings and introductions. The first four volumes focus on the teaching of basic functions and topics of conversation, training the students' abilities to use language structures for communication. The last two volumes cultivate students' abilities to comprehend and communicate at a higher level, especially their abilities to use paragraphs to communicate. Functional items are included throughout the six volumes in order to constantly improve the learner's listening, speaking, reading and writing skills. Some pictures and

culturally authentic materials are also used, such as selections from timetables, menus, advertisements, announcements, newspapers and classic works.

3. Unlike the vast majority of previous textbooks, *New Practical Chinese Reader* emphasizes the systematic study of Chinese characters. In view of the difficulties encountered by students lacking a background in Chinese characters, the first two volumes stress the rules of learning Chinese characters, studying easy forms such as basic strokes, character components and single-component characters first before moving on to difficult ones. The first six lessons of Volume One separate the study of characters from the text. The teaching of characters starts with the introduction of 60 common, easily learnt characters. These characters are frequently used as components of other characters. Some character components are also taught. The goal of this approach is to let students learn multi-component characters by mastering their components first.

4. Transcending the limits of campus life, *New Practical Chinese Reader* distinguishes itself from most previous Chinese textbooks even at the beginning stage by including a broader range of interesting materials. The first four volumes develop a series of attractive stories, narrating the lives of the three international students mentioned above, including their friendship, love stories and teacher-student relationships with the Chinese students Song Hua, Wang Xiaoyun, the journalist Lu Yuping, the tour guide Xiaoyanzi, as well as several Chinese language teachers. Volumes One and Two interweave campus life with daily life, introducing customs and culture closely associated with the expression and comprehension of Chinese. The third and fourth volumes concentrate on topics of interest to students, illustrating cultural differences between China and the West. The last two volumes introduce various aspects of Chinese society, highlighting traditional and contemporary Chinese culture.

5. *New Practical Chinese Reader* abandons the mechanical, monotonous and inflexible formulae of previous teaching materials and can suit the needs of students at different levels. It increases the language input, the amount of vocabulary and exercises, while adopting a module structure that balances the relationship between core material and supplementary contents. By guaranteeing the teaching of core material, it increases the amount of supplementary contents so that students can learn according to their individual needs, and teachers can use the textbook to suit the different levels of their students.

Furthermore, to help students better learn the rules of Chinese and develop their communication skills, innovations are also made in this set of textbooks in teaching word structure, morpheme and discourse.

The Layout of Volumes One to Four of *New Practical Chinese Reader*

■ Textbooks

Text   This section supplies the topics and scenes of each lesson. For the most part, Volumes One and Two use dialogue form (with two paragraphs in each lesson), strengthening listening and speaking practice and providing an overall foundation for the four basic skills in Chinese. The pronunciation section in lessons one to six emphasizes the texts annotated in *pinyin*, while lessons seven to fourteen focus on Chinese characters with *pinyin* written beneath them. In the second volume, *pinyin* disappears, and there are only tone marks. From the third volume onward, tone marks are no longer used. In this way, learners gradually free themselves from *pinyin*.

New Words   This part of each lesson analyzes the morphemes (Chinese characters) that form new words with the aim of improving learners' comprehension and memory. At the same time, students can master the use of new words by practicing them in phrases. Supplementary words can be learned according to the learners' individual abilities.

Notes   For the most part, notes contain explanations of new words, develop grammatical points taught previously, or introduce necessary cultural background. English translations are provided to help students comprehend sentences containing grammar that will be dealt with in latter lessons.

Conversation Practice   (excluding Lessons 1–6), **Drills and Practice** (excluding Lessons 7–14)   We hope students will thoroughly master the key sentences illustrating the fundamental language structures and functions in the text. By practicing phrases, doing pattern drills, and taking part in dialogues and communicative exercises, students can successfully move from doing mechanical exercises to proficient communication.

Reading Comprehension and Paraphrasing   Exercises of this kind ensure the review of some of the sentence patterns and lexical items already taught, thereby developing the students' discourse abilities in both oral and written forms. From the second volume on, the contents of reading texts are expanded so as to strengthen the students' reading comprehension.

Phonetics and Pronunciation Drills   (in Lessons 1–6)   In view of the peculiarities of Chinese pronunciation and the special difficulties presented to foreign learners with English as their mother tongue, the texts focus on the principal features of the Chinese pronunciation system, phonetics and spelling rules. Students can gradually achieve a good foundation in pronunciation by doing the exercises for spelling, the four tones, sound discriminations, tone discriminations, tone sandhi, tone combinations, practice on disyllabic and polysyllabic words, and reading aloud classroom expressions.

Grammar   The grammar explanations take into account the special features of the Chinese language and the difficulties encountered by native speakers of English in learning them. They do not attempt to treat Chinese grammar comprehensively but articulate the most important grammatical structures and rules for sentence formation. There are two review lessons in each volume that help learners review the grammatical points taught before.

Chinese Characters   The text first introduces character components, later combining them to form characters. Rules for constructing and writing characters are also given to facilitate the learning of Chinese writing.

Cultural Note   At first, a cultural note in English is provided so that students can gain insight into cultural information related to their language studies. With the improvement of learners' Chinese proficiency, cultural note is more and more incorporated into the Chinese texts.

■ Workbooks

The Workbooks are designed for students to use after class. In addition to exercises for studying Chinese characters, phonetics, sentence patterns and words, they also include general exercises for listening, speaking, reading, and writing.

■ Instructor's Manuals

Suggestions are made in the Instructor's Manuals regarding the goals and methods of teaching and supply explanations of each lesson's contents. They also supply the instructors with more knowledge about phonetics, grammar and vocabulary. Unit tests and keys to the tests and some exercises of Workbooks are provided.

Acknowledgements

Sponsored by the National Office for Teaching Chinese as a Foreign Language (hereinafter referred to as NOTCFL), this set of teaching materials is one part of a key research project undertaken by the Beijing Language and Culture University. Ms. Yan Meihua, the director-general of the NOTCFL, Professor Jiang Mingbao and Ms. Li Guiling from the NOTCFL were responsible for planning and organizing this project. The President of the Beijing Language and Culture University, Professor Qu Delin, and the Chairman of the Council for University Affairs, Researcher Wang Lujiang, guaranteed the smooth implementation of this project undertaken by our university. In order to obtain an understanding of Chinese teaching overseas, we made a study trip to six Canadian universities with Chinese language programs before compiling this set of teaching materials. Special thanks go to Ms. Xu Lin, Educational Consul of the Chinese Consulate General in Vancouver, whose work helped us establish our partnership with the Asian Studies Department of the University of British Columbia. Our thanks are also due to Mr. Song Yongbo from the Teaching Bureau of the NOTCFL, for his assistance during the whole project.

We are very grateful to McGill University, University of Montreal, University of Toronto, University of British Columbia, Simon Fraser University and University of Victoria for the great hospitality they offered us during our study trip as well as the valuable suggestions provided by our colleagues from these institutions. Chinese language instructors from Queen's University, Huron College of the University of Western Ontario, York University, Langara College, Douglas College, and Comosen College also enthusiastically participated in our forum on Chinese textbooks. It is our pleasure to give special thanks to Dr. Robert Shanmu Chen, Chinese Coordinator of the Asian Studies Department of U.B.C., Mr. Zheng Zhining from the same department, Dr. Helen Wu of University of

Toronto, and Mr. Wang Renzhong of McGill University, who agreed to be on the Canadian Consulting Group for our teaching materials.

Dr. Robert S. Chen and Mr. Zheng Zhining were in charge of the Canadian party of this joint project, which would have never succeeded without their continuous organization and coordination. They are also responsible for the final proofreading of both the Chinese and English texts of all the six volumes. Dr. Robert S. Chen, Dr. Cheng Maorong, Dr. He Donghui, Dr. Li Tianming, Mr. Zheng Zhining and Ms. Xia Wei, all of which are from U.B.C., spent much time and effort translating the original Chinese text into English. Dr. Cheng Maorong, Dr. He Donghui, Dr. Li Tianming, Dr. Mou Huaichuan, Ms. Lin Huimin, Ms. Lü Mingzhu, Ms. Xia Wei, Ms. Yang Liqiong and Mr. Zheng Zhining participated in the proofreading of the Chinese texts. Mr. Allen Haaheim and Mr. Paul Crowe of U.B.C.. edited and proofread the first version of the English translations, while Professor Jerry D. Schmidt proofread the final version of all the English translations. Dr. Cheng Maorong, Dr. He Donghui, Ms. Lin Huimin, Ms. Xia Wei, Ms. Yang Liqiong and Mr. Zheng Zhining did trial teaching of sample lessons from the six volumes at the Asian Studies Department of U.B.C.. We appreciate all these people for their efforts.

Special thanks are also due to the Director and General Editor of Beijing Language and Culture University Press, Professor Wang Jianqin, Editors Wang Hongyu and Wang Biao, and Painter Yang Keqian who did much hard work to facilitate the publication of our textbooks.

The chief compiler of this textbook series is Prof. Liu Xun. The other compilers include Associate Prof. Zhang Kai, Associate Prof. Liu Shehui, Associate Prof. Chen Xi, Ms. Zuo Shandan, and Ms. Shi Jiawei. Shi Jiawei and Liu Xun were in charge of writing Volumes One and Two. Volumes Three and Four were largely written by Liu Shehui and Chen Xi, and Volumes Five and Six mainly by Zhang Kai and Zuo Shandan.

We sincerely hope teachers and students using our materials to offer their valuable criticisms and suggestions to enable us to improve these textbooks in the future.

Compilers
January 2002
Beijing Language and Culture University

Welcome to *New Practical Chinese Reader* (the 2nd Edition)!

This textbook features several imaginary characters to make your Chinese learning experience more enjoyable: international students Ding Libo, Lin Na, and Ma Dawei; Chinese teachers Mr. Yang, Ms. Chen, and Professor Zhang; Chinese students Song Hua, and Wang Xiaoyun; and Chinese reporter Lu Yuping. They, together with the help of your instructor, will act as tour guides for your adventure, guiding you and your classmates into the fascinating world of Chinese, the language with the largest number of speakers in the world today. Now let's get to know our companions for this journey.

人 物 介 绍

Introduction to the Main Characters in the Text

丁力波 Dīng Lìbō
A Canadian student, aged 21, male. His father is Gu Bo, his mother is Ding Yun.

马大为 Mǎ Dàwéi
An American student, aged 22, male.

林娜 Lín Nà
A British student, aged 19, female.

宋华 Sòng Huá
A Chinese student, aged 20, male.

陆雨平 Lù Yǔpíng
A Chinese reporter, aged 26, male.

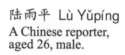

王小云 Wáng Xiǎoyún
A Chinese student, aged 20, female.

张教授 Zhāng jiàoshòu
A Chinese professor, aged 48, male.

陈老师 Chén lǎoshī
A Chinese teacher, aged 30, female.

杨老师 Yáng lǎoshī
A Chinese teacher, aged 32, male.

第一课

Lesson 1

Nǐ   hǎo
你   好
How do you do?

This lesson begins by introducing some sounds unique to the Chinese language, including tones. The Chinese writing system dates back more than 3,000 years, and it is especially intriguing to see how Chinese characters developed since their basically pictographic origins in ancient China. By the end of the lesson, you will be able to express some everyday greetings in Chinese.

一、课文   Text

🎧 1 （一）

Lù Yǔpíng：   Lìbō， nǐ hǎo.^①
陆雨平：   力波，你 好。

Lìbō：   Nǐ hǎo， Lù Yǔpíng.
力波：   你 好， 陆 雨平。

打招呼
Saying hello

生词 New Words

1. nǐ	你	Pr	you
2. hǎo	好	A	good, well, fine, OK
3. Lù Yǔpíng	陆雨平	PN	(name of a Chinese reporter)
4. Lìbō	力波	PN	(name of a Canadian student)

注释   Notes

① Nǐ hǎo.

"Hello!", "How do you do?"

This is the most common form of greeting in Chinese. It can be used at any time of the day when meeting people for the first time or for people you know. The response to this greeting form is also "Nǐ hǎo. (你好。)".

 （二）

Lìbō： Lín Nà, nǐ hǎo ma? ②
力波： 林 娜，你 好 吗?

Lín Nà： Wǒ hěn hǎo, nǐ ne? ③
林娜： 我 很 好，你 呢?

Lìbō： Yě hěn hǎo. ④
力波： 也 很 好。

生词 New Words

1. ma	吗	QPt	*(a particle used for a question expecting a yes-no answer)*
2. wǒ	我	Pr	I, me
3. hěn	很	Adv	very
4. ne	呢	QPt	*(a modal particle used for elliptical questions)*
5. yě	也[1]	Adv	too, also
6. Lín Nà	林娜	PN	(name of a British student)

注释　Notes

② Nǐ hǎo ma?

　　"How are you?"

　　This is also a form of greeting, often used after you have not seen someone for some time, and the response is usually "Wǒ hěn hǎo (我很好)" or other similar polite, conventional verbal exchanges.

---

[1] : Students are required to master the characters in red in each lesson.

③ Nǐ ne?

"And (how are) you?"

④ Yě hěn hǎo.

"(I am) fine (literally, very good), too."

This is an elliptical sentence, with the subject "wǒ (我)" omitted. In spoken Chinese, when the context is explicit and there is no ambiguity, the subject is often omitted. One may also say "Hěn hǎo. (很好。)" to answer the question "Nǐ hǎo ma? (你好吗？)".

二、练习　Exercises

语音 练习　Pronunciation Drills

声母 Initials:	b	p	m	n	l	h
韵母 Finals:	a	o	e	i	u	ü
	ao	en	ie	in	ing	uo

1 拼音　*Pinyin*

bā	bō	bī	bū	bīn	bīng
pā	pō	pī	pū	pīn	pīng
mā	mō	mī	mū		
nē	nāo	niē			
lē	lāo	liē	luō		
hē	hāo	huō			

2　四声　The four tones

ā	á	ǎ	à	
nī	ní	nǐ	nì	
hāo	háo	hǎo	hào	nǐ hǎo
lī	lí	lǐ	lì	
bō	bó	bǒ	bò	Lìbō
līn	lín	lǐn	lìn	
nā	ná	nǎ	nà	Lín nà
lū	lú	lǔ	lù	
yū	yú	yǔ	yù	
pīng	píng			Lù Yǔpíng
wō		wǒ	wò	
	hén	hěn	hèn	wǒ hěn hǎo
yē	yé	yě	yè	yě hěn hǎo

3　辨音　Sound discrimination

bā —— pā
(eight)　(lie on one's
　　　　stomach)

nǚ —— nǔ
(female)　(to exert)

wǔ —— hǔ
(five)　(tiger)

bīng —— bīn
(ice)　(guest)

piě —— biě
(left-falling　(shrivelled)
stroke)

huǒ —— wǒ
(fire)　(I)

4　辨调　Tone discrimination

mǎ —— mā
(horse)　(mom)

mù —— mǔ
(wood)　(mother)

yī —— yí
(one)　(aunt)

yě —— yè
(also)　(night)

lì —— lǐ
(strength)　(in)

mén —— mèn
(door)　(depressed)

5　三声变调　Third-tone sandhi

nǐ hǎo　　　　hěn hǎo　　　　yě hǎo　　　　yě hěn hǎo

6　朗读下列课堂用语　Read the following classroom expressions aloud

Nǐ hǎo.　　　　　　　　Nǐmen hǎo.

会话 练习　Conversation Practice 4

核心句 KEY SENTENCES

1. Nǐ hǎo.　　　　3. Wǒ hěn hǎo, nǐ ne?
2. Nǐ hǎo ma?　　4. Yě hěn hǎo.

（一）打招呼　Saying hello

1. 完成下列会话　Complete the following dialogue

Lín Nà：Lìbō, nǐ hǎo!

Lìbō：_____.

2. 看图会话　Make dialogues based on the pictures

❶ A: _____.

　 B: _____.

❷ A: _____.

　 B: _____.

（二）问候　Greetings

1. 完成下列会话　Complete the following dialogue

Mǎlì: Nǐ hǎo ma?

Lù Yì: _____, _____?

Mǎlì: Wǒ yě hěn hǎo.

2. 情景会话 Situational dialogue

You run into a Chinese friend whom you haven't seen for a long time. What will you say to him / her?

5 （三）听述 Listen and repeat

A：你好吗？

B：我很好，你呢？

A：我也很好。

三、语音 Phonetics

1 声母和韵母 Initials and finals

A syllable in the common speech of modern Chinese usually consists of an initial, which is a consonant that begins the syllable, and a final, which constitutes the rest of the syllable. For example, in the syllable "píng", "p" is the initial and "ing" is the final. A syllable can stand without an initial, such as "yě", but a syllable must have a final. In the common speech of modern Chinese, there are 21 initials and 38 finals altogether.

2 发音要领(1) Key points of pronunciation (1)

Initials: m, n, l, h   are pronounced similarly to their counterparts in the English language.

         b   like "p" in "speak" (unaspirated, voiceless).

         p   like "p" in "park" (aspirated, voiceless).

Note: Particular attention should be paid to the pronunciation of the aspirated and unaspirated consonants: b-p.

Finals: e   like "er" in "her".

       ie   like "ye" in "yes".

       -ng   (final) a nasalised sound like the "ng" in "bang" without pronouncing the "g".

Note: The pronunciation of the "e" in a compound final is different from that of the simple final "e".

③ 声调　Tones

Chinese is a tonal language in which the tones convey differences in meaning.

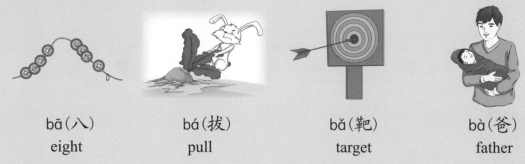

bā（八）　　　bá（拔）　　　bǎ（靶）　　　bà（爸）
eight　　　　　pull　　　　　target　　　　　father

In common speech there are four basic tones, represented respectively by the following tone marks:

　　" ˉ " for the first tone,

　　" ˊ " for the second tone,

　　" ˇ " for the third tone,

　　and " ˋ " for the fourth tone.

When a syllable contains only a single vowel, the tone mark is placed directly above the vowel letter as in "lǜ" and "hěn". The dot over the vowel "i" should be dropped if the tone mark is placed above it, as in "nǐ", "nín" and "píng". When the final of the syllable is composed of two or more vowels, the tone mark should be placed above the vowel pronounced with the mouth widest open (e.g. hǎo).

The openness of the mouth for the vowels, from the widest to the smallest is as follows:

a　o　e　i　u　ü

④ 三声变调（1）　Third-tone sandhi (1)

A third tone, when immediately followed by another third tone, should be pronounced in the second tone, but with the tone mark " ˇ " remaining unchanged. For example:

　　Nǐ hǎo.　→　Ní hǎo.　　　　　Wǒ hěn hǎo. → Wó hén hǎo.

　　hěn hǎo　→　hén hǎo　　　　　Yě hěn hǎo. → Yé hén hǎo.

⑤ 拼写规则（1）　Spelling rules (1)

At the beginning of a syllable, "i" is written as "y" (e.g. iě → yě). "i" is written as "yi" when it forms a syllable all by itself (e.g. ī → yī).

At the beginning of a syllable, "u" is written as "w" (e.g. uǒ → wǒ). "u" is written as "wu" when it forms a syllable all by itself (e.g. ǔ → wǔ).

When "ü" is at the beginning of a syllable or forms a syllable by itself, a "y" is added to it and the two dots over it are omitted (e.g. ǚ → yǔ).

四、语法　Grammar

■ 汉语的语序　Word order in Chinese

The main characteristic of Chinese grammar is that it lacks of morphological changes in person, tense, gender, number, and case in the strict sense. The word order, however, is very important to convey different grammatical meanings. The subject of a sentence is usually placed before the predicate. For example:

Subject	Predicate
Nǐ 你	hǎo. 好。
Wǒ 我	hěn hǎo. 很　好。
Lìbō 力波	yě hěn hǎo. 也　很　好。

五、汉字　Chinese Characters

Chinese characters originated from pictures. The history of their formation is very long, dating back to remote antiquity. Present-day Chinese characters, which evolved from ancient Chinese characters, are square-shaped. Here are some examples illustrating their long evolution:

Picture	Oracle Bone Inscription	Small Seal Character	Official Script	Traditional Chinese in Regular Script	Simplified Chinese in Regular Script
				馬	马

1 汉字基本笔画 Basic strokes of Chinese characters

Chinese characters are written by combining various kinds of "strokes". These strokes can be divided into "basic" strokes and "combined" strokes.

Basic Stroke	Name	Example	Way to Write
、 ↘	diǎn	门	The dot is written from top to bottom-right, as in the first stroke of "门".
一 →	héng	一	The horizontal stroke is written from left to right.
丨 ↓	shù	木	The vertical stroke is written from top to bottom, as in the second stroke of "木".
丿 ↙	piě	力	The left-falling stroke is written from top to bottom-left, as in the second stroke of "力".
乀 ↘	nà	八	The right-falling stroke is written from top to bottom-right, as in the second stroke of "八".
㇀ ↗	tí	我	The upward stroke is written from bottom-left to top-right, as in the fourth stroke of "我".

2 认写基本汉字 Learn and write basic Chinese characters

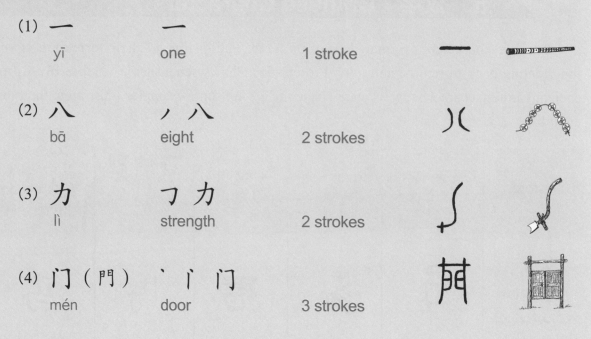

(1) 一   一
    yī   one   1 stroke

(2) 八   丿八
    bā   eight   2 strokes

(3) 力   フ力
    lì   strength   2 strokes

(4) 门（門）   丶冂门
    mén   door   3 strokes

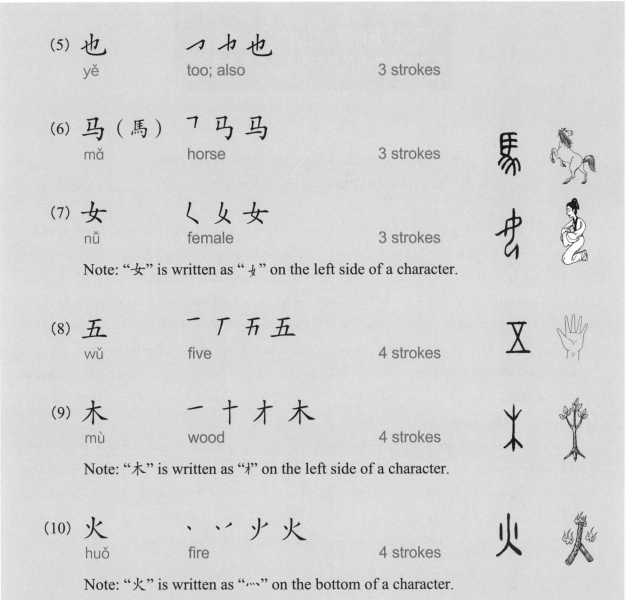

(5) 也　　　　フ 力 也

　　yě　　　too; also　　　　3 strokes

(6) 马（馬）　フ 马 马

　　mǎ　　　horse　　　　　3 strokes

(7) 女　　　　く 女 女

　　nǚ　　　female　　　　3 strokes

Note: "女" is written as "女" on the left side of a character.

(8) 五　　　　一 丁 五 五

　　wǔ　　　five　　　　　4 strokes

(9) 木　　　　一 十 才 木

　　mù　　　wood　　　　4 strokes

Note: "木" is written as "才" on the left side of a character.

(10) 火　　　、 丶 少 火

　　huǒ　　　fire　　　　　4 strokes

Note: "火" is written as "灬" on the bottom of a character.

3 认写课文中的汉字　Learn and write the Chinese character in the text

林 lín

　　林 → 才 + 木　　　　　8 strokes

The Chinese Language (*Hanyu*) and "Common Speech" (*Putonghua*)

The Chinese language (*Hanyu*), the major language of the Chinese people with a history of more than 5,000 years, is one of the oldest languages in the world. In spite of its old age, Chinese is now one of the most widely used living languages. The language is spoken in many regions of China, as well as in many overseas Chinese communities, especially in Singapore and Malaysia. And there are more than a billion native speakers of Chinese worldwide. It is one of the working languages of the United Nations.

Chinese belongs to the Sino-Tibetan language family. Among the 56 ethnic groups in China, the *Han*, *Hui*, *Manchu* and other ethnic groups, constituting 94% of the population of China, speak Chinese.

Chinese includes variants from seven main dialect groups. The northern or Mandarin dialect covers three fourths of China's territory and includes two thirds of its population. Standard Chinese is also known by its official designation, *Putonghua*, literally "common speech". *Putonghua* is based on the northern dialect, using the dialect of Beijing as the basis for its pronunciation and modern vernacular literature for its grammatical structure.

第二课

Lesson 2

Nǐ máng ma
你 忙 吗
Are you busy?

By the end of this lesson, you will be able to greet others and express your needs in Chinese.

一、课文 Text

🎧6 （一）

Lín Nà: Lù Yǔpíng, nǐ hǎo ma?
林娜： 陆 雨平，你 好 吗？

问候别人
Greetings

Lù Yǔpíng: Wǒ hěn hǎo. Nǐ bàba、māma hǎo ma?①
陆雨平： 我 很 好。你 爸爸、妈妈 好 吗？

Lín Nà: Tāmen dōu hěn hǎo.② Nǐ máng ma?
林娜： 他们 都 很 好。你 忙 吗？

Lù Yǔpíng: Wǒ bù máng. Nǐ nán péngyou ne?
陆雨平： 我 不 忙。你 男 朋友 呢？

Lín Nà: Tā hěn máng.
林娜： 他 很 忙。

📖 生词 New Words

1. máng	忙	A	busy
*2. ma	吗[1]	QPt	(a particle used for questions expecting a yes-no answer)
3. bàba	爸爸	N	dad
4. māma	妈妈	N	mom
5. tāmen	他们	Pr	they, them
tā	他	Pr	he, him

[1]: Words marked by an asterisk have appeared in previous lessons.

men	们	Suf	(*used after pronouns* 我, 你, 他, 它 *or certain nouns to denote plurality*)
6. dōu	都	Adv	both, all
7. bù	不	Adv	not, no
8. nán	男	A	male
9. péngyou	朋友	N	friend
*10. ne	呢	MdPt	(*a modal particle used for elliptical questions*)

注释　Notes

① Nǐ bàba、 māma hǎo ma?

"How are your mom and dad?"

nǐ bàba —— your dad, nǐ māma —— your mom, nǐ nán péngyou —— your boyfriend.

② Tāmen dōu hěn hǎo.

"They are both fine (literally, very good)."

🎧 **7** （二）

问需要
Asking what someone wants

Dīng Lìbō: Gēge, nǐ yào kāfēi ma? ③
丁力波: 哥哥，你 要 咖啡 吗？

Gēge: Wǒ yào kāfēi.
哥哥: 我 要 咖啡。

Dìdi: Wǒ yě yào kāfēi. ④
弟弟: 我 也 要 咖啡。

Dīng Lìbō: Hǎo, wǒmen dōu
丁力波: 好， 我们 都

hē kāfēi. ⑤
喝 咖啡。

生词 New Words

1. gēge	哥哥	N	elder brother
2. yào	要	V	to want
3. kāfēi	咖啡	N	coffee
4. dìdi	弟弟	N	younger brother
5. wǒmen	我们	Pr	we, us
6. hē	喝	V	to drink
7. Dīng	丁	PN	(a surname)

注释　Notes

③ Nǐ yào kāfēi ma?

"Do you want some coffee?"

"Nǐ yào……ma?（你要……吗？）" is a sentence pattern commonly used when asking what the other party wants, whereas "Wǒ yào…… (我要……)" is used to express what "I" want.

④ Wǒ yě yào kāfēi.

"I want some coffee, too."

⑤ Wǒmen dōu hē kāfēi.

"We all drink coffee."

二、练习 Exercises

语音 练习 Pronunciation Drills 8

声母 Initials：d t g k f

韵母 Finals：ei ou an ang eng iao iou (-iu)

1 拼音 *Pinyin*

dē	dōu	dān	dāng
tē	tōu	tān	tāng
gē	gōu	gān	gāng
kē	kōu	kān	kāng
bēi	bān	bēng	biāo
pēi	pān	pēng	piāo
fēi	fān	fēng	diū
hēi	hān	hēng	niū

2 四声 The four tones

tā		tǎ	tà	
mēn	mén		mèn	tāmen
wō		wǒ	wò	wǒmen
nī	ní	nǐ	nì	nǐmen
nān	nán	nǎn	nàn	
pēng	péng	pěng	pèng	
yōu	yóu	yǒu	yòu	nán péngyou
bū	bú	bǔ	bù	
	máng	mǎng		bù máng
gē	gé	gě	gè	gēge
dī	dí	dǐ	dì	dìdi
hē	hé		hè	
kā		kǎ		
fēi	féi	fěi	fèi	hē kāfēi

3 辨音 Sound discrimination

dà —— tà
(big) (to step on)

kě —— gě
(may) (a surname)

kǒu —— gǒu
(mouth) (dog)

dōu —— duō
(all) (many)

gēn —— gēng
(to follow) (to plough)

dīng —— tīng
(nail) (to listen)

4 辨调   Tone discrimination

dāo —— dào	tǔ —— tù	yòu —— yǒu
(knife) (to arrive)	(soil) (rabbit)	(again) (to have)

ní —— nǐ	liù —— liǔ	kàn —— kǎn
(nun) (you)	(six) (willow)	(to see) (to cut)

5 轻声   Neutral tone

bàba   māma   gēge   dìdi

nǐmen   wǒmen   tāmen

……hǎo ma?   Nǐ ne?   Nǐ nán péngyou ne?

6 双音节连读   Practice on disyllabic words

yǐnliào (drinks)   yéye (grandpa)

kělè (coke)   mèimei (younger sister)

hànbǎo (hamburger)   fāyīn (pronunciation)

píngguǒ (apple)   hēibǎn (blackboard)

7 朗读下列课堂用语   Read the following classroom expressions aloud

Tīng wǒ fāyīn.   Listen to my pronunciation.

Kàn hēibǎn.   Look at the blackboard.

会话练习 Conversation Practice ₉

核心句 KEY SENTENCES

1. Tāmen dōu hěn hǎo.   4. Nǐ yào kāfēi ma?

2. Nǐ máng ma?   5. Wǒ yào kāfēi.

3. Wǒ bù máng.   6. Wǒmen dōu hē kāfēi.

（一）问候别人　Greetings

(1) A：Dà Lín，nǐ máng ma?

B：_____. Nǐ ne?

A：_____.

(2) A：Nǐ bàba、māma hǎo ma?

B：_____. Nǐ gēge ne?

A：_____.

(3) A：Nǐ dìdi hǎo ma?

B：_____. Nǐ_____ne?

A：_____.

（二）问需要　Asking what someone wants

1. 完成下列会话　Complete the following dialogues

(1) A：Nín yào kāfēi ma?

B：Wǒ yào kāfēi.

A：Nǐ ne?

C：_____.

(2) A：Nǐ yào kělè (coke) ma?

B：_____.

A：Nǐ ne?

C：_____.

2. 看图会话　Make dialogues based on the pictures

❶ A：_____?

B：_____.

❷ A：_____?

B：_____.

10 （三）听述 Listen and repeat

A：你爸爸、妈妈都好吗？

B：他们都很好。

三、语音 Phonetics

1 轻声 Neutral tone

In the common speech of modern Chinese, there are a number of syllables which are unstressed and are pronounced in a "weak" tone. This is known as the neutral tone and is indicated by the absence of a tone mark. For example:

吗 ma   呢 ne   们 men

2 发音要领（2） Key points of pronunciation (2)

Initials: f   is pronounced similarly to its counterpart in the English language.

d   like "t" in "stay" (unaspirated).

t   like "t" in "tag" (aspirated).

g   a soft unaspirated "k" sound like "k" in "skate".

k   like "k" in "kangaroo" (aspirated).

Note: Particular attention should be paid to the pronunciation of the aspirated and unaspirated consonants: d-t, g-k.

Finals: ei   like "ay" in "play".

ou   like "o" in "so".

an   like "an" in "can" (without stressing the "n").

3 拼写规则（2） Spelling rules (2)

The compound final "iou" is written as "-iu" when it comes after an initial and the tone mark is placed on "u". For example: liù (six).

四、语法　Grammar

1 形容词谓语句　Sentences with an adjectival predicate

Adjectives in Chinese can function directly as predicates. This kind of sentence is called a sentence with an adjectival predicate. Adjectives in this kind of sentence can be modified by adverbs such as "很", "也", and "都". The negative form of sentences with an adjectival predicate is generated by placing the negative adverb "不" before the adjective that functions as the predicate. For example: "我不忙".

Subject	Predicate
Nǐ 你	hǎo. 好。
Tā 他	hěn　máng. 很　忙。
Wǒ 我	bù　máng. 不　忙。
Tāmen 他们	dōu　hěn　hǎo. 都　很　好。

Note: Adverbs such as "很", "也", and "都" must be placed before the adjective they modify.

2 用"吗"的是非问句　"Yes-no" question with "吗"

A declarative sentence can be changed into a "yes-no" question by adding the question particle "吗" at the end of it.

Statement	Question
Nǐ hǎo. 你 好。 →	Nǐ hǎo ma? 你 好 吗？
Tā bàba、māma dōu hǎo. 他爸爸、妈妈 都 好。 →	Tā bàba、māma dōu hǎo ma? 他爸爸、妈妈 都 好 吗？
Tā máng. 她 忙。 →	Tā máng ma? 她 忙 吗？
Wǒ yào kāfēi. 我 要 咖啡。 →	Nǐ yào kāfēi ma? 你 要 咖啡 吗？

五、汉字　Chinese Characters

1 认写基本汉字　Learn and write basic Chinese characters

(1)　丁　　　一 丁
　　dīng　　　nail　　　　2 strokes

(2)　刀　　　フ 刀
　　dāo　　　knife　　　2 strokes

Note: "刀" is written as "刂" on the right side of a character.

(3)　又　　　フ 又
　　yòu　　　again　　　2 strokes

Note: "又" was originally a pictograph of "the right hand".

(4)　大　　　一 ナ 大
　　dà　　　big　　　　3 strokes

(5)　口　　　丨 冂 口
　　kǒu　　　mouth　　　3 strokes

(6)　土　　　一 十 土
　　tǔ　　　earth　　　3 strokes

Note: "土" is written as "𧘇" on the left side of a character.

(7)　六　　　丶 二 宀 六
　　liù　　　six　　　　4 strokes

(8)　不　　　一　丆　不　不

bù　　　　no, not　　　　　　　4 strokes

(9)　尼　　　一　乛　尸　尸　尼

ní　　　　nun　　　　　　　　5 strokes

(10)　可　　　一　丆　亓　可　可

kě　　　　can, may　　　　　　5 strokes

2　认写课文中的汉字　Learn and write the Chinese characters in the texts

(1)　吗 ma （嗎）

吗 → 口 ＋ 马　　　　　　6 strokes

("口" denotes the meaning of speaking, "马" denotes the pronunciation.)

(2)　呢 ne

呢 → 口 ＋ 尼　　　　　　8 strokes

("口" denotes the meaning of speaking, "尼" denotes the pronunciation.)

(3)　妈妈 māma （媽媽）

妈 → 女 ＋ 马　　　　　　6 strokes

("女" denotes the meaning of woman, "马" denotes the pronunciation.)

(4)　哥哥 gēge

哥 → 可 ＋ 可　　　　　　10 strokes

Chinese Characters and Simplified Characters

The Chinese character is the only ideograph still in daily use in the world today. Unlike the alphabetic systems used by most languages, Chinese is made up of characters, the majority of which are "pictophonetic". Most consist of a component indicating the sound of the character, the phonetic, combined with a semantic component, the significance of the radical, which shows the category of meaning to which the character belongs.

Chinese characters are monosyllables, and generally each character represents a single morpheme. The total number of Chinese characters is estimated at over 40,000, of which only 5,000 – 8,000 are frequently used, while 3,000 are normally adequate for everyday situations.

A considerable number of Chinese characters are composed of numerous strokes and are therefore complicated to write. With a view to facilitating writing, people have made continuous attempts to simplify the writing system. The simplification of Chinese characters includes two aspects: to reduce the number of characters, and to reduce the number of strokes. What are known as "simplified characters" refer to those characters that have been thus simplified; traditional characters, on the other hand, are those that retain their earlier forms.

The use of simplified characters is now official policy in the People's Republic of China, while traditional characters are restricted mainly to academic use or aesthetic purposes. Simplified characters have the advantages of being easier to learn, memorize, read and write. Here are two examples:

mother	媽 (traditional)	妈 (simplified)
door	門 (traditional)	门 (simplified)

Simplified characters are used in this textbook.

第三课

Lesson

3

Tā shì nǎ guó rén

她 是 哪 国 人

Which country does she come from?

Now, would you like to use Chinese to learn more about the people you meet? This lesson will show you how to ask a person's occupation and nationality, as well as how to introduce your friends and family to others. In addition, you will learn compound characters originated from basic characters.

一、课文　Text

🎧11 （一）

Gēge: Lìbō, nà shì shéi?
哥哥：力波，那是 谁？

Dīng Lìbō: Nà shì wǒmen lǎoshī.
丁力波：那 是 我们 老师。

Gēge: Tā shì nǎ guó rén?①
哥哥：她 是 哪 国 人？

Dīng Lìbō: Tā shì Zhōngguó rén.②
丁力波：她 是 中国 人。

Wǒmen lǎoshī dōu shì Zhōngguó rén.
我们 老师 都 是 中国 人。

> 认指人
> **Identifying people**

> 问国籍
> **Asking someone's nationality**

生词 New Words

1. tā	她	Pr	she, her
2. shì	是	V	to be
3. nǎ	哪	QPr	which
4. guó	国	N	country, nation
5. rén	人	N	people, person
6. nà	那	Pr	that
7. shéi	谁	QPr	who, whom
8. lǎoshī	老师	N	teacher
*9. dōu	都	Adv	both, all
10. Zhōngguó	中国	PN	China

注释　Notes

① Tā shì nǎ guó rén?

"What's her nationality?"

There are two Chinese characters for the third person singular "tā": one is "他" and can be used for a male; the other is "她" and refers to a female.

② Tā shì Zhōngguó rén.

"She is Chinese."

To indicate the nationality of an individual, the character "rén（人）" is usually placed after the name of his/her motherland. For example:

Zhōngguó（中国　China）— Zhōngguó rén（中国人　Chinese people）

🎧 12　（二）

Dīng Lìbō:　Chén lǎoshī, nín hǎo![3] Zhè shì wǒ gēge,[4] tā shì wàiyǔ
丁力波:　陈　老师，您好！　这　是　我　哥哥，他　是　外语

lǎoshī.
老师。

【介绍】

Introducing people

Chén lǎoshī：　Nǐ　hǎo.
陈老师：　你　好。

Dīng Lìbō：　Zhè　shì　wǒ　péngyou.
丁力波：　这　是　我　朋友。

Chén lǎoshī：　Nǐ　hǎo!　Nǐ　yě　shì　lǎoshī　ma?
陈老师：　你　好！　你　也　是　老师　吗？

Péngyou：　Nín　hǎo!　Wǒ　bú　shì　lǎoshī,　wǒ　shì　yīshēng.
朋友：　您　好！　我　不　是　老师，　我　是　医生。

Chén lǎoshī：　Lìbō,　zhè　shì　nǐ　nǎinai　ma?
陈老师：　力波，这　是　你　奶奶　吗？

Dīng Lìbō：　Bú　shì,　tā　shì　wǒ　wàipó.⑤
丁力波：　不　是，她　是　我　外婆。

Chén lǎoshī：　Wàipó,　nín　hǎo!
陈老师：　外婆，　您　好！

Wàipó：　Nín　hǎo,
外婆：　您　好，

Chén　lǎoshī.
陈　老师。

生词 New Words

1.	nín	您	Pr	you (polite form)
2.	zhè	这	Pr	this
*3.	tā	他	Pr	he, him
4.	wàiyǔ	外语	N	foreign language
*5.	nǐ	你	Pr	you
6.	yīshēng	医生	N	doctor, physician
7.	nǎinai	奶奶	N	(paternal) grandmother
8.	wàipó	外婆	N	(maternal) grandmother
9.	Chén	陈	PN	(a surname)

注释　Notes

③ Chén lǎoshī, nín hǎo!

In China, a person's position or occupation, such as the director of a factory, manager, section head, engineer, movie director, or teacher, is frequently used as a title to address people in preference to such expressions as Mr. or Miss. Surnames always precede the titles. It is considered impolite for a student to address a teacher directly by his / her personal name. "Surname ＋ teacher" is the most proper form of address frequently used for a teacher, e.g., "Chén lǎoshī（陈老师）".

"nín（您）" is the polite form of "你", commonly used to refer to an elderly or a senior person during a conversation or to a person of the same generation when speaking on a formal occasion. People in Beijing are quite fond of using this form of address.

④ Zhè shì wǒ gēge.

"This is my elder brother."

When introducing someone to a person, we often use the sentence pattern "Zhè shì……（这是……）". "shì（是）" is pronounced as a weak syllable.

⑤ Lìbō, zhè shì nǐ nǎinai ma?—— Bú shì, tā shì wǒ wàipó.

The Chinese language uses many words to refer to individuals in a family so that their specific relationship to other members of the family is made clear. Different words are used depending on whether a relative is on the mother's or wife's side or on the father's or husband's side. Some examples are "yéye（爷爷）" and "nǎinai（奶奶）" used by a child to address the parents of his / her father, differentiated from "wàigōng（外公）" and "wàipó（外婆）" or "lǎoye（姥爷）" and "lǎolao（姥姥）" used to address his / her mother's parents.

 二、练习　Exercises

语音 练习　Pronunciation Drills 13

声母 Initials：zh ch sh r
韵母 Finals：-i[ʅ]
　　　　　　ai uai ong

1 拼音 *Pinyin*

zhā	chā	shā	
zhī	chī	shī	rī
zhē	chē	shē	rēng
zhāi	chāi	shāi	rāng
zhōu	chōu	shōu	
zhuō	chuō	shuō	
zhuāi	chuāi	shuāi	
zhōng	chōng		

2 四声 The four tones

chā	chá	chǎ	chà	
	rú	rǔ	rù	
zhē	zhé	zhě	zhè	
shī	shí	shǐ	shì	zhè shì
lāo	láo	lǎo	lào	lǎoshī
chēn	chén	chěn	chèn	Chén lǎoshī
wāi		wǎi	wài	
yū	yú	yǔ	yù	wàiyǔ
yī	yí	yǐ	yì	
shēng	shéng	shěng	shèng	yīshēng
zhōng		zhǒng	zhòng	
guō	guó	guǒ	guò	Zhōngguó
	rén	rěn	rèn	Zhōngguó rén

3 辨音　Sound discrimination

zhōng —— chōng
(middle)　(to pour boiling water on)

shēng —— shāng
(to be born)　(injury)

rì —— rè
(sun)　(hot)

bǐ —— pǐ
(dagger)　(*a measure word for horses*)

dǒng —— tǒng
(to understand)　(bucket)

ròu —— ruò
(meat)　(weak)

4 辨调　Tone discrimination

shí —— shǐ
(ten)　(arrow)

zhě —— zhè
(person, thing)　(this)

rén —— rèn
(person)　(to recognize)

pái —— pài
(to arrange)　(to send)

chéng —— chēng
(city)　(to weigh)

zhuǎi —— zhuài
(to waddle)　(to drag)

5 半三声　Half third tone

lǎoshī　nǎinai　wǒmen　nǐmen

wǒ gēge　wǒ péngyou　wǒ nǎinai

nǐ wàipó　nǐ bàba　nǎ guó rén

hǎo ma　nǐ máng　hěn máng

nǐ yào　wǒ yào　yě yào　kělè

6 声调组合　Combination of tones

- + -
kāfēi

- + ′
Zhōngguó

- + ˇ
hēibǎn
(blackboard)

- + ﹨
shēngdiào
(tones)

- + ｡ [1]
tāmen

yīshēng

hē chá
(to drink tea)

shēntǐ
(body)

chīfàn
(to eat a meal)

gēge

- - - - -

′ + -
túshū
(books)

′ + ′
chángcháng
(often)

′ + ˇ
niúnǎi
(milk)

′ + ﹨
liúlì
(fluent)

′ + ｡
péngyou

chénggōng
(success)

yínháng
(bank)

píngguǒ
(apple)

chídào
(late)

yéye
(paternal grandfather)

[1]: " ｡ " here represents the neutral tone.

7 双音节连读　Practice on disyllabic words

gōngren　(worker)　　　　　Yīngguó　(England, UK)

shāngrén　(merchant)　　　Déguó　(Germany)

lǜshī　(lawyer)　　　　　　Měiguó　(USA)

gànbu　(cadre)　　　　　　Fǎguó　(France)

nóngmín　(farmer)　　　　　Rìběn　(Japan)

8 朗读下列课堂用语　Read the following classroom expressions aloud

Dǎ kāi shū.　　　　Open the book.

Gēn wǒ niàn.　　　Read after me.

Nǐmen niàn.　　　　Read out.

Dǒng bu dǒng?　　Do you understand?

Dǒng le.　　　　　Yes, I / we understand.

会话 练习　Conversation Practice 14

核心句　KEY SENTENCES

1. Nà shì shéi?
2. Nà shì wǒmen lǎoshī.
3. Tā shì nǎ guó rén?
4. Tā shì Zhōngguó rén.
5. Zhè shì wǒ péngyou.
6. Nǐ yě shì lǎoshī ma?
7. Wǒ bú shì lǎoshī, wǒ shì yīshēng.

（一）认指人　Identifying people

1. 看图会话　Make dialogues based on the pictures

❶ A: Nà shì shéi?

　　B: Nà shì＿＿＿＿＿＿＿＿.

❷ A：Tā shì shéi?

　B：Tā shì_____.

（二）问国籍　Asking someone's nationality

1. 完成下列会话　Complete the following dialogues

(1) A：Nín shì nǎ guó rén?

　　B：_____.

　　A：Tā ne?

　　B：_____.

(2) A：Nín shì Yīngguó rén ma?

　　B：Bú shì, _____. Nín shì nǎ guó rén?

　　A：_____.

2. 看图会话　Make dialogues based on the pictures

A：_____?

B：_____.

（三）介绍 Introducing people

1. 完成下列会话 Complete the following dialogues

(1) A：Zhè shì Lín yīshēng. Zhè shì Chén lǎoshī.

B：_____.

C：Nín hǎo，Lín yīshēng.

(2) A：Zhè shì _____. Zhè shì _____.

B：_____.

C：_____.

2. 情景会话 Situational dialogue

Introduce your teacher and classmates.

15 （四）听述 Listen and repeat

那是谁？那是陈老师。她是中国人。

这是我朋友，他不是老师，他是医生。

三、语音 Phonetics

1 三声变调(2) Third-tone sandhi (2)

A third tone, when followed by a first, second or fourth tone, or most neutral tone syllables, usually becomes a half third tone, that is, a tone that only falls but does not rise. The tone mark is unchanged. For example:

nǐ gēge   wǒ yào   Nǐ máng ma?

2 "不"的变调 Tone sandhi of "不"

"不（bù）" is a fourth tone syllable by itself. But it becomes a second tone when followed by a fourth tone. For example:

bù hē   bù máng   bù hǎo   bú shì   bú yào

3 发音要领(3)　Key points of pronunciation (3)

Initials: zh　like "j" in "jerk", but with the tip of the tongue curled farther back, unaspirated.

　　　　ch　like "ch" in "church", but with the tip of the tongue curled farther back, aspirated.

　　　　sh　like "sh" in "ship", but with the tip of the tongue curled farther back.

　　　　r　as in "right" in English, but with lips unrounded, and the tip of the tongue curled farther back. Always pronounce the Chinese /r/ sound with a nice smile!

Finals: ai　like "y" in "sky".

　　　　-i [ʅ]　"-i [ʅ]" in "zhi", "chi", "shi" and "ri" is pronounced differently from the simple final "i [i]". After pronouncing the initials "zh", "ch", "sh" and "r", do not move your tongue. Care must be taken not to pronounce the simple final "i [i]", which is never found after "zh", "ch", "sh" or "r".

四、汉字　Chinese Characters

1 认写基本汉字　Learn and write basic Chinese characters

(1) 人　　　丿 人

rén　　　　people, person　　　2 strokes

Note: On the left side of a character, "人" is written as "亻".

(2) 十　　　一 十

shí　　　　ten　　　　2 strokes

(3) 匕　　　ノ 匕

bǐ　　　　dagger　　　2 strokes

(4) 中　　　丨 口 口 中

zhōng　　　middle　　　4 strokes

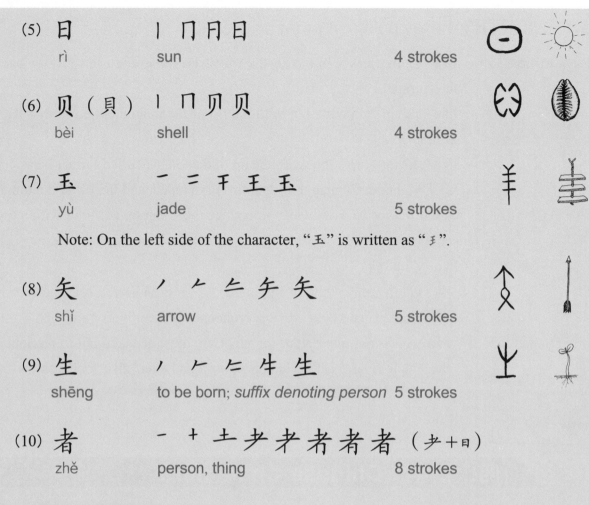

(5) 日   丨 冂 月 日
rì   sun   4 strokes

(6) 贝（貝）丨 冂 贝 贝
bèi   shell   4 strokes

(7) 玉   一 二 干 王 玉
yù   jade   5 strokes

Note: On the left side of the character, "玉" is written as "王".

(8) 矢   丿 亠 亠 午 矢
shǐ   arrow   5 strokes

(9) 生   丿 亠 亡 牛 生
shēng   to be born; *suffix denoting person* 5 strokes

(10) 者   一 十 土 少 耂 者 者 者 （耂 + 日）
zhě   person, thing   8 strokes

2 认写课文中的汉字 Learn and write the Chinese characters in the texts

(1) 她 tā
她 → 女 + 也   6 strokes
(The "female" side "女" denotes something related to a woman.)

(2) 他 tā
他 → 亻 + 也   5 strokes
(The "standing person" side "亻" denotes something related to a person.)

(3) 们 men（們）   5 strokes
们 → 亻 + 门 (The meaning side is "亻", and the phonetic side is "门".)

(4) 你 nǐ
你 → 亻 + 尔（尔：丿 亇 亇 尔 尔）   7 strokes
(The "standing person" side "亻" denotes something related to a person.)

阝 (yòu'ěrdāor, the "right-ear" side) ㇌ 阝 2 strokes

刅 (nàzìpángr, the "that" side) ㇆ ㇆ ⺕ 刅 4 strokes

(5) 那 nà

那 → 刅 + 阝 6 strokes

(6) 哪 nǎ 9 strokes

哪 → 口 + 那 (The meaning side is "口", and the phonetic side is "那".)

(7) 娜 nà 9 strokes

娜 → 女 + 那 (The meaning side is "女", and the phonetic side is "那".)

耂 (lǎozìtóur, the "old" top) 一 十 土 耂 4 strokes

巾 (jīnzìr, the "towel" character) 丨 冂 巾 3 strokes

刂 (shīzìpángr, the "teacher" side) 丨 刂 2 strokes

(8) 都 dōu

都 → 者 + 阝 10 strokes

(9) 老师 lǎoshī (老師)

老 → 耂 + 匕 6 strokes

师 → 刂 + 一 + 巾 6 strokes

囗 (guózìkuàngr, the "country" frame "囗" denotes the boundary of a country.)

丨 冂 囗 3 strokes

(10) 中国 Zhōngguó (中國)

国 → 囗 + 玉 8 strokes

匚 (qūzìkuàngr, the "district" frame) 一 匚 2 strokes

(11) 医生 yīshēng (醫生)

医 → 匚 + 矢 (一 ㇀ ㇀ ㇀ ㇀ ㇀ 医) 7 strokes

(12) 是 shì

是 → 日 + 𤴓 9 strokes

Scheme for the Chinese Phonetic Alphabet

Chinese differs from other alphabetic languages in that its written form is not directly related to its pronunciation. In order to provide phonetic notation for Chinese characters and to facilitate the consultation of dictionaries, phonologists drafted the "Scheme for the Chinese Phonetic Alphabet", and in 1958 the Chinese government passed an act to promote the application of this scheme, commonly known as the *pinyin* ("arranged sounds") system. *Pinyin* has adopted the Latin alphabet to transcribe Chinese sounds and four diacritical tone marks to indicate the different tones of Chinese characters. *Pinyin* is now widely used for the study of the Chinese language, and has aided the popularization of standard Chinese (*Putonghua*).

第四课

Lesson

4

Rènshi nǐ hěn gāoxìng

认识 你 很 高兴

Nice to meet you!

In this lesson, you will learn to ask someone's name politely, how to introduce yourself, and how to ask for permission. The pronunciations of the Chinese initials introduced in this lesson may seem unfamiliar to you. Don't be discouraged, however, for with daily practice, you will surely be able to master them.

一、课文 Text

🎧 16 （一）

请求允许
Asking for permission

| Yáng lǎoshī: | Kěyǐ jìnlai ma?① |
| 杨老师： | 可以 进来 吗？ |

| Lín Nà: | Qǐng jìn!② Yáng lǎoshī, |
| 林娜： | 请 进！ 杨 老师， |

nín hǎo. Zhè shì wǒ
您 好。 这 是 我

péngyou, tā shì jìzhě.
朋友， 他 是 记者。

问姓名
Asking someone's name

| Yáng lǎoshī: | Qǐngwèn,　nín guìxìng?③ |
| 杨老师： | 请问，　您 贵姓？ |

| Lù Yǔpíng: | Wǒ xìng Lù, jiào Lù Yǔpíng.④ |
| 陆雨平： | 我 姓 陆， 叫 陆 雨平。 |

| Yáng lǎoshī: | Nǐ hǎo, Lù xiānsheng, rènshi nǐ hěn gāoxìng.⑤ |
| 杨老师： | 你 好， 陆 先生， 认识 你 很 高兴。 |

| Lù Yǔpíng: | Yáng lǎoshī, rènshi nín wǒ yě hěn gāoxìng. |
| 陆雨平： | 杨 老师， 认识 您 我 也 很 高兴。 |

生词 New Words

1. rènshi	认识	V	to know (somebody)
2. gāoxìng	高兴	A	happy, pleased
gāo	高	A	tall
3. kěyǐ	可以	OpV	may
4. jìnlai	进来	VC	to come in
jìn	进	V	to enter

lái	来	V	to come
5. qǐng	请	V	please
*6. nín	您	Pr	you (polite form)
*7. péngyou	朋友	N	friend
8. jìzhě	记者	N	reporter
9. qǐngwèn	请问	V	May I ask...?
wèn	问	V	to ask
10. guìxìng	贵姓	IE	your surname (polite form)
xìng	姓	V/N	one's surname is… / surname
11. jiào	叫	V	to be called
12. xiānsheng	先生	N	Mr.; sir
13. Yáng	杨	PN	(a surname)

注释　Notes

① Kěyǐ jìnlai ma?

    "May I come in?"

② Qǐng jìn!

    "Come in, please!"

    "Qǐng（请）……" is an expression used for making polite requests.

③ Qǐngwèn, nín guìxìng?

    "May I have your surname?"

    This is a polite way of asking someone's surname. In China, when meeting someone for the first time, it is considered more polite to ask his / her surname rather than his / her full name. Notice that "guì（贵）" can only be used in combination with "nǐ（你）" or "nín（您）", and not with "wǒ（我）" or "tā（他/她）".

④ Wǒ xìng Lù, jiào Lù Yǔpíng.

    "My surname is Lu, and my full name is Lu Yuping."

    When answering the question "Nín guìxìng?", one can either give one's surname by saying "Wǒ xìng……（我姓……）", or give one's full name by saying "Wǒ jiào……（我叫……）" or say both "Wǒ xìng……, jiào……（我姓……，叫……）"

    Note that in Chinese, one's surname always comes before his given name.

⑤　Rènshi nǐ hěn gāoxìng.

　　"(I'm) glad to meet (literally, know) you."

🎧 17　(二)

Lín Nà： Wǒ shì Yǔyán Xuéyuàn de xuésheng.⑥ Wǒ xìng Lín, jiào
林娜：　我 是 语言 学院 的 学生。 我 姓 林, 叫

Lín Nà. Wǒ shì Yīngguó rén. Nǐ xìng shénme?⑦
林娜。我 是 英国 人。你 姓 什么?

Mǎ Dàwéi： Wǒ xìng Mǎ, jiào Mǎ Dàwéi.
马大为：　我 姓 马, 叫 马 大为。

Lín Nà： Nǐ shì Jiānádà rén ma?
林娜：　你 是 加拿大人 吗?

自我介绍
Introducing oneself

Mǎ Dàwéi： Wǒ bú shì Jiānádà rén, wǒ shì Měiguó rén, yě shì Yǔyán
马大为：　我 不 是 加拿大人, 我 是 美国 人, 也 是 语言

Xuéyuàn de xuésheng. Wǒ xuéxí Hànyǔ.
学院 的 学生。 我 学习 汉语。

生词 New Words

1. yǔyán	语言	N	language
2. xuéyuàn	学院	N	institute, college
xué	学	V	to learn, to study 学语言
3. de	的	StPt	(a possessive or modifying particle)
4. xuésheng	学生	N	student
5. shénme	什么	QPr	what
6. xuéxí	学习	V	to learn, to study 学习语言
7. Hànyǔ	汉语	N	Chinese (language)
8. Yīngguó	英国	PN	Great Britain, England
9. Mǎ Dàwéi	马大为	PN	(name of an American student)

| 10. Jiānádà | 加拿大 | PN | Canada |
| 11. Měiguó | 美国 | PN | the United States of America |

补充生词 Supplementary Words

1. Fǎguó	法国	PN	France
2. Déguó	德国	PN	Germany
3. Éluósī	俄罗斯	PN	Russia
4. Rìběn	日本	PN	Japan

注释 Notes

⑥ Wǒ shì Yǔyán Xuéyuàn de xuésheng.

"I am a student at (literally, of) the Language Institute."

⑦ Nǐ xìng shénme?

"What's your surname?"

This informal way of asking someone's surname is appropriate when an adult is speaking to a child, or when young people are talking with each other.

 二、练习 Exercises

语音 练习 Pronunciation Drills 18

声母 Initials：j q x
韵母 Finals：ia ian iang
uei (-ui) uen (-un) üe üan

1 拼音 *Pinyin*

jī	qī	xī
jiā	qiā	xiā
jiān	qiān	xiān
jiāng	qiāng	xiāng
jīn	qīn	xīn
jīng	qīng	xīng
jū	qū	xū
juē	quē	xuē
juān	quān	xuān
guī	kuī	huī
zhūn	chūn	tūn

2 四声 The four tones

jī	jí	jǐ	jì	
zhē	zhé	zhě	zhè	jìzhě
qīng	qíng	qǐng	qìng	
jīn		jǐn	jìn	qǐng jìn
guī		guǐ	guì	
xīng	xíng	xǐng	xìng	guìxìng
xiān	xián	xiǎn	xiàn	
shēng	shéng	shěng	shèng	xiānsheng
yū	yú	yǔ	yù	
yān	yán	yǎn	yàn	yǔyán
xuē	xué	xuě	xuè	
yuān	yuán	yuǎn	yuàn	xuéyuàn

xī	xí	xǐ	xì	xuéxí
hān	hán	hǎn	hàn	Hànyǔ
jiā	jiá	jiǎ	jià	Jiānádà

3 辨音　Sound discrimination

jiāo —— qiāo　　　yuè —— yè　　　duì —— tuì
(to teach) (to knock)　(month) (night)　(right) (to move back)

tián —— tíng　　　yán —— yáng　　　zhǐ —— chǐ
(field)　(to stop)　(speech) (sheep)　(only) (ruler)

4 辨调　Tone discrimination

shǒu —— shòu　　　xià — xiā　　　shuǐ —— shuì
(hand)　(thin)　　(down) (shrimp)　(water) (to sleep)

xīn —— xìn　　　bái —— bǎi　　　xiǎo —— xiào
(heart) (letter)　(white) (hundred)　(small) (to laugh)

5 声调组合　Combination of tones

ˇ + ˉ	ˇ + ´	ˇ + ˇ	ˇ + ˋ	ˇ + ˳
lǎoshī	yǔyán	kěyǐ	qǐng jìn	wǒmen
Běijīng	lǚxíng	yǔfǎ	kǎoshì	jiějie
(Beijing)	(to travel)	(grammar)	(exam)	(elder sister)

- -

ˋ + ˉ	ˋ + ´	ˋ + ˇ	ˋ + ˋ	ˋ + ˳
Lìbō	wàipó	Hànyǔ	guìxìng	mèimei
				(younger sister)
miànbāo	liànxí	bàozhǐ	zhùyì	kèqi
(bread)	(exercise)	(newspaper)	(to pay attention to)	(courtesy)

6　双音节连读　Practice on disyllabic words

tàitai (Mrs.)　　　　　Yīngyǔ (English)

xiǎojie (Miss)　　　　Fǎyǔ (French)

nǚshì (madam)　　　　Déyǔ (German)

jīnglǐ (manager)　　　Éyǔ (Russian)

tóngshì (colleague)　　Rìyǔ (Japanese)

7　朗读下列课堂用语　Read the following classroom expressions aloud

Zhùyì fāyīn.　　　　　　Pay attention to your pronunciation.

Zhùyì shēngdiào.　　　　Pay attention to your tones.

Duì bu duì?　　　　　　Is it right?

Duì le.　　　　　　　　It's right.

Bú duì.　　　　　　　　It's not right.

会话 练习　Conversation Practice　19

核心句　KEY SENTENCES

1. Kěyǐ jìnlai ma?

2. Qǐng jìn!

3. Nín guìxìng?

4. Wǒ xìng Lù, jiào Lù Yǔpíng.

5. Rènshi nǐ hěn gāoxìng.

6. Wǒ shì Yǔyán Xuéyuàn de xuésheng.

7. Wǒ xuéxí Hànyǔ.

（一）请求允许　Asking for permission

看图会话　Make a dialogue based on the picture

A: _____?

B: _____.

（二）问姓名   Asking someone's name

完成下列会话 Complete the following dialogues

(1) A：Nín guìxìng?

  B：Wǒ xìng _____， jiào _____.

  A：Wǒ jiào _____. _____ wǒ hěn gāoxìng.

  B：_____.

(2) A：Nǐ xìng shénme?

  B：_____.

(3) A：Tā xìng shénme?

  B：_____.

(4) A：Tā jiào shénme?

  B：_____.

（三）自我介绍   Introducing oneself

情景会话 Situational dialogue

  Ask everyone to introduce himself / herself in a meeting by imitating Dialogue II in the text.

（四）听述   Listen and repeat

请进!

您贵姓?

我叫马大为，是语言学院的学生。我学习汉语，杨先生是我们的老师。

陆雨平是我朋友，他是记者。认识他，我很高兴。

三、语音　Phonetics

1 发音要领(4)　Key points of pronunciation (4)

Initials: j　is an unaspirated voiceless palatal affricate. To pronounce this sound, first raise the front of the tongue to the hard palate and press the tip of the tongue against the back of the lower teeth, and then loosen the tongue to let the air squeeze out through the channel. The sound is unaspirated and the vocal cords do not vibrate.

q　is an aspirated voiceless palatal affricate. It is pronounced in the same manner as "j", but it is aspirated.

x　is a voiceless palatal fricative. To pronounce it, first raise the front of the tongue toward (but not touching) the hard palate and then let the air squeeze out. The vocal cords do not vibrate.

Note: The finals that can be combined with "j", "q" and "x" are limited to "i", "ü" and compound finals that start with "i" or "ü".

2 拼写规则(3)　Spelling rules (3)

(1) When the compound final "uei" is combined with initials, it is simplified to "-ui" and the tone mark is written over "i". For example: guì.

(2) When the compound final "uen" is combined with initials, it is simplified to "-un". For example: lùn.

(3) When "ü" is combined with "j", "q" and "x", the two dots over it are omitted. For example: xué. "y" is added to the compound finals which start with "ü" and the two dots over it are omitted. For example: yǔyán, xuéyuàn.

Note: "j", "q" and "x" are never combined with "u" and "a".

四、语法　Grammar

■ "是"字句(1)　Sentences with "是" (1)

In an "A 是 B" sentence, the verb "是" is used to connect the two parts. Its negative form is made by putting "不" before the verb "是". If the sentence is not particularly emphatic, "是" is read softly.

Note：The adverb "不" must be placed before "是".

Subject	Predicate			
	Adv	是	N / NP	QPt
Tā 他		shì 是	lǎoshī. 老师。	
Mǎ Dàwéi 马 大为	bú 不	shì 是	lǎoshī. 老师。	
Tā 她		shì 是	xuésheng 学生	ma? 吗？

五、汉字　Chinese Characters

1　笔顺规则　Rules of stroke order

Example	Stroke Order	Rule to Write
十	一 十	Horizontal before vertical
人	丿 人	Left-falling before right-falling
妈	女 妈	From left to right
只	口 只	From top to bottom
月	几 月	From outside to inside
国	冂 囯 国	Outside before inside and inside before enclosing
小	亅 小 小	Middle before two sides

2　认写基本汉字　Learn and write basic Chinese characters

(1) 七　一 七

qī　　seven　　　　2 strokes

Note: It means "cut" orginally.

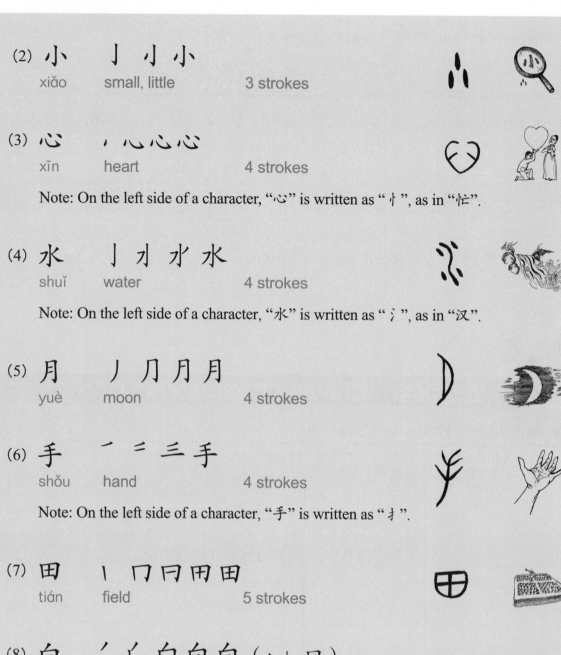

(2) 小　　丿 小 小
xiǎo　　small, little　　　　3 strokes

(3) 心　　丶 心 心 心
xīn　　heart　　　　4 strokes

Note: On the left side of a character, "心" is written as "忄", as in "忙".

(4) 水　　丿 才 水 水
shuǐ　　water　　　　4 strokes

Note: On the left side of a character, "水" is written as "氵", as in "汉".

(5) 月　　丿 刀 月 月
yuè　　moon　　　　4 strokes

(6) 手　　一 二 三 手
shǒu　　hand　　　　4 strokes

Note: On the left side of a character, "手" is written as "扌".

(7) 田　　丨 冂 日 用 田
tián　　field　　　　5 strokes

(8) 白　　丿 亻 白 白 白　(丿 + 日)
bái　　white　　　　5 strokes

(9) 只　　丶 冂 口 尸 只　(口 + 八)
zhǐ　　only　　　　5 strokes

(10) 言　　丶 亠 二 言 言 言 言
yán　　speech　　　　7 strokes

Note: On the left side of a character, "言" is written as "讠", as in "认识".

3 认写课文中的汉字　Learn and write the Chinese characters in the texts

　　(1) 认识 rènshi （認識）

　　　　认 → 讠 + 人　　　　　　　　　　　4 strokes

　　　　（"讠", the meaning side plus the phonetic side, "人".）

　　　　识 → 讠 + 只　　　　　　　　　　　7 strokes

　　　　（"讠", the meaning side, denotes language-related behavior.）

　　(2) 语言 yǔyán （語言）

　　　　语 → 讠 + 五 + 口　　　　　　　　9 strokes

　　　　氵 (sāndiǎnshuǐr, the "three-drops-of-water" side) 丶丶氵　3 strokes

　　(3) 汉语 Hànyǔ （漢語）

　　　　汉 → 氵 + 又　　　　　　　　　　　5 strokes

　　(4) 您 nín

　　　　您 → 你 + 心　　　　　　　　　　　11 strokes

　　　　ナ (yǒuzìtóur, the "to have" top) 一ナ　　2 strokes

　　(5) 朋友 péngyou

　　　　朋 → 月 + 月　　　　　　　　　　　8 strokes

　　　　友 → ナ + 又　　　　　　　　　　　4 strokes

　　(6) 贵姓 guìxìng （貴姓）

　　　　贵 → 中 + 一 + 贝　　　　　　　　9 strokes

　　　　姓 → 女 + 生　　　　　　　　　　　8 strokes

　　(7) 叫 jiào

　　　　叫 → 口 + 丩　　　　　　　　　　　5 strokes

　　(8) 的 de

　　　　的 → 白 + 勺　　　　　　　　　　　8 strokes

文化知识 **Cultural Note**

Chinese Dictionaries

The *Xinhua Zidian* (New Chinese Dictionary) and *Xiandai Hanyu Cidian* (Modern Chinese Dictionary) are among the most widely used dictionaries in China nowadays. The first is a pocket-sized dictionary, containing over 8,000 entries. The second is a medium-sized dictionary including more than 56,000 entries. The encyclopedic *Cihai* (Sea of Words) and the detailed *Ciyuan* (Sources of Words) are both large dictionaries, often issued in multi-volume sets. There are also many dictionaries specially designed for international students who want to study Chinese language and culture.

Unlike most dictionaries used in Western countries, in which entries are arranged alphabetically, Chinese dictionaries are organized in a number of different ways. They can be compiled alphabetically (using *pinyin* or another romanization system), by the number of strokes used to write the character in question, or by the radical of the character. Many dictionaries published before the 1920s order their entries according to the radical, whereas modern dictionaries are often arranged alphabetically and include radical and stroke-number indexes.

Dictionaries for Foreigners

第五课

Lesson 5

Cāntīng zài nǎr

餐厅 在 哪儿

Where is the dining hall?

By the end of this lesson, you should be able
to ask for directions, look for someone, express
gratitude and regret, and say goodbye in Chinese.
Remember to keep practicing your pronunciation
and tones every day.

一、课文 Text

 21 (一)

Mǎ Dàwéi: Qǐngwèn, zhè shì Wáng Xiǎoyún
马大为: 请问, 这是王 小云

de sùshè ma?
的 宿舍 吗?

找人
Looking for someone

Nǚ xuésheng: Shì. Qǐng jìn, qǐng zuò.
女学生: 是。请 进, 请 坐。

Mǎ Dàwéi: Xièxie. Wáng Xiǎoyún zài ma?①
马大为: 谢谢。王 小云 在 吗?

Nǚ xuésheng: Tā bú zài.
女学生: 她 不 在。

Mǎ Dàwéi: Tā zài nǎr?②
马大为: 她 在 哪儿?

Nǚ xuésheng: Duìbuqǐ, wǒ bù zhīdào.③
女学生: 对不起,我 不 知道。

Mǎ Dàwéi: Méi guānxi. Hǎo, zàijiàn.
马大为: 没 关系。好, 再见。

告别
Saying goodbye

Nǚ xuésheng: Zàijiàn.
女学生: 再见。

chén kǎi jié

生词 New Words

1. cāntīng	餐厅	N	dining hall
2. zài	在	V	to be (here, there), to be (in, on, at)
3. nǎr	哪儿	QPr	where
*4. qǐngwèn	请问	V	May I ask...?
wèn	问	V	to ask
*5. zhè	这	Pr	this
6. sùshè	宿舍	N	dormitory
7. nǚ	女	A	female
*8. xuésheng	学生	N	student
*9. jìn	进	V	to enter
10. zuò	坐	V	to sit
11. xièxie	谢谢	V	to thank
12. duìbuqǐ	对不起	IE	I'm sorry
*13. wǒ	我	Pr	I, me
14. zhīdao	知道	V	to know
15. méi guānxi	没关系	IE	never mind, it doesn't matter
*16. hǎo	好	A	good, well, fine, OK
17. zàijiàn	再见	IE	goodbye
zài	再	Adv	again
18. Wáng Xiǎoyún	王小云	PN	(name of a Chinese student)

注释　Notes

① Wáng Xiǎoyún zài ma?

　　"Is Wang Xiaoyun in?"

② Tā zài nǎr?

　　"Where is she?"

③ Duìbuqǐ, wǒ bù zhīdào.

　　"duìbuqǐ (对不起)" is a phrase commonly used in asking for excuses or making apologies, and the response to it is usually "méi guānxi (没关系)".

🎧 22 （二）

Mǎ Dàwéi： Xiǎojie, qǐngwèn cāntīng zài nǎr?④
马大为： 小姐，请问　餐厅　在哪儿？

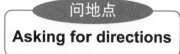

Xiǎojie： Zài èr céng èr líng sì hào.⑤
小姐： 在 二 层 二 〇 四 号。

Mǎ Dàwéi： Xièxie.
马大为： 谢谢。

道谢
Expressing thanks

Xiǎojie： Búyòng xiè.⑥
小姐： 不用　谢。

＊　　＊　　＊　　＊　　＊　　＊

Sòng Huá： Dàwéi, wǒmen zài zhèr.
宋华： 大为，我们　在 这儿。

Mǎ Dàwéi： Duìbuqǐ, wǒ láiwǎn le.⑦
马大为： 对不起，我 来晚 了。

道歉
Making an apology

Wáng Xiǎoyún： Méi guānxi.
王小云： 没　关系。

生词 New Words

1. xiǎojie	小姐	N	Miss, young lady
2. èr	二	Nu	two
3. céng	层	M	story, floor
4. líng	〇/零	Nu	zero

5. sì	四	Nu	four
6. hào	号	N	ordinal number
7. búyòng	不用	Adv	need not
8. zhèr	这儿	Pr	here
9. wǎn	晚	A	late
10. le	了	Pt	(*a modal particle, aspect particle*)
11. Sòng Huá	宋华	PN	(name of a Chinese student)

注释　Notes

④ Cāntīng zài nǎr?

　　"Where is the dining hall?"

⑤ Zài èr céng èr líng sì hào.

　　"It's in No. 204 on the second floor." In Chinese, the ground floor of a building is considered to be the first floor.

⑥ Búyòng xiè.

　　"Don't mention it."

　　This phrase is used as a response to an expression of gratitude. One may also say, "Bú xiè(不谢)".

⑦ Duìbuqǐ，wǒ láiwǎn le.

　　"Sorry, I am late."

二、练习　Exercises

语音 练习　Pronunciation Drills　23

声母 Initials：z　c　s

韵母 Finals：-i[1]　er

　　　　　　iong　ua　uan　uang　ün

1 拼音 *Pinyin*

zā	cā	sā
zī	cī	sī
zū	cū	sū
zuān	cuān	suān
zuī	cuī	suī
zūn	cūn	sūn
zhuāng	chuāng	shuāng
jiōng	qiōng	xiōng
jūn	qūn	xūn
guā	kuā	huā

2 四声 The four tones

zāi		zǎi	zài	zài
cān	cán	cǎn	càn	
tīng	tíng	tǐng	tìng	cāntīng
sī		sǐ	sì	
cēng	céng		cèng	sì céng
	ér	ěr	èr	èr hào
wēn	wén	wěn	wèn	qǐngwèn
xiē	xié	xiě	xiè	xièxie
jiān		jiǎn	jiàn	zàijiàn
wān	wán	wǎn	wàn	láiwǎn le
yōng	yóng	yǒng	yòng	búyòng
wāng	wáng	wǎng	wàng	
yūn	yún	yǔn	yùn	Wáng Xiǎoyún
sōng	sóng	sǒng	sòng	
huā	huá		huà	Sòng Huá

3 辨音　Sound discrimination

zǐ —— cǐ	qiě —— jiě	jiàn —— qiàn
(son)　(here; this)	(and)　(elder sister)	(to see)　(to owe)

qīng —— jīng	kuài —— kuà	huān —— huāng
(blue, green)　(eye)	(quick)　(to stride)	(happy)　(hurried)

4 辨调　Tone discrimination

sì —— sī	jǐng —— jīng	èr —— ér
(four)　(silk)	(well)　(eye)	(two)　(son)

yǒng —— yòng	wén —— wèn	xióng —— xiōng
(brave)　(to use)	(written language)　(to ask)	(bear)　(elder brother)

5 韵母er和儿化韵　Final "er" and retroflex ending

èr (two)	zhèr (here)
érzi (son)	nàr (there)
ěrduo (ear)	nǎr (where)
nǚ'ér (daughter)	wánr (to play)

6 声调组合　Combination of tones

– + –	– + ′	– + ∨	– + ＼	– + 。
cāntīng	Yīngguó	jīnglǐ (manager)	gāoxìng	xiānsheng
fēijī (plane)	shēngcí (new word)	qiānbǐ (pencil)	gōngzuò (to work)	xiūxi (to rest)
kāichē (to drive a car)	huānyíng (to welcome)	kāishǐ (to start)	shāngdiàn (shop)	qīzi (wife)

／ ＋ ‐	／ ＋ ／	／ ＋ ˇ	／ ＋ ＼	／ ＋ ◦
míngtiān (tomorrow)	xuéxí	yóuyǒng (to swim)	xuéyuàn	shénme
shíjiān (time)	huídá (to answer)	píjiǔ (beer)	zázhì (magazine)	míngzi (name)
zuótiān (yesterday)	zúqiú (football)	cídiǎn (dictionary)	cídài (tape)	háizi (child)

7 双音节连读   Practice on disyllabic words

jiàoshì (classroom)   Hélán (the Netherlands)

lǐtáng (auditorium)   Āijí (Egypt)

cāochǎng (playground)   Yuènán (Vietnam)

cèsuǒ (restroom)   Tàiguó (Thailand)

yīyuàn (hospital)   Yìndù (India)

8 多音节连读   Practice on polysyllabic words

túshūguǎn (library)   Xīnjiāpō (Singapore)

shíyànshì (laboratory)   Fēilǜbīn (the Philippines)

bàngōngshì (office)   Xīnxīlán (New Zealand)

tǐyùguǎn (gymnasium)   Àodàlìyà (Australia)

wàishìchù (Foreign Affairs Department)   Mǎláixīyà (Malaysia)

tíngchēchǎng (parking lot)   Yìndùníxīyà (Indonesia)

9 朗读下列课堂用语   Read the following classroom expressions aloud

Qǐng niàn kèwén.   Please read the text.

Qǐng niàn shēngcí.   Please read the new words.

Wǒ shuō, nǐmen tīng.   Listen to me.

会话 练习　Conversation Practice　 24

核心句　KEY SENTENCES

1. Qǐng jìn, qǐng zuò.
2. Wǒ bù zhīdào.
3. Zàijiàn.
4. Qǐngwèn, cāntīng zài nǎr?

5. Xièxie.
6. Búyòng xiè.
7. Duìbuqǐ.
8. Méi guānxi.

（一）找人　Looking for someone

1. 完成下列会话　Complete the following dialogues

(1) A：Qǐngwèn， Lín Nà zài ma?

　　 B：＿＿＿＿＿＿＿＿＿＿＿＿＿.

　　 A：Tā zài nǎr?

　　 B：Duìbuqǐ, ＿＿＿＿＿＿＿＿＿＿＿＿＿.

　　 A：Méi guānxi. Zàijiàn!

　　 B：＿＿＿＿＿＿＿＿＿＿＿＿＿.

(2) A：＿＿＿＿＿＿＿＿＿＿＿＿＿?

　　 B：Zài. Qǐng jìn.

2. 看图会话　Make dialogues based on the pictures

❶ Xuésheng：＿＿＿＿＿＿＿＿＿?
　 Yáng lǎoshī：＿＿＿＿＿＿＿.

❷ Lín Nà：Lìbō zài ma?

Mǎ Dàwéi：_____.

Lín Nà：_____?

Mǎ Dàwéi：_____.

Lín Nà：_____.

Mǎ Dàwéi：_____.

（二）问地点   Asking for directions

1. 完成下列会话   Complete the following dialogues

(1) A：Qǐngwèn, cèsuǒ zài nǎr?

　　B：_____.

　　A：Xièxie.

　　B：_____.

(2) A：Qǐngwèn, jiàoshì zài nǎr?

　　B：Duìbuqǐ, _____.

2. 情景会话   Situational dialogue

In an unfamiliar building:

(1) You are looking for the elevator (电梯, diàntī).

(2) You are looking for Mr. Yang's office.

（三）道歉　Making an apology

看图会话　Make dialogues based on the pictures

❶ A：_____．

　 B：_____．

❷ A：_____．

　 B：_____．

（四）问职业　Asking about someone's occupation

完成下列会话　Complete the following dialogues

(1) A：Nín shì lǎoshī ma?

　　B：Bú shì, wǒ shì _____．

　　A：Nín ne?

　　C：Wǒ yě shì xuésheng, wǒ xuéxí Hànyǔ．

(2) A：_____?

　　B：Shì, wǒ shì wàiyǔ lǎoshī．

　　A：Nǐ _____?

　　C：Wǒ bú shì wàiyǔ lǎoshī. Wǒ shì _____．

🎧 25　（五）听述　Listen and repeat

A：请问，他的宿舍在哪儿？

B：在三层三一〇号。

A：谢谢。

A：请问，您认识陈老师吗？

B：对不起，我不认识。

A：没关系。再见。

B：再见。

三、语音 Phonetics

1 儿化韵 Retroflex ending

The final "er" sometimes does not form a syllable by itself, but is attached to another final to form a retroflex final. A retroflex final is represented by the letter "r" added to the final. In writing, "儿" is added to the character in question, as in "nǎr 哪儿".

2 发音要领(5) Key points of pronunciation (5)

Initials: z like "ds" in "beds".

c like "ts" in "cats", with aspiration.

s pronounced the same as "s" in "see" in English.

Final: -r like "er" in "sister" (American pronunciation).

四、语法 Grammar

■ 用疑问代词的问句 Questions with an interrogative pronoun

Statement	Question
Nà shì wǒmen lǎoshī. 那 是 我们 老师。 →	Nà shì shéi? 那 是 谁?
Wǒ xìng Mǎ. 我 姓 马。 →	Nǐ xìng shénme? 你 姓 什么?
Cāntīng zài èr céng. 餐厅 在 二 层。 →	Cāntīng zài nǎr? 餐厅 在 哪儿?
Tā shì Zhōngguó rén. 她 是 中国 人。 →	Tā shì nǎ guó rén? 她 是 哪 国 人?

The word order in a question with an interrogative pronoun is the same as that in a declarative sentence. In this kind of sentence, a question pronoun simply replaces the part of the sentence to which the interrogative pronoun corresponds.

五、汉字　Chinese Characters

1 汉字复合笔画（1）　Combined character strokes (1)

Stroke	Name	Example	Way to Write
㇖	hénggōu	你	The horizontal stroke with a hook, is written like the fourth stroke in "你".
㇕	héngzhé	马	The horizontal stroke with a downward turn, is written like the first stroke in "马".
㇇	héngpiě	又	The horizontal stroke with a downward turn to the left, is written like the first stroke in "又".
㇆	héngzhégōu	门	The horizontal stroke with a downward turn and a hook, is written like the third stroke in "门".
㇍	héngzhétí	语	The horizontal stroke with a downward turn，and then an upward turn to the right, is written like the second stroke in "语".
㇚	shùgōu	丁	The vertical stroke with a hook, is written like the second stroke in "丁".

2 认写基本汉字　Learn and write basic Chinese characters

(1) 二　　一 二
　　èr　　　　two　　　　　　2 strokes

(2) 儿（兒）　丿 儿
　　ér　　　　son　　　　　　2 strokes

(3) 子　　㇇ 了 子
　　zǐ　　　　son　　　　　　3 strokes

(4) 井　　一 二 丰 井
jǐng　　well　　4 strokes

(5) 文　　丶 ﹀ 亠 文
wén　　written language　　4 strokes

(6) 见（見）　　丨 冂 贝 见
jiàn　　to see　　4 strokes

(7) 且　　丨 冂 月 月 且
qiě　　and　　5 strokes

Note: "且" is the original character for "祖" (zǔ, ancestor). When it became a loaned function word, "祖" substitutes for the original character.

(8) 四　　丨 冂 冂 四 四
sì　　four　　5 strokes

(9) 我　　丿 二 于 手 我 我 我
wǒ　　I, me　　7 strokes

(10) 青　　一 二 丰 丰 圭 青 青 青
qīng　　blue, green　　8 strokes

3 认写课文中的汉字　Learn and write the Chinese characters in the texts

才（zàizìtóur, the "location" top）　一 ナ 才　　3 strokes

(1) 在 zài

在 → 才 + 土　　6 strokes

(2) 坐 zuò

坐 → 人 + 人 + 土　　7 strokes

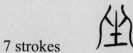

(3) 请问 qǐngwèn （請問）

请 → 讠 ＋ 青　　　　　　10 strokes

(The meaning side is "讠", and the phonetic side is "青".)

问 → 门 ＋ 口　　　　　　6 strokes

辶 (zǒuzhīr, the "walking" bottom)　丶 讠 辶　　　3 strokes

(4) 这 zhè （這）

这 → 文 ＋ 辶　　　　　　7 strokes

(5) 进 jìn （進）

进 → 井 ＋ 辶　　　　　　7 strokes

(6) 再见 zàijiàn （再見）

再 → 一 ＋ 冂 ＋ 土（一 丆 丏 丙 再 再）　6 strokes

⺌ (xuézìtóur, the "study" top)　丶 丶 ⺍ ⺌ ⺌　5 strokes

(7) 学生 xuésheng （學生）

学 → ⺌ ＋ 子　　　　　　8 strokes

(8) 好 hǎo

好 → 女 ＋ 子　　　　　　6 strokes

(9) 小姐 xiǎojie

姐 → 女 ＋ 且　　　　　　8 strokes

冂 (zhōuzìkuàngr, the "border" frame)　丿 冂　2 strokes

(10) 不用 búyòng

用 → 冂 ＋ 丰（丰：一 二 丰）　5 strokes

Chinese People's Daily Meals

The Chinese believe "food is the paramount necessity of the people", therefore, they eat abundant food in their daily meals.

The Chinese differ in their eating habits due to the vast territory of this country. However, generally speaking, northerners are keen on wheaten food, while southerners are partial to cooked rice. Traditional Chinese food includes gruel, wonton, *mantou* (steamed bread), *baozi* (steamed twisted roll), *youtiao* (deep fried twisted dough stick), *shaobing* (sesame seed cake), eggs and soybean milk; in some places, people eat noodles, *mifen* (rice-flour noodles), *tangyuan* (dumplings made of glutinous rice flour) and *jianbing* (fried pancake rolled up in egg filling) instead. Moreover, each food in itself is rich in variety. Most southerners eat cooked rice and soup for their lunch and supper, while northerners' favorite is wheaten food. Cooked vegetables, which are liked by both southerners and northerners, are various beyond count. Besides eating cooked rice, wheaten food and cooked vegetables, in some other places, people are used to eating gruel instead.

Nowadays, as people's pace of life continues to increase, besides the traditional Chinese food, many people choose fast and convenient Western food for breakfast, such as bread and milk; they have also begun to eat Westernized fast food for lunch, such as McDonald's and KFC. Since people enjoy their supper time with their family members and have more time to prepare, they cook food they like.

With the development of the Chinese economy, in most places, people can not only enjoy Chinese dishes rich in local flavor, but can also taste food from around the world, such as that in Western countries, Japan, Korea and Southeast Asia. As a result, their daily meals are greater in profusion.

youtiao

jianbing

tangyuan

baozi

wonton

mantou

第六课

Lesson

6

● 复习　Review

Wǒmen qù yóuyǒng, hǎo ma
我们　去　游泳，好　吗
Let's go swimming, shall we?

In this lesson, you will learn what to say when you don't understand what another person said. You will also learn how to make suggestions, how to accept or decline suggestions, and how to make comments. This lesson also provides a review of the pronunciation and tones covered so far.

一、课文　Text

🎧 26　（一）

Wáng Xiǎoyún:　Lín Nà, zuótiān de jīngjù zěnmeyàng? ①
王小云：　　　林　娜，　昨天　的　京剧　怎么样？

評论
Making comments

Lín Nà:　Hěn yǒu yìsi.　Jīntiān tiānqì hěn hǎo, wǒmen qù
林娜：　很　有意思。今天　天气　很　好，　我们　去

yóuyǒng, hǎo ma? ②
游泳，　好　吗？

建议
Making suggestions

Wáng Xiǎoyún:　Tài hǎo le! Shénme shíhou qù? ③
王小云：　　　太　好　了！什么　时候　去？

Lín Nà:　Xiànzài qù, kěyǐ ma? ④
林娜：　现在　去，可以　吗？

Wáng Xiǎoyún:　Kěyǐ.
王小云：　　　可以。

生词 New Words

1. qù	去	V	to go	
2. yóuyǒng	游泳	VO	to swim	
3. zuótiān	昨天	N	yesterday	

4. jīngjù	京剧	N	Beijing opera
5. zěnmeyàng	怎么样	QPr	how is ...
6. yǒu yìsi	有意思	IE	interesting
7. jīntiān	今天	N	today
tiān	天	N	day
8. tiānqì	天气	N	weather
9. tài	太	Adv	too, extremely
*10. shénme	什么	QPr	what
11. shíhou	时候	N	time, moment
12. xiànzài	现在	N	now

注释 Notes

① Zuótiān de jīngjù zěnmeyàng?

"How was yesterday's Beijing opera?"

"······zěnmeyàng? （······怎么样？）" is an expression commonly used to ask for someone's opinion. Among the roughly 300 forms of opera in China, Beijing opera has enjoyed the greatest popularity and has the most extensive influence. As a unique art form representing Chinese culture, it is loved by many people all over the world.

② Wǒmen qù yóuyǒng, hǎo ma?

"Shall we go swimming?"

"······, hǎo ma? （······，好吗？）" is a pattern used when making a suggestion.

③ Tài hǎo le! Shénme shíhou qù?

"That's great! When are we going?"

"Tài hǎo le! （太好了！）" is an expression used to express satisfaction and approval. It is also used to express happy agreement with a suggestion. You may also use "hǎo（好）" or "xíng（行）" as a response.

④ Xiànzài qù, kěyǐ ma?

"Is it OK to go right now?"

"······, kěyǐ ma? （······，可以吗？）" is another expression used to make a suggestion. If you agree with a suggestion, you may say "kěyǐ（可以）" or "hǎo（好）".

🎧 27 （二）

Dīng Lìbō: Yáng lǎoshī, míngtiān nín yǒu shíjiān ma?⑤
丁力波：杨 老师， 明天 您 有 时间 吗？

Yáng lǎoshī: Duìbuqǐ, qǐng zài shuō yí biàn.⑥
杨老师：对不起， 请 再 说 一 遍。

> 请求重复
> **Asking someone to repeat something**

Dīng Lìbō: Míngtiān nín yǒu shíjiān ma? Wǒmen qù dǎ qiú, hǎo ma?
丁力波：明天 您 有 时间 吗？我们 去 打 球，好 吗？

Yáng lǎoshī: Hěn bàoqiàn, míngtiān wǒ hěn máng, kǒngpà bù xíng.⑦
杨老师：很 抱歉， 明天 我 很 忙， 恐怕 不 行。

Xièxie nǐmen.
谢谢 你们。

> 婉拒
> **Refusing or declining politely**

生词 New Words

1. míngtiān	明天	N	tomorrow
2. yǒu	有	V	to have
3. shíjiān	时间	N	time
4. shuō	说	V	to say, to speak
5. biàn	遍	M	(for action) a time
6. dǎ qiú	打球	V O	to play ball games
dǎ	打	V	to play
qiú	球	N	ball
7. bàoqiàn	抱歉	A	sorry

*8. máng	忙	A	busy
9. kǒngpà	恐怕	Adv	afraid that...
10. xíng	行	V	to be OK
*11. xièxie	谢谢	V	to thank
12. nǐmen	你们	Pr	you (pl.)

注释　Notes

⑤ Míngtiān nín yǒu shíjiān ma?

"Do you have time tomorrow?"

⑥ Qǐng zài shuō yí biàn.

"Pardon? Would you please say it again?"

This phrase is used when the speaker's words were not heard clearly and you would like him / her to repeat.

⑦ Hěn bàoqiàn，míngtiān wǒ hěn máng，kǒngpà bù xíng.

"I'm sorry, but I'll be very busy tomorrow. I'm afraid I can't."

"kǒngpà bù xíng（恐怕不行）" is a phrase to express a polite refusal.

二、练习　Exercises

语音 复习　Pronunciation Review 28

1 拼音　*Pinyin*

zhī	chī	zī	cī
jū	qū	gū	kū
bēn	pēng	tān	dāng
zhōng	chōng	gān	kāng
zān	cāng	jīn	qīng
zhā	chā	zū	cū
gē	kē	jī	qī

2 四声   The four tones

yōu	yóu	yǒu	yòu	
yōng		yǒng	yòng	yóuyǒng
zuō	zuó	zuǒ	zuò	
tiān	tián	tiǎn	tiàn	zuótiān
jīn		jǐn	jìn	jīntiān
	míng	mǐng	mìng	míngtiān
qī	qí	qǐ	qì	tiānqì
xiān	xián	xiǎn	xiàn	xiànzài
jīng		jǐng	jìng	
jū	jú	jǔ	jù	jīngjù
bāo	báo	bǎo	bào	
qiān	qián	qiǎn	qiàn	bàoqiàn
kōng		kǒng	kòng	kǒngpà
xīng	xíng	xǐng	xìng	bù xíng

3 辨音   Sound discrimination

jiǔ —— xiǔ   sī —— shī   cùn —— zùn
(nine) (rotten)   (private) (teacher)   (inch)   (to press with
                                                  one's finger)

qì —— jì   duì —— tuì   guǎn —— juǎn
(air) (to remember) (to exchange) (to move back)   (pipe)   (to roll up)

4 辨调   Tone discrimination

wáng —— wàng   kàn —— kǎn   gōng —— gòng
(to die) (to forget)   (to see) (to cut)   (labor)   (together)

sān —— sǎn   shēn —— shèn   guāi —— guǎi
(three) (umbrella)   (body) (kidney)   (well-behaved) (to turn)

5 声调组合　Combination of tones

ˇ + ˉ	ˇ + ˊ	ˇ + ˇ	ˇ + ˋ	ˇ + ˚
lǎoshī	yǔyán	kěyǐ	kǒngpà	jiějie
yǔyīn (pronunciation)	dǎ qiú	yǔfǎ (grammar)	qǐngwèn	zěnme (how)
xiǎoshuō (novel)	qǐchuáng (to get up)	fǔdǎo (coach)	nǚshì (madam)	yǐzi (chair)

- -

ˋ + ˉ	ˋ + ˊ	ˋ + ˇ	ˋ + ˋ	ˋ + ˚
shàng bān (to go to work)	sì céng (the fourth floor)	wàiyǔ	bàoqiàn	xièxie
qìchē (car)	kèwén (text)	diànyǐng (movie)	huìhuà (conversation)	mèimei (younger sister)
lùyīn (recording)	fùxí (to review)	diànnǎo (computer)	Hànzì (Chinese character)	kèqi (polite)

6 双音节连读　Practice on disyllabic words

duànliàn (to have physical training)　　chànggē (to sing a song)

chīfàn (to eat a meal)　　tiàowǔ (to dance)

shàngkè (to have lessons)　　xǐzǎo (to take a bath)

xiàkè (class is over)　　shuìjiào (to sleep)

7 多音节连读　Practice on polysyllabic words

shuō Hànyǔ (to speak Chinese)　　kàn lùxiàng (to watch the video)

niàn shēngcí (to read the new words)　　zuò liànxí (to do exercises)

xiě Hànzì (to write Chinese characters)　　fānyì jùzi (to translate a sentence)

tīng lùyīn (to listen to the recording)　　yòng diànnǎo (to use a computer)

8 朗读下面的唐诗 Read the following poem aloud

Dēng Guàn Què Lóu
登 鹳 雀 楼   On the Stork Tower

(Táng) Wáng Zhīhuàn
（唐） 王 之涣   (Tang Dynasty) Wang Zhihuan

Bái rì yī shān jìn,
白 日 依 山 尽，   The sun along the mountain bows;

Huáng Hé rù hǎi liú.
黄 河 入 海 流。   The Yellow River seawards flows.

Yù qióng qiān lǐ mù,
欲 穷 千 里 目，   You will enjoy a grander sight;

gèng shàng yì céng lóu.
更 上 一 层 楼。   By climbing to a greater height.

9 朗读下列课堂用语 Read the following classroom expressions aloud

Qǐng kàn shū.   Please read your book.

Qǐng xiě Hànzì.   Please write the Chinese characters.

Qǐng zài niàn yí biàn.   Please read it again.

Wǒmen tīngxiě.   Let's do dictation.

会话练习 Conversation Practice 29

核心句 KEY SENTENCES

1. Zuótiān de jīngjù zěnmeyàng?
2. Jīntiān tiānqì hěn hǎo, wǒmen qù yóuyǒng, hǎo ma?
3. Tài hǎo le! Shénme shíhou qù?
4. Xiànzài qù, kěyǐ ma?
5. Kěyǐ.
6. Míngtiān nín yǒu shíjiān ma?
7. Duìbuqǐ, qǐng zài shuō yí biàn.
8. Hěn bàoqiàn, kǒngpà bù xíng.

（一）评论　Making comments

看图会话　Make dialogues based on the pictures

❶ A：Qǐngwèn, zhè shì shénme?

　　B：Zhè shì wǔshù.

　　A：Wǔshù zěnmeyàng?

　　B：＿＿＿＿＿＿＿＿＿＿.

❷ A：Zhè shì shénme?

　　B：Zhè shì xióngmāo.

　　A：Xióngmāo zěnmeyàng?

　　B：＿＿＿＿＿＿＿＿＿＿.

（二）建议　Making suggestions; 婉拒　Refusing or declining politely

看图会话　Make dialogues based on the pictures

❶ A：＿＿＿＿＿＿＿＿, hǎo ma?

　　B：Tài hǎo le! ＿＿＿＿＿＿＿?

　　A：＿＿＿＿＿＿＿＿, kěyǐ ma?

　　B：＿＿＿＿＿＿＿＿.

❷ A：＿＿＿＿＿＿＿＿, hǎo ma?

　　B：Shénme shíhou qù?

　　A：＿＿＿＿＿＿＿＿＿, kěyǐ ma?

　　B：Duìbuqǐ, ＿＿＿＿＿＿, ＿＿＿＿＿＿.

　　A：Méi guānxi.

tiàowǔ
to dance

（三）请求重复   Asking someone to repeat something

看图会话 Make a dialogue based on the picture

A：_____?

B：Duìbuqǐ, _____.

A：_____?

🎧30 （四）模仿下面的会话进行练习   Imitate the following dialogues

(1) A：Nín hǎo!

B：Nín hǎo!

A：Qǐngwèn, nín guìxìng?

B：Wǒ xìng Lǐ, jiào Lǐ Mǎlì. Qǐngwèn, nín xìng shénme?

A：Wǒ xìng Sòng, jiào Sòng Huá. Nín shì nǎ guó rén?

B：Wǒ shì Měiguó rén, shì Běijīng Dàxué (Peking University) de xuésheng.

A：Rènshi nín hěn gāoxìng.

B：Rènshi nín, wǒ yě hěn gāoxìng.

(2) A：Lìbō, nǐ hǎo ma?

C：Wǒ hěn hǎo. Sòng Huá, nǐ ne?

A：Wǒ hěn máng. Nǐ wàipó hǎo ma?

C：Xièxie, tā hěn hǎo. Nǐ bàba、māma dōu hǎo ma?

A：Tāmen dōu hěn hǎo. Mǎlì, zhè shì wǒ
   péngyou, Dīng Lìbō.

C：Nǐ hǎo.

A：Zhè shì Mǎlì.

B：Nǐ hǎo. Wǒ jiào Mǎlì, shì Běijīng Dàxué
   de xuésheng. Wǒ xuéxí Hànyǔ. Qǐngwèn,
   nǐ shì Měiguó rén ma?

C：Bú shì, wǒ shì Jiānádà rén.

(3) A：Tā shì shéi?

　　B：Tā shì wǒmen lǎoshī.

　　A：Tā shì Zhōngguó rén ma?

　　B：Tā shì Zhōngguó rén. Tā xìng Chén.

　　A：Nà shì shéi?

　　B：Tā jiào Lù Yǔpíng.

　　A：Tā yě shì lǎoshī ma?

　　B：Tā bú shì lǎoshī. Tā shì jìzhě.

(4) A：Xiānsheng, qǐngwèn, bàngōngshì zài nǎr?

　　B：Zài wǔ céng.

　　*　*　*　*　*

　　A：Chén lǎoshī zài ma?

　　C：Shéi? Duìbuqǐ, qǐng zài shuō yí biàn.

　　A：Chén Fāngfāng lǎoshī zài ma?

　　C：Tā zài.

　　A：Xièxie.

　　C：Bú xiè.

(5) A：Kěyǐ jìnlai ma?

　　B：Wáng xiānsheng, nín hǎo. Qǐng jìn, qǐng zuò.

　　A：Duìbuqǐ, wǒ lái wǎn le.

　　B：Méi guānxi. Nín yào kāfēi ma?

　　A：Wǒ bú yào. Xièxie. Míngtiān wǒmen qù kàn jīngjù, hǎo ma?

　　B：Duìbuqǐ, míngtiān wǒ hěn máng, kǒngpà bù xíng.

（五）听述　Listen and repeat

对不起，请再说一遍！

很抱歉，明天我没有时间，恐怕不行。

三、语音   Phonetics

1 "一" 的变调   Tone sandhi of "一"

Normally "一" is pronounced in the first tone when it stands by itself, at the end of a word, phrase or sentence, or when it is used as an ordinal number. However, "一" is pronounced in the fourth tone when it precedes a first tone, second tone or third tone syllable. It is read in the second tone when it precedes a fourth tone.

$$yī + \begin{cases} - \\ ^\prime \\ ^\vee \end{cases} \rightarrow yì + \begin{cases} - & \text{For example: yì bēi (a cup of)} \\ ^\prime & \text{For example: yì píng (a bottle of)} \\ ^\vee & \text{For example: yì zhǒng (a type of)} \end{cases}$$

$$yī + \quad ^\backslash \quad \rightarrow yí + \quad ^\backslash \quad \text{For example: yí biàn (once)}$$

2 普通话声母韵母拼合总表
Table of Combinations of Initials and Finals in Common Speech

There are more than 400 meaningful syllables in the common speech of modern Chinese. If we add the four tones to these, we can distinguish more than 1,200 syllables. The syllables from Lesson 1 to Lesson 6 are shown in the table on the next page.

四、语法   Grammar

■ 动词谓语句   Sentences with a verbal predicate

The main part of the predicate in a sentence with a verbal predicate is a verb. The object usually follows the verb. One of its negative forms is made by placing the adverb "不" before the verb.

普通话声母韵母拼合总表
Table of Combinations of Initials and Finals in Common Speech

Initials \ Finals	a	o	e	-i[ɿ]	-i[ʅ]	er	ai	ei	ao	ou	an	en	ang	eng	i	ia	ie	iao	iou (iu)	ian	in	iang	ing	u	ua	uo	uai	uei (ui)	uan	uen (un)	uang	ueng	ong	ü	üe	üan	ün	iong
	a	o	e			er	ai	ei	ao	ou	an	en	ang	eng	yi	ya	ye	yao	you	yan	yin	yang	ying	wu	wa	wo	wai	wei	wan	wen	wang	weng		yu	yue	yuan	yun	yong
b	ba	bo					bai	bei	bao		ban	ben	bang	beng	bi		bie	biao		bian	bin		bing	bu														
p	pa	po					pai	pei	pao	pou	pan	pen	pang	peng	pi		pie	piao		pian	pin		ping	pu														
m	ma	mo	me				mai	mei	mao	mou	man	men	mang	meng	mi		mie	miao	miu	mian	min		ming	mu														
f	fa	fo						fei		fou	fan	fen	fang	feng										fu														
d	da		de				dai	dei	dao	dou	dan	den	dang	deng	di		die	diao	diu	dian			ding	du		duo		dui	duan	dun			dong					
t	ta		te				tai		tao	tou	tan		tang	teng	ti		tie	tiao		tian			ting	tu		tuo		tui	tuan	tun			tong					
n	na		ne				nai	nei	nao	nou	nan	nen	nang	neng	ni		nie	niao	niu	nian	nin	niang	ning	nu		nuo			nuan				nong	nü	nüe			
l	la		le				lai	lei	lao	lou	lan		lang	leng	li	lia	lie	liao	liu	lian	lin	liang	ling	lu		luo			luan	lun			long	lü	lüe			
g	ga		ge				gai	gei	gao	gou	gan	gen	gang	geng										gu	gua	guo	guai	gui	guan	gun	guang		gong					
k	ka		ke				kai	kei	kao	kou	kan	ken	kang	keng										ku	kua	kuo	kuai	kui	kuan	kun	kuang		kong					
h	ha		he				hai	hei	hao	hou	han	hen	hang	heng										hu	hua	huo	huai	hui	huan	hun	huang		hong					
j															ji	jia	jie	jiao	jiu	jian	jin	jiang	jing											ju	jue	juan	jun	jiong
q															qi	qia	qie	qiao	qiu	qian	qin	qiang	qing											qu	que	quan	qun	qiong
x															xi	xia	xie	xiao	xiu	xian	xin	xiang	xing											xu	xue	xuan	xun	xiong
zh	zha		zhe		zhi		zhai	zhei	zhao	zhou	zhan	zhen	zhang	zheng										zhu	zhua	zhuo	zhuai	zhui	zhuan	zhun	zhuang		zhong					
ch	cha		che		chi		chai		chao	chou	chan	chen	chang	cheng										chu	chua	chuo	chuai	chui	chuan	chun	chuang		chong					
sh	sha		she		shi		shai	shei	shao	shou	shan	shen	shang	sheng										shu	shua	shuo	shuai	shui	shuan	shun	shuang							
r			re		ri				rao	rou	ran	ren	rang	reng										ru		ruo		rui	ruan	run			rong					
z	za		ze	zi			zai	zei	zao	zou	zan	zen	zang	zeng										zu		zuo		zui	zuan	zun			zong					
c	ca		ce	ci			cai		cao	cou	can	cen	cang	ceng										cu		cuo		cui	cuan	cun			cong					
s	sa		se	si			sai		sao	sou	san	sen	sang	seng										su		suo		sui	suan	sun			song					

Subject	Predicate			
	Adv / Time	V	O	吗？
Nǐ 你		yào 要	kāfēi 咖啡	ma? 吗？
Wǒmen 我们	dōu 都	xuéxí 学习	Hànyǔ. 汉语。	
Cāntīng 餐厅		zài 在	nǎr? 哪儿？	
Wǒ 我	bù 不	zhīdào. 知道。		
Wǒ 我		xìng 姓	Lù. 陆。	
Tā 她		jiào 叫	Lín Nà. 林娜。	
Nín 您	míngtiān 明天	yǒu 有	shíjiān 时间	ma? 吗？

五、汉字　Chinese Characters

1 汉字复合笔画（2）　Combined character strokes (2)

Stroke	Name	Example	Way to Write
⌐	shùzhé	山	The vertical stroke with a horizontal turn to the right, is written like the second stroke in "山".
⌐	shùtí	以	The vertical stroke with an upward turn to the right, is written like the first stroke in "以".
勹	shùzhézhé-gōu	马	The vertical stroke with a horizontal turn to the right, and then a downward turn and a hook, is written like the second stroke in "马".

Stroke	Name	Example	Way to Write
乙	héngzhéwān-gōu	九	The horizontal stroke with a downward turn to the left, and then a horizontal turn to the right and an upward hook, is written like the second stroke in "九".
ㄥ	piězhé	么	The downward stroke to the left, and then a horizontal turn to the right, is written like the second stroke in "么".
ㄑ	piědiǎn	女	The downward stroke to the left and then an extended dot to the right, is written like the first stroke in "女".

2 笔画组合 Combination of strokes

The relationship between strokes in a Chinese character can be essential to its meaning. There are three ways to combine strokes in a character.

(1) Adjacent (not attached) like "八", "儿", "二", "小";

(2) Crossing like "十", "大", "九", "夫";

(3) Connecting like "厂", "丁", "人", "山", "天".

3 认写基本汉字 Learn and write basic Chinese characters

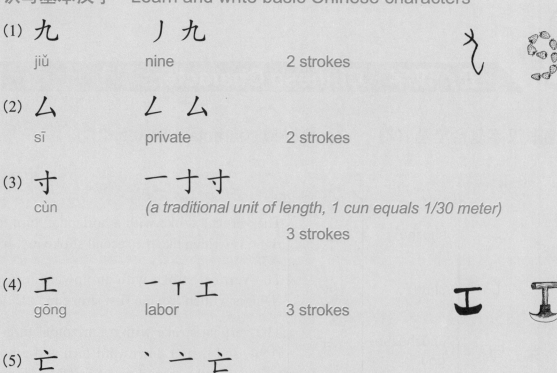

(1) 九   丿九
    jiǔ   nine   2 strokes

(2) 厶   ㄥ 厶
    sī   private   2 strokes

(3) 寸   一 寸 寸
    cùn   (a traditional unit of length, 1 cun equals 1/30 meter)
                                       3 strokes

(4) 工   一 丁 工
    gōng   labor   3 strokes

(5) 亡   丶 亠 亡
    wáng   to die   3 strokes

(6) 三　　　一 二 三

sān　　　three　　　3 strokes

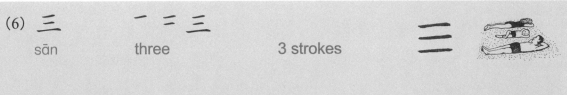

(7) 气（氣）　ノ ケ 仁 气

qì　　　air　　　4 strokes

(8) 立　　　丶 一 ヒ 六 立

lì　　　to stand　　　5 strokes

(9) 身　　　ノ イ 丹 自 自 身 身

shēn　　　body　　　7 strokes

Note: On the left side or in the middle of a character, "身" is written as "身".

(10) 兑　　　丶 丷 丷 凸 兮 兮 兑

duì　　　to exchange　　　7 strokes

4 认写课文中的汉字　Learn and write the Chinese characters in the texts

(1) 去 qù

去 → 土 ＋ ム　　　5 strokes

(2) 有意思 yǒu yìsi

有 → 广 ＋ 月　　　6 strokes
意 → 立 ＋ 日 ＋ 心　　　13 strokes
思 → 田 ＋ 心　　　9 strokes

(3) 天气 tiānqì （天氣）

天 → 一 ＋ 大　　　4 strokes

(4) 太 tài

太 → 大 ＋ 丶　　　4 strokes

(5) 什么 shénme （甚麼）

什 → 亻 + 十   4 strokes

么 → 丿 + 厶   3 strokes

(6) 时候 shíhou （時候）

时 → 日 + 寸   7 strokes

（"日", the "sun" side denotes time.）

候 → 亻 + 丨 + ⊐ + 矢   10 strokes

（丿 亻 忄 忭 佇 佇 佇 候 候）

(7) 现在 xiànzài （現在）

现 → 王 + 见   8 strokes

(8) 明天 míngtiān

明 → 日 + 月   8 strokes

（"日", the "sun" side and "月", the "moon" side denote light.）

(9) 时间 shíjiān （時間）

间 → 门 + 日   7 strokes

(10) 说 shuō （说）

说 → 讠 + 兑   9 strokes

忄 （shùxīnpángr, the "standing heart" side） 丶 丶 忄   3 strokes

（On the left side of a character, "心" is written as "忄".）

(11) 忙 máng

忙 → 忄 + 亡   6 strokes

(12) 谢谢 xièxie （謝謝）

谢 → 讠 + 身 + 寸   12 strokes

Beijing Opera

Beijing opera is a branch of traditional Chinese musical drama. It took shape in Beijing about 150 years ago and has been popular ever since. Beijing opera is a theatrical art synthesizing recitation, instrumental music, singing, dancing, acrobatics and martial arts, and featuring symbolic motions and stage design. The highly formulaic and suggestive movements of the actors are accompanied by the rhythmic beats of gongs and drums, or the haunting melodies of traditional instruments. All contribute to its uniqueness as a performing art. Beijing opera is deeply rooted in Chinese culture and still strongly appeals to many Chinese.

Today, Beijing opera can be enjoyed at Mei Lanfang Grand Theater, Chang'an Theater, or any of several other theaters in Beijing. Foreigners can also learn a bit about Beijing opera through the Chinese film *Farewell My Concubine* (《霸王别姬》Bàwáng Bié Jī).

The first six lessons of this textbook provide an overview of the phonetic system of Chinese language, which consists of 21 initials, 38 finals, and four basic tones. There are only a little over 1,200 ways of combining initials and finals in Chinese. Now that you can use *pinyin*, you should be able to read any Chinese syllable correctly.

A major goal of language learning is to acquire the ability to communicate in that language. For this purpose, you have learned how to respond to a number of basic social situations. In addition, you have met with more than 100 words and expressions, have learned 40 key sentences and have studied 22 sentences of classroom Chinese expressions.

So far, you have acquired 60 basic Chinese characters as well as more than 50 new words formed from them. You have also learned some rules of stroke order for Chinese characters. This elementary vocabulary will be useful when you start to learn compound words and continue to build your vocabulary.

第七课

Lesson

7

Nǐ rènshi bu rènshi tā
你 认识 不 认识 他
Do you know him?

From this lesson on, apart from continuing to work on improving your Chinese pronunciation, you will learn to talk about everyday situations using a greater variety of Chinese expressions than before. You will experiment with a larger number of Chinese sentences, and will further explore the culture, customs, and habits of Chinese-speaking peoples. This lesson will help you with making your acquaintances, discussing your studies, and asking questions in a new way.

一、课文 Text

🎧 31 （一）

林娜： 力波， 明天 开学， 我 很 高兴。 你 看， 他
Lín Nà: Lìbō, míngtiān kāixué, wǒ hěn gāoxìng. Nǐ kàn, tā

是 不 是 我们 学院 的 老师？
shì bu shì wǒmen xuéyuàn de lǎoshī?

丁力波： 我 问 一下。① 请问， 您 是 我们 学院
Dīng Lìbō: Wǒ wèn yíxià.   Qǐngwèn, nín shì wǒmen xuéyuàn

的 老师 吗？②
de lǎoshī ma?

张教授： 是， 我 是 语言 学院 的 老师。
Zhāng jiàoshòu: Shì, wǒ shì Yǔyán Xuéyuàn de lǎoshī.

丁力波： 您 贵姓？
Dīng Lìbō: Nín guìxìng?

初次见面

**Meeting someone for
the first time**

张教授： 我 姓 张， 我们
Zhāng jiàoshòu: Wǒ xìng Zhāng, wǒmen

认识 一下， 这 是 我 的 名片。
rènshi yíxià, zhè shì wǒ de míngpiàn.

丁力波： 谢谢。（看名片）啊， 您 是 张 教授。③ 我
Dīng Lìbō: Xièxie.   À, nín shì Zhāng jiàoshòu. Wǒ

张介元 ｜教授

语言学院经济系

地址：语言学院 26 楼 301 号
电话：62257892

叫 丁 力波， 她 叫
jiào Dīng Lìbō,   tā jiào

林 娜。 我们 都 是
Lín Nà. Wǒmen dōu shì

语言 学院 的 学生。
Yǔyán Xuéyuàn de xuésheng.

林娜： 您 是 语言 学院 的 教授， 认识 您，
Lín Nà: Nín shì Yǔyán Xuéyuàn de jiàoshòu, rènshi nín,

我们　很　高兴。
wǒmen　hěn　gāoxìng.

张教授：　认识　你们，　我　也　很　高兴。　你们　都
Zhāng jiàoshòu:　Rènshi　nǐmen,　wǒ　yě　hěn　gāoxìng.　Nǐmen　dōu

好　吗？
hǎo　ma?

林娜：　谢谢，　我们　都　很　好。　张　　教授，　您
Lín Nà:　Xièxie,　wǒmen　dōu　hěn　hǎo.　Zhāng　jiàoshòu,　nín

忙　不　忙？
máng　bu　máng?

张教授：　我　很　忙。　好，　你们　请　坐，　再见！
Zhāng jiàoshòu:　Wǒ　hěn　máng.　Hǎo,　nǐmen　qǐng　zuò,　zàijiàn!

丁力波：
Dīng Lìbō:　再见！
Zàijiàn!

林娜：
Lín Nà:

生词 New Words

1. 开学	kāixué	VO	school opens, term begins
开	kāi	V	to open, to start
*2. 很	hěn	Adv	very

*3.	高兴	gāoxìng	A	happy, pleased
	高	gāo	A	tall
4.	看	kàn	V	to watch, to look at 看老师，看这儿
*5.	问	wèn	V	to ask 问老师，问朋友
6.	一下	yíxià	Nu-M	*(used after a verb to indicate a short, quick, random, informal action)*
				介绍一下，认识一下，问一下，看一下
*7.	学院	xuéyuàn	N	institute, college 语言学院，汉语学院
8.	名片	míngpiàn	N	business card 我的名片，老师的名片
9.	啊	à	Int	ah, oh
10.	教授	jiàoshòu	N	professor
	教	jiào	V	to teach, to instruct
11.	丁力波	Dīng Lìbō	PN	(name of a Canadian student)
12.	张	Zhāng	PN	(a surname)

注释　Notes

① 我问一下。

　　"一下" is used after a verb to indicate that an action is of short duration, or indicate an attempt. It can soften the tone of an expression so that it sounds less formal. For example: "认识一下"，"介绍一下"，"去一下"，"进来一下"，"说一下"，"坐一下".

　　"我来介绍一下" and "我们认识一下" are expressions commonly used when people meet each other for the first time.

② 您是我们学院的老师吗？

　　To indicate the place or organization where one works, plural pronouns are often used as modifiers. For example, the following phrases are used: "他们学院"，"你们系"，"我们国家 (guójiā, country) "，rather than "他学院"，"你系"，"我国家".

③ 啊，您是张教授。

　　"啊" is read in the fourth tone, indicating a sudden understanding or expressing admiration.

🎧 32 （二）

丁力波： 林 娜，那 是 谁？
Dīng Lìbō: Lín Nà, nà shì shéi?

林娜： 那 是 马 大为。 你 认识 不 认识 他？
Lín Nà: Nà shì Mǎ Dàwéi. Nǐ rènshi bu rènshi tā?

丁力波： 我 不 认识 他。
Dīng Lìbō: Wǒ bú rènshi tā.

林娜： 我 来 介绍 一下。 你 好， 大为， 这 是 我
Lín Nà: Wǒ lái jièshào yíxià. Nǐ hǎo, Dàwéi, zhè shì wǒ

朋友——
péngyou—

丁力波： 你 好！ 我 姓 丁， 叫 丁 力波。 请问， 你 叫
Dīng Lìbō: Nǐ hǎo! Wǒ xìng Dīng, jiào Dīng Lìbō. Qǐngwèn, nǐ jiào

什么 名字？④
shénme míngzi?

马大为： 我 的 中文 名字 叫 马 大为。⑤ 你 是 不 是
Mǎ Dàwéi: Wǒ de Zhōngwén míngzi jiào Mǎ Dàwéi. Nǐ shì bu shì

中国 人？
Zhōngguó rén?

丁力波： 我 是 加拿大 人。 我 妈妈 是 中国 人， 我
Dīng Lìbō: Wǒ shì Jiānádà rén. Wǒ māma shì Zhōngguó rén, wǒ

爸爸 是 加拿大 人。 你 是 哪 国 人？
bàba shì Jiānádà rén. Nǐ shì nǎ guó rén?

马大为： 我 是 美国 人。你 学习 什么 专业？
Mǎ Dàwéi: Wǒ shì Měiguó rén. Nǐ xuéxí shénme zhuānyè?

丁力波： 我 学习 美术 专业， 你 呢？
Dīng Lìbō: Wǒ xuéxí měishù zhuānyè, nǐ ne?

马大为：我 学习 文学 专业。
Mǎ Dàwéi: Wǒ xuéxí wénxué zhuānyè.

现在 我 学习 汉语。
Xiànzài wǒ xuéxí Hànyǔ.

林娜：现在 我们 都 学习 汉语，也 都 是 汉语 系
Lín Nà: Xiànzài wǒmen dōu xuéxí Hànyǔ, yě dōu shì Hànyǔ xì

的 学生。
de xuésheng.

谈专业
Talking about one's major

生词 New Words

*1. 谁	shéi	QPr	who, whom
*2. 来	lái	V	to come
3. 介绍	jièshào	V	to introduce 介绍林娜，介绍语言学院
4. 名字	míngzi	N	name 你的名字，叫什么名字
5. 中文	Zhōngwén	N	Chinese 中文名字，中文名片
*6. 爸爸	bàba	N	dad
*7. 学习	xuéxí	V	to learn, to study 学习中文，学习汉语
学	xué	V	to learn, to study 学中文，学语言
8. 专业	zhuānyè	N	major, speciality 中文专业，汉语专业，语言专业
9. 美术	měishù	N	fine arts 学习美术，美术专业
美	měi	A	beautiful
10. 文学	wénxué	N	literature 中国文学，文学专业
11. 系	xì	N	faculty, department 汉语系，语言系，中文系
*12. 马大为	Mǎ Dàwéi	PN	(name of an American student)
*13. 加拿大	Jiānádà	PN	Canada
*14. 美国	Měiguó	PN	the United States of America

补充生词 Supplementary Words

1. 物理	wùlǐ	N	physics
2. 化学	huàxué	N	chemistry
3. 数学	shùxué	N	mathematics
4. 音乐	yīnyuè	N	music
5. 历史	lìshǐ	N	history
6. 哲学	zhéxué	N	philosophy
7. 经济	jīngjì	N	economics
8. 教育	jiàoyù	N	education
9. 选修	xuǎnxiū	V	to take an elective course
10. 文化	wénhuà	N	culture

注释　Notes

④ 你叫什么名字？

　　This is a casual way to ask someone's name, applicable to an adult talking with a child, or used among youngsters. The answer is usually one's full name. For example: "我叫丁力波". You may also answer by giving your surname first, and then your full name. For example: "我姓丁，叫丁力波".

⑤ 我的中文名字叫马大为。

　　A noun can be placed directly before a noun as its attributive modifier. For example: "中文名字", "汉语老师", "中国人". To render a non-Chinese name into Chinese, we may choose two or three characters based on the pronunciation or meaning of the original name. David March, for example, may be rendered into Chinese as "马大为", and Natalie Lynn as "林娜"; the surname "White" can be translated as "白", and a girl by the name of Amy can be called "爱美". Both "中文" and "汉语" refer to the Chinese language. "中文" has a broader meaning, referring to the Chinese language in both its written and spoken forms. Originally, "汉语" referred only to the spoken language of the Han people. Today, it is often used to refer to both the written and spoken forms of the Han language. These words are now used interchangeably by most people.

二、练习 Exercises

练习与运用 Drills and Practice 33

核心句 KEY SENTENCES

1. 他是不是我们学院的老师？

2. 你认识不认识他？

3. 我来介绍一下。

4. 我的中文名字叫马大为。

5. 你学习什么专业？

6. 我学习美术专业，你呢？

7. 现在我们都学习汉语，也都是汉语系的学生。

---

1. 熟读下列词组 Read the following phrases until you learn them by heart

（1）看一下　说一下　介绍一下　认识一下　学习一下

（2）认识不认识　知道不知道　学习不学习　是不是　看不看
　　问不问　要不要　在不在　去不去　说不说

（3）我爸爸　你妈妈　我朋友　她男朋友　我们老师　你们学院

（4）我的名片　他的名字　我们学院的老师　语言学院的学生　中文系的教授

（5）中国人　加拿大人　美国人　中国老师　加拿大朋友　美国学生
　　男朋友　女朋友　男老师　女老师　男（学）生　女（学）生
　　男人　女人

---

2. 句型替换 Pattern drills

（1）A：那是谁？

　　B：那是我朋友。

　　A：他/她姓什么？

　　B：他/她姓马。

她男朋友	张
加拿大学生	丁
英国记者	林

（2）A：谁是王小姐？

B：她/他是王小姐。

A：王小姐叫什么名字？

B：王小姐叫王玉文。

宋先生	宋华
张老师	张林生
林小姐	林娜

（3）A：他/她是你们老师吗？

B：他/她不是我们老师，

　　他/她是我朋友。

你学生	我朋友
中文老师	美术老师
张教授	杨老师

（4）A：你是不是中国人？

B：不是，我是加拿大人。

A：他也是加拿大人吗？

B：是，他也是加拿大人。

老师	学生
美国学生	英国学生
中文系的学生	美术系的学生

（5）A：这是不是你的名片？

B：这不是我的名片。

A：这是谁的名片？

B：这是她的名片。

丁力波	马大为
张教授	王医生
你们老师	他们老师

（6）A：你认识不认识马大为？

B：我认识马大为。

A：他/她是哪国人？

B：他/她是加拿大人。

林小姐	英国
王医生	中国
白教授	美国

（7）A：他<u>不是汉语系的学生</u>，你呢？
　　B：<u>我也不是汉语系的学生</u>。
　　A：<u>谁是汉语系的学生</u>？
　　B：<u>林娜 是汉语系的学生</u>。

是语言学院的教授　张先生
忙　　　　　　　　陆雨平
学习物理(wùlǐ)　　王波

（8）A：你的专业是不是汉语？
　　B：不是。
　　A：你学习什么专业？
　　B：我学习<u>美术</u>专业，你呢？
　　A：我学习<u>文学</u>专业。

数学(shùxué)　　历史(lìshǐ)
化学(huàxué)　　哲学(zhéxué)
音乐(yīnyuè)　　经济(jīngjì)

3. 看图造句　Make sentences according to the pictures

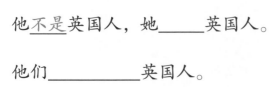

他<u>是</u>学生，她<u>也</u>是学生。

他们<u>都</u>是学生。

他<u>是</u>老师，她＿＿＿＿老师。

他们＿＿＿＿＿＿老师。

他<u>不是</u>英国人，她＿＿＿＿英国人。

他们＿＿＿＿＿＿英国人。

她们<u>是</u>中国人，她_____中国人。

她们_____中国人。

❷

A：今天天气<u>好不好</u>？

B：今天天气很好。

A：他_____？

B：他很忙。

A：他_____？

B：他不高兴。

4. 会话练习 Conversation practice

【初次见面 Meeting someone for the first time】

（1）A：请问，您贵姓？

B：我姓_____，叫_____。您呢？

A：我叫_____。这是我的名片。

B：谢谢。

（2）A：我们认识一下。我叫_____。你叫什么名字？

B：我叫 David March。我的中文名字叫马大为。

（3）A：请问，您是哪国人？

B：我是_____。你呢？

A：我是_____。

（4）A：请问，您是不是中国人？

B：我不是_____，我是_____。

（5）A：我介绍一下，这是＿＿＿＿，他是＿＿＿＿（国）人，是＿＿＿＿。

这是＿＿＿＿＿，她是＿＿＿＿（国）人，是＿＿＿＿＿。

B：认识你很高兴。

C：＿＿＿＿＿＿＿＿＿。

（6）你们好！我姓丁，叫丁力波，是加拿大人。我的专业是美术。现在我学习汉语，是语言学院汉语系的学生。认识你们，我很高兴。

【谈专业　Talking about one's major】

（1）A：小丁，你是不是汉语系的学生？

B：我是汉语系的学生。你学习什么专业？

A：我学习教育（jiàoyù）专业。你哥哥的专业是什么？

B：我哥哥的专业是＿＿＿＿＿。

（2）A：你们明天开学吗？

B：我们明天开学。

A：你的专业是不是汉语？

B：不是，我的专业是美术。

A：你选修（xuǎnxiū）什么？

B：我选修中国文化（wénhuà）。

5. 交际练习 Communication exercises

（1）You come across a student whom you don't know. How do you carry out a conversation with him / her in order to know more about him / her?

（2）Two of your friends do not know each other. How do you introduce them to each other?

（3）How do you introduce yourself in a meeting?

（4）How do you ask about your new friend's major?

（5）Fill in your information in the Student's Registration Form, then ask your friend's information and fill in the form for him / her.

学生登记表 Students' Registration Form

姓名 name	性别 sex	年龄 age	国籍 nationality	学院/系
丁力波	男	21	加拿大	语言学院汉语系
林娜	女	20	英国	语言学院汉语系
马大为	男	22	美国	语言学院汉语系

阅读与复述 Reading Comprehension and Paraphrasing

他们是不是学生?

是,他们都是语言学院的学生。你不认识他们,我介绍一下。他们都有中国姓,有中文名字。这是林娜,她是英国人。他是美国人,他姓马,他的中文名字很有意思,叫大为。他叫丁力波,爸爸是加拿大人,妈妈是中国人,他是加拿大人。马大为的专业是文学,丁力波的专业是美术。现在他们都学习汉语。

那是语言学院的汉语老师:女老师姓陈,男老师姓杨。他们都是汉语系的老师,也都是中国人。张教授也是语言学院的老师,他很忙。你看,这是张教授的名片。

王小姐不是老师,她是语言学院的医生。

三、语法 Grammar

1 表领属关系的定语 Attributives expressing possession

In Chinese, an attributive must be placed before the word it modifies. When a pronoun or a noun is used as an attributive to express possession, the structural particle "的" is usually required.

$$NP \ / \ Pr \ + \ 的 \ + \ N$$

我	的	名片
哥哥	的	咖啡
语言学院	的	老师

When a personal pronoun functions as an attributive and the modified word is a noun referring to a relative or the name of a work unit, the "的" between the attributive and the word it modifies may be omitted. For example: "我妈妈", "你爸爸", "他们家", "我们学院".

2　正反疑问句　V / A-not-V / A questions

A question can also be formed by juxtaposing the affirmative and negative forms of the main element of the predicate (verb or adjective) in a sentence.

$$V/A + 不 + V/A + O$$

Subject	Predicate		
	V / A	不　V / A	O
你	忙	不　　忙?	
你们	认识	不认识	他?
力波	是	不是	中国人?

The response to such a question may be a complete sentence (affirmative or negative) or a sentence with its subject or object omitted. One may respond with "是" (affirmative answer) or "不是" (negative answer) at the beginning of an answer to a "是不是" question. For example:

（1）（我）很忙。　　　　（我）不忙。

（2）（我们）认识（他）。　（我们）不认识（他）。

（3）（陆雨平）是中国人。　是，陆雨平是中国人。

　　　（力波）不是中国人。　不是，力波不是中国人。

3　用"呢"构成的省略式问句　Abbreviated questions with "呢"

An abbreviated question with "呢" is made by adding "呢" directly after a pronoun or a noun. The meaning of the question, however, must be clearly indicated in the previous sentence.

$$Pr / NP + 呢?$$

我<u>很好</u>，你呢？　　　　　（你呢？　　　＝你好吗？）

你<u>不忙</u>，你男朋友呢？　（你男朋友呢？　＝你男朋友忙吗？）

你是<u>加拿大人</u>，他呢？　（他呢？　　　＝他是加拿大人吗？）

林娜<u>学习汉语</u>，马大为呢？（马大为呢？　＝马大为学习汉语吗？）

4　副词"也"和"都"的位置　The position of the adverbs "也" and "都"

The adverbs "也" and "都" must occur after the subject and before the predicative verb or adjective. For example: "她也是加拿大人", "他们都是加拿大人". One cannot say "也她是加拿大人", "都他们是加拿大人".

If both "也" and "都" modify the predicate, "也" must be put before "都".

$$也 / 都 + V / A$$

Subject	Predicate	
	Adv	V / A
丁力波		是加拿大人。
丁力波		认识他。
丁力波	很	忙。
她	也	是加拿大人。
她	也	认识他。
她	也很	忙。
他们	都	是加拿大人。
他们	都	认识他。
他们	都很	忙。
我们	也都	是加拿大人。
我们	也都	认识他。
我们	也都很	忙。

In a negative sentence, "也" must occur before "不". "都" may be put before or after "不", but the meanings of "都 不" and "不 都" are different.

也 / 都　+　不　+　V / A

Subject	Predicate	
	Adv	V　/　A
她	不	是老师。
你	也不	是老师。
我们	都不	是老师。(none of us)
我们	不都	是老师。(not all of us)

四、汉字　Chinese Characters

1 汉字的部件　Chinese character components

There are three aspects as to the structure of a Chinese character: the strokes, the components and the whole character. For example, the character "木" consists of four strokes: "一", "丨", "丿", "乀". It is a basic character and is also used as a component for some other characters. For example, "林" consists of two "木" characters. The components are the core structure of a Chinese character. Chinese characters can be divided into character-parts and non-character-parts. For example, "院" can be divided into the following three parts: "阝", "宀" and "元", of which "元" is a character-part, while "阝" and "宀" are the non-character-parts. The key to learning Chinese characters well is to master their components.

2 认写基本汉字　Learn and write basic Chinese characters

(1) 开（開）　一 二 于 开

kāi　　　　　　　　to open　　　　　　4 strokes

Note: "开" looks like the bar or the bolt of a door; when the "二" in "开" is removed, the door opens.

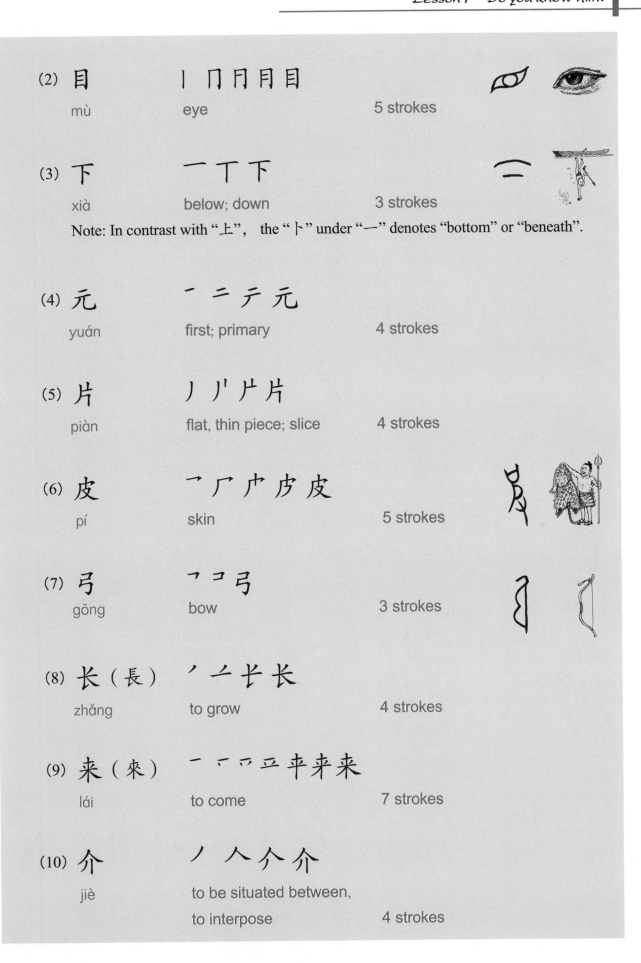

(2) 目　　　｜ 冂 月 月 目

mù　　　eye　　　5 strokes

(3) 下　　　一 丁 下

xià　　　below; down　　　3 strokes

Note: In contrast with "上", the "卜" under "一" denotes "bottom" or "beneath".

(4) 元　　　一 二 テ 元

yuán　　　first; primary　　　4 strokes

(5) 片　　　丿 丿' 尸 片

piàn　　　flat, thin piece; slice　　　4 strokes

(6) 皮　　　一 厂 广 皮 皮

pí　　　skin　　　5 strokes

(7) 弓　　　フ コ 弓

gōng　　　bow　　　3 strokes

(8) 长（長）　丿 二 长 长

zhǎng　　　to grow　　　4 strokes

(9) 来（來）　一 一 冂 卫 平 来 来

lái　　　to come　　　7 strokes

(10) 介　　　丿 人 介 介

jiè　　　to be situated between,
　　　to interpose　　　4 strokes

(11)　父　　　丶 八 分 父

　　　fù　　　　father　　　　　　　　　　　　4 strokes

(12)　巴　　　フ フ 巴 巴

　　　bā　　　　to wait anxiously; to cling to;
　　　　　　　　a suffix　　　　　　　　　　4 strokes

Note: "巴" stands on the right side or at the bottom of a Chinese character, and denotes the pronunciation of the character.

(13)　习（習）　フ コ 习

　　　xí　　　　to study　　　　　　　　　　3 strokes

(14)　专（專）　一 二 专 专

　　　zhuān　　　special　　　　　　　　　　4 strokes

Note that the third stroke of "专" is one stroke, not two strokes.

(15)　业（業）　丨 刂 刂 业 业

　　　yè　　　　business, trade　　　　　　　5 strokes

(16)　羊　　　丶 丷 丷 兰 兰 羊　　

　　　yáng　　　sheep, goat　　　　　　　　6 strokes

(17)　术（術）　一 十 才 木 术

　　　shù　　　　art, skill　　　　　　　　　5 strokes

Note that "术" has one more dot than "木".

(18)　系　　　一 工 至 玄 至 系 系　　

　　　xì　　　　department, system　　　　7 strokes

(19)　为（爲）　丶 丷 为 为

　　　wéi　　　　to act, to do　　　　　　　4 strokes

3 认写课文中的汉字 Learn and write the Chinese characters in the texts

彳 (shuānglìrénr, "亻" is called the "single-standing-person" side; "彳" is called the "double-standing-person" side.) ノ ㇒ 彳 3 strokes

艮 gèn ㇇ ㇕ ㇛ 㔾 艮 艮 6 strokes

(1) 很 hěn

很 → 彳 + 艮 9 strokes

亠 (jīngzìtóur, the "capital" top) 丶 亠 2 strokes

(2) 高兴 gāoxìng (高興)

高 → 亠 + 口 + 冂 + 口 10 strokes

兴 → ⺍ + 一 + 八 6 strokes

龵 (kànzìtóur, in a multi-component character, the vertical stroke with a hook "亅" in "手" is written as a downward stroke to the left "ノ".)

一 二 三 龵 4 strokes

(3) 看 kàn

看 → 龵 + 目 9 strokes

(Holding a hand "手" above one's eyes "目" to gaze.)

阝 (zuǒ'ěrdāor, the "left-ear" side) ㇋ 阝 2 strokes

(4) 学院 xuéyuàn (學院)

院 → 阝 + 宀 + 元 9 strokes

(5) 名片 míngpiàn

名 → 夕 + 口 6 strokes

(6) 啊 à

啊 → 口 + 阝 + 可 10 strokes

子 (zǐzìpángr, the "son" side) (The horizontal stroke in the character "子" is written as an upward stroke, when the character becomes the left side component of another character.)　フ了子　　　　　　　3 strokes

攵 (fǎnwénpángr, the "tapping" side) (The dot in "文" is written as "丿", a downward stroke to the left, when the character becomes the right side component of another character.)　丿⺊夂攵　　　　　4 strokes

爫 (zhǎozìtóur, the "claw" top)　丿⺀⺈爫　　　　　　4 strokes

冖 (tūbǎogàir, the "bald cover" top)　丶冖　　　　　　2 strokes

(7) 教授 jiàoshòu

教 → 耂 + 孑 + 攵　　　　　11 strokes
授 → 扌 + 爫 + 冖 + 又　　11 strokes

(8) 丁力波 Dīng Lìbō

波 → 氵 + 皮　　　　　　　8 strokes

(9) 张 zhāng（張）

张 → 弓 + 长　　　　　　　7 strokes
(The meaning side is "弓", and the phonetic side is "长".)

隹 zhuī　　丿亻亻亻仁仹隹隹　　　8 strokes

(10) 谁 shéi（誰）

谁 → 讠 + 隹　　　　　　　10 strokes

纟（糹）(jiǎosīpángr, the "entangled silk" side）　乚纟纟　3 strokes

(11) 介绍 jièshào（介紹）

绍 → 纟 + 刀 + 口　　　　　8 strokes

宀 (bǎogàitóur, the "roof" top)　丶丷宀　　　　3 strokes

(12) 名字 míngzi

字 → 宀 + 子　　　　6 strokes

(13) 爸爸 bàba

爸 → 父 + 巴　　　　8 strokes

("父" suggests the meaning and "巴" denotes the pronunciation.)

羊 (měizìtóur, the "beautiful" top)　丶丷⺍⺌⺍羊　　6 strokes

(14) 美术 měishù（美術）

美 → 羊 + 大　　　　9 strokes

(15) 加拿大 Jiānádà

加 → 力 + 口　　　　5 strokes

拿 → 人 + 丶 + 口 + 手　　　10 strokes

(Hands are joined together to denote the meaning of "taking".)

Chinese Names

Chinese names are made up of two parts: family names (*xing*) and given names (*ming*). Family names always precede given names in Chinese, which is similar to Japanese names. While family names generally come from the father's side (nowadays we also find family names which come from the mother's side), parents choose given names for their children.

There are over 1,000 Chinese family names. Li, Wang, Liu, and Chen are among the most popular ones. Li is the most common surname. There are about 100 million people who have this surname.

The majority of family names in Chinese consist of a single character, but there are some, such as Ouyang and Sima, that have two, and hence are known as disyllabic or double-character family names (*fuxing*). In China's mainland, women retain their family names after marriage. On the other hand, it is common to have single-character or double-character given names, such as in Song Hua and Lu Yuping. Due to the limited number of characters used in family names as well as in given names, it is not unusual for people to have identical names in China.

The Most Common Chinese Surnames

李 (Lǐ)	王 (Wáng)	张 (Zhāng)	刘 (Liú)
陈 (Chén)	杨 (Yáng)	赵 (Zhào)	黄 (Huáng)
周 (Zhōu)	吴 (Wú)	徐 (Xú)	孙 (Sūn)
胡 (Hú)	朱 (Zhū)	高 (Gāo)	林 (Lín)
何 (Hé)	郭 (Guō)	马 (Mǎ)	罗 (Luó)

第八课

Lesson 8

Nǐmen jiā yǒu jǐ kǒu rén

你们 家 有 几 口 人

How many people are there in your family?

This lesson will teach you to describe your family members, and how to talk about your university and department. You will learn to count to 100, and ask questions related to numbers and amount. Finally, we will introduce you to measure words, a grammatical category particularly well-developed in the Chinese language.

一、课文 Text

🎧 34 (一)

林娜: 这 是 不 是 你们 家
Lín Nà: Zhè shì bu shì nǐmen jiā

的 照片?
de zhàopiàn?

王小云: 是 啊。①
Wáng Xiǎoyún: Shì a.

林娜: 我 看 一下。你们 家 有 几 口 人?
Lín Nà: Wǒ kàn yíxià. Nǐmen jiā yǒu jǐ kǒu rén?

王小云: 我们 家 有 四 口 人。
Wáng Xiǎoyún: Wǒmen jiā yǒu sì kǒu rén.

谈家庭
Talking about one's family

这 是 我 爸爸、我
Zhè shì wǒ bàba、 wǒ

妈妈, 这 是 我 哥哥 和 我。② 你们 家 呢?
māma, zhè shì wǒ gēge hé wǒ. Nǐmen jiā ne?

林娜: 我 有 妈妈, 有 一 个 姐姐 和 两 个 弟弟。③
Lín Nà: Wǒ yǒu māma, yǒu yí ge jiějie hé liǎng ge dìdi.

我们 家 一共 有 六 口 人。
Wǒmen jiā yígòng yǒu liù kǒu rén.

王小云: 这 是 五 口 人, 还 有 谁?④
Wáng Xiǎoyún: Zhè shì wǔ kǒu rén, hái yǒu shéi?

林娜: 还 有 贝贝。
Lín Nà: Hái yǒu Bèibei.

王小云: 贝贝 是 你 妹妹 吗?
Wáng Xiǎoyún: Bèibei shì nǐ mèimei ma?

林娜：不，贝贝是我的小狗。
Lín Nà: Bù, Bèibei shì wǒ de xiǎo gǒu.

王小云：小　狗也是一口人吗？
Wáng Xiǎoyún: Xiǎo gǒu yě shì yì kǒu rén ma?

林娜：贝贝是　我们　的好　朋友，　当然　是　我们　家
Lín Nà: Bèibei shì wǒmen de hǎo péngyou, dāngrán shì wǒmen jiā

的人。我有一　张　贝贝的　照片，　你看！
de rén. Wǒ yǒu yì zhāng Bèibei de zhàopiàn, nǐ kàn!

王小云：真　可爱。
Wáng Xiǎoyún: Zhēn kě'ài.

林娜：你们家有　小　狗吗？
Lín Nà: Nǐmen jiā yǒu xiǎo gǒu ma?

王小云：我们　家　没有　小　狗。林　娜，你有　没有　男
Wáng Xiǎoyún: Wǒmen jiā méiyǒu xiǎo gǒu. Lín Nà, nǐ yǒu méiyǒu nán

朋友？
péngyou?

林娜：我　有男　朋友。
Lín Nà: Wǒ yǒu nán péngyou.

| 问职业 |
| **Asking about someone's occupation** |

王小云：他做　什么　工作？
Wáng Xiǎoyún: Tā zuò shénme gōngzuò?

林娜：他　是　医生。
Lín Nà: Tā shì yīshēng.

生词 New Words

1.	家	jiā	N	family, home 我们家，你们家，他们家
2.	几	jǐ	Qpr	how many, how much
3.	口	kǒu	M	(a measure word mainly for the number of people in a family) 几口人，五口人
4.	照片	zhàopiàn	N	picture, photo 我的照片，我们家的照片

5.	和	hé	Conj	and 爸爸和妈妈，哥哥和我，你和他
6.	个	gè	M	(*a measure word for general use*) 九个系，几个弟弟，一个朋友，五个医生，七个学院
7.	姐姐	jiějie	N	elder sister
8.	两	liǎng	Nu	two 两口人，两个姐姐，两个老师，两个系
*9.	弟弟	dìdi	N	younger brother
10.	一共	yígòng	Adv	altogether 一共有六口人
11.	还	hái	Adv	in addition; still 还有，还要，还认识
12.	妹妹	mèimei	N	younger sister
13.	小	xiǎo	A	little, small 小弟弟，小妹妹
14.	狗	gǒu	N	dog 小狗，我的小狗
15.	当然	dāngrán	Adv	of course 当然是，当然去
*16.	张	zhāng	M	(*a measure word for flat objects*) 两张名片
17.	真	zhēn	A /Adv	real; really 真的，真忙，真高兴，真有意思
18.	可爱	kě'ài	A	lovely, cute 真可爱，可爱的贝贝，可爱的小狗
	爱	ài	V	to love 爱爸爸，爱妈妈，爱弟弟妹妹
19.	没	méi	Adv	not 没有
*20.	男	nán	A	male
21.	做	zuò	V	to do, to be, to make
22.	工作	gōngzuò	V/ N	to work; work, job 工作一年；做什么工作
*23.	王小云	Wáng Xiǎoyún	PN	(name of a Chinese student)
24.	贝贝	Bèibei	PN	(name of a dog)

注释　Notes

① 是啊。

　　"啊" is a modal particle expressing affirmation.

② 这是我哥哥和我。

　　The conjunction "和" is generally used to connect pronouns, nouns or noun phrases, e.g. "他和她", "哥哥和弟弟", "我们老师和你们老师", "和"cannot be used to connect two clauses, and is seldom used to connect two verbs.

③ 我有一个姐姐和两个弟弟。

When the numeral "2" is used with a measure word in Chinese, the character "两" is used instead of "二", for example: "两张照片", "两个人" (we do not say "二张照片", "二个人"). When the numeral "2" is used alone, as in "一，二，三，……", or when it is used in a multi-digit number, we still use "二", even if it is followed by a measure word, for example: "十二", "二十二", "九十二个人", "二百".

④ 还有谁?

One of the uses of "还" is to make an additional remark. For example:

我有两个姐姐，还有一个弟弟。
我认识马大为，还认识他朋友。

🎧 35 （二）

林娜： 语言　学院　大 不 大?
Lín Nà: Yǔyán Xuéyuàn dà bu dà?

谈学校
Talking about one's school

王小云： 不 太 大。⑤
Wáng Xiǎoyún: Bú tài dà.

林娜： 语言　学院　有　多少　个 系?
Lín Nà: Yǔyán Xuéyuàn yǒu duōshao ge xì?

王小云： 有 十二 个 系。
Wáng Xiǎoyún: Yǒu shí'èr ge xì.

林娜： 你 喜欢　你们　外语 系 吗?
Lín Nà: Nǐ xǐhuan nǐmen wàiyǔ xì ma?

王小云： 我 很 喜欢　外语 系。
Wáng Xiǎoyún: Wǒ hěn xǐhuan wàiyǔ xì.

林娜： 你们　外语 系 有　多少　老师?
Lín Nà: Nǐmen wàiyǔ xì yǒu duōshao lǎoshī?

王小云： 外语 系 有 二十八 个　中国　老师, 十一 个
Wáng Xiǎoyún: Wàiyǔ xì yǒu èrshíbā ge Zhōngguó lǎoshī, shíyī ge

外国　老师。你们　系 呢?
wàiguó lǎoshī. Nǐmen xì ne?

林娜： 我们　汉语 系 很 大。我们　系 的 老师 也 很
Lín Nà: Wǒmen Hànyǔ xì hěn dà. Wǒmen xì de lǎoshī yě hěn

多， 有 一百 个。他们 都 是 中国 人。
duō，yǒu yìbǎi ge. Tāmen dōu shì Zhōngguó rén.

我们 系 没有 外国 老师。
Wǒmen xì méiyǒu wàiguó lǎoshī.

生词 New Words

1.	大	dà	A	big, large 大照片，不太大
2.	多少	duōshao	QPr	how many, how much 多少人，多少教授
	多	duō	A	many, much
	少	shǎo	A	few, less
3.	喜欢	xǐhuan	V	to like 喜欢汉语，喜欢老师
*4.	外语	wàiyǔ	N	foreign language 外语学院，外语老师
	外	wài	N	foreign, outside
	语	yǔ	N	language
5.	外国	wàiguó	N	foreign country 外国人，外国朋友，外国学生
6.	百	bǎi	Nu	hundred 一百，二百，三百，四百，八百

补充生词 Supplementary Words

1.	位	wèi	M	(a polite measure word for persons)
2.	车	chē	N	vehicle
3.	电脑	diànnǎo	N	computer
4.	词典	cídiǎn	N	dictionary
5.	孩子	háizi	N	child
6.	助教	zhùjiào	N	teaching assistant
7.	系主任	xìzhǔrèn	N	director of the department
8.	律师	lǜshī	N	lawyer
9.	工程师	gōngchéngshī	N	engineer

10.	爷爷	yéye	N	(paternal) grandfather
11.	外公	wàigōng	N	(maternal) grandfather
12.	年	nián	N	year
13.	前	qián	N	ago
14.	英语	Yīngyǔ	N	English
15.	常常	chángcháng	Adv	often

注释　Notes

⑤ 不太大。

　　The adverb "太" can be used in a negative construction."不太" means "不很……"，so "不太大"means "不很大", and "不太忙" means "不很忙". However, when "太" is used in an affirmative construction, such as "太大（了）", "太小（了）" or "太忙（了）", it often means "too much" or "excessively".

二、练习　Exercises

练习与运用　Drills and Practice 36

核心句　KEY SENTENCES

1. 你们家有几口人？
2. 这是五口人，还有谁？
3. 你有没有男朋友？
4. 我有男朋友。
5. 他做什么工作？
6. 你们外语系有多少老师？
7. 外语系有二十八个中国老师。

1. 熟读下列词组 Read the following phrases until you learn them by heart

（1）我们家　我们系　我们学院　我们老师
　　　你们家　你们系　你们学院　你们老师
　　　他们家　他们系　他们学院　他们老师

（2）我爸爸　我妈妈　我哥哥　我弟弟　我姐姐　我妹妹　我朋友
　　　你爸爸　你妈妈　你哥哥　你弟弟　你姐姐　你妹妹　你朋友

（3）中国老师　中国学生　中国朋友　中国教授　中国医生　中国人
　　　外国老师　外国学生　外国朋友　外国教授　外国医生　外国人

（4）我们的名片　我们家的小狗　我们学院的学生　我们系的外国老师
　　　他的照片　　他们家的照片　他们学院的老师　他们系的中国老师

（5）我和你　　　我们系和你们系　　我们系的老师和你们系的老师
　　　你们和他们　汉语学院和外语学院　汉语学院的学生和外语学院的学生

（6）两口人　　　　四口人　　　　　五口人　　　　　八口人

　　　十二张照片　　二十三张照片　　七十张名片　　　一百张名片

　　　八个学院　　　十个系　　　　　二十六位老师　　九百个学生

　　　两位教授　　　四位记者　　　　八十九个学生　　三十七个人

　　　几口人　　　　几张照片　　　　几个弟弟　　　　几个系

　　　多少人　　　　多少（张）照片　多少（个）朋友　多少（个）系

2. 句型替换　Pattern drills

（1）A：你有名片吗?
　　　B：我没有名片。你呢?
　　　A：我也没有名片。

●小狗
车(chē)
电脑(diànnǎo)
汉语词典(cídiǎn)

（2）A：他有没有中国朋友?
　　　B：他有中国朋友。
　　　A：他有几个中国朋友?
　　　B：他有两个中国朋友。

弟弟　　　●
姐姐
孩子 (háizi)

（3）A：你们系的外国学生多不多?
　　　B：我们系的外国学生不太多。
　　　A：你们系有多少外国学生?
　　　B：我们系有二十个外国学生。

●教授　　　　　3
　外国老师　　　2
　助教(zhùjiào)　7
　中国学生　　　15

（4）A：你们家有几口人？

　　　B：我们家有六口人。

　　　A：你爸爸做什么工作？

　　　B：他是教授。

3	记者	⬤
6	外语系系主任(xìzhǔrèn)	
4	律师 (lǜshī)	
5	工程师 (gōngchéngshī)	

（5）A：他们有几个孩子？

　　　B：他们有两个孩子，都很可爱。

　　　A：都是男孩子吗？

　　　B：不是，他们有一个男孩子和一个
　　　　女孩子。

3	1	2
4	2	2
5	2	3

3. 与你的同学口头做算术题　Solve the following math problems verbally

（1）E.g.　1＋2＝？　⟶　A：一加（jiā, plus）二是多少？

　　　　　　　　　　　　　B：一加二是三。

　　3＋7＝?　　　　　28＋22＝?

　　42＋35＝?　　　　56＋12＝?

（2）E.g.　15－12＝？　⟶　A：十五减（jiǎn, minus）十二是多少？

　　　　　　　　　　　　　B：十五减十二是三。

　　36－16＝?　　　　47－29＝?

　　53－38＝?　　　　90－69＝?

（3）E.g.　4×3＝？　⟶　A：四乘（chéng, times）三是多少？

　　　　　　　　　　　　　B：四乘三是十二。

　　4×5＝?　　　　　3×9＝?

　　6×7＝?　　　　　8×4＝?

4. 会话练习　Conversation practice

【谈家庭　Talking about one's family】

（1）A：你们家有几口人？

　　　B：＿＿＿＿＿＿＿＿＿。

A：你有没有哥哥和姐姐？

B：我有＿＿＿＿＿＿，没有＿＿＿＿。你呢？

A：我有一个＿＿＿＿，两个＿＿＿＿。

（2）A：你爸爸、妈妈做什么工作？

B：我爸爸是＿＿＿＿，妈妈是＿＿＿＿。你爸爸、妈妈呢？

A：我爸爸是＿＿＿＿，妈妈不工作。

B：你爷爷 (yéye) 和外公 (wàigōng) 呢？

A：我爷爷是＿＿＿＿，外公是＿＿＿＿。

（3）A：你哥哥做什么工作？

B：他是学生。

A：他学习什么专业？

B：他学习＿＿＿＿。

【谈学校　Talking about one's school】

（1）A：你们学院大不大？

B：＿＿＿＿＿＿＿＿＿＿＿＿＿。

A：你们学院有多少个系？

B：＿＿＿＿＿＿＿＿＿＿＿＿＿。

A：你们学院有多少个专业？

B：＿＿＿＿＿＿＿＿＿＿＿＿＿。

A：你喜欢你的专业吗？

B：我当然喜欢。

（2）A：你们系的老师多不多？

B：我们系的老师＿＿＿＿＿。

A：你们系有没有外国老师？

B：我们系有外国老师。

A：你们系的外国老师＿＿＿＿＿？

B：我们系的外国老师很少。

（3）A：你们汉语系的学生多不多？

　　　B：我们系的学生＿＿＿＿＿＿＿＿＿＿。

　　　A：你们系的男（学）生多吗？

　　　B：我们系的男（学）生很少，女（学）生＿＿＿＿＿＿＿＿＿。

　　　A：你喜欢不喜欢你们系？

　　　B：我很喜欢。

5. 交际练习　Communication exercises

（1）Introduce your family to your good friend.

（2）Talk about your friend's family.

（3）One of your friends inquires about your department. How do you answer him / her?

● 阅读与复述 Reading Comprehension and Paraphrasing

　　丁力波是加拿大学生。他家有五口人：爸爸、妈妈、哥哥、弟弟和他。他妈妈姓丁，叫丁云，是中国人。他爸爸叫古波（Gǔ Bō），是加拿大人。二十年（nián）前（qián），古波在加拿大认识了丁云，那时候，丁云学习英语（Yīngyǔ），古波学习汉语。

　　现在，丁云和古波都是汉语教授。他们有三个男孩子，没有女孩子。现在，丁力波和他哥哥、弟弟都在北京（Běijīng, Beijing）。丁力波是语言学院的学生，他学习汉语。他很喜欢语言学院。语言学院不太大，有十二个系。汉语系有一百个中国老师，学生都是外国人。外语系的学生是中国人，外语系有很多外国老师。丁力波的中国朋友都是外语系的学生。丁力波的哥哥学习历史专业，他弟弟的专业是经济。

　　他们的外婆也在北京。他们常常（chángcháng）去外婆家，他们很爱外婆。

三、语法　Grammar

1　11～100 的称数法　Numbers from 11 to 100

11 十一	12 十二	13 十三	……	19 十九	20 二十
21 二十一	22 二十二	23 二十三	……	29 二十九	30 三十
31 三十一	32 三十二	33 三十三	……	39 三十九	40 四十
⋮	⋮	⋮		⋮	⋮
81 八十一	82 八十二	83 八十三	……	89 八十九	90 九十
91 九十一	92 九十二	93 九十三	……	99 九十九	100 一百

2　数量词作定语　Numeral-measure words as attributives

In modern Chinese, a numeral alone cannot directly function as an attributive to modify a noun but must be combined with a measure word. All nouns have their own particular measure words, for example:

Nu	+	M	+	N
五		口		人
一		个		姐姐
十二		个		系
二十		张		照片

"个" is the most commonly used measure word, applied before nouns referring to people, things and units. (It is read in the neutral tone). "张" is usually used before nouns of objects with a flat surface such as paper, photographs, and business cards. The measure word "口" is used to express the number of people in a family when it is combined with "人". For example: "五口人". In other cases, "个" should be used. For example: "我们班有二十个人". One cannot say "我们班有二十口人".

3　"有"字句　Sentences with "有"

The sentence taking the verb "有" as the main element of the predicate usually expresses possession. Its negative form is formed by adding the adverb "没" before "有". (Note: "不" cannot be used here.) Its V-not-V form is "有没有".

(没) 有 + O

第八课　你们家有几口人
Lesson 8　How many people are there in your family?

123

Subject	Predicate		
	（没）有	Object	Particle
我	有	姐姐。	
你	有	名片	
语言学院	有	十二个系。	吗？
她	没有	男朋友。	
我们系	没有	外国老师。	
你	有没有	照片？	
你们家	有没有	小狗？	

If the subject of a sentence with "有" is a noun indicating a work unit, place or location, this kind of sentence with "有" is similar to the English sentence pattern of "There is / are...".

4 用"几"或"多少"提问　Questions with "几" or "多少"

The question pronouns "几" and "多少" are used to ask about numbers. "几" is often used to ask about numbers less than 10, and a measure word is needed between it and the noun. "多少" may be used to ask about any number, and the measure word after it is optional.

几 ＋ M ＋ N

A: 你们家有几口人？

B: 我家有五口人。

多少（＋ M）＋ N

A: 你们系有多少（个）学生？

B: 我们系有五百个学生。

四、汉字　Chinese Characters

1 汉字的结构(1)　Structure of Chinese characters (1)

Structurally speaking, Chinese characters fall into two categories: the single-component characters and the multi-component characters. All of the basic Chinese characters we have learned so far are single-component characters, such as "人", "手", "刀", "马", "牛", "羊", "日", "月", "水", "木", "上", "下". The multi-component characters consist of two or more components, such as "爸", "妈", "你", "们", "哪", "语". The order of writing components in a character is similar to the order of writing the strokes of a character. There are three basic types of configuration for multi-component characters:

The left-right structure ①

a. Equal left-right (the numbers indicate the order of writing the components)

| 1 | 2 | 朋 |

b. Small left-big right

| 1 | 2 | 汉 |

| 1 | 2 / 3 | 语 |

c. Big left-small right

| 1 | 2 | 那 |

| 1/2 | 3 | 都 |

2 认写基本汉字　Learn and write basic Chinese characters

(1) 几（幾）　　丿 几
jǐ　　how many　　2 strokes

(2) 禾　　一 二 千 禾 禾
hé　　standing grain　　5 strokes

(3) 个（個）　　丿 人 个
gè　　(a measure word)　　3 strokes

(4) 两（兩）　　一 厂 厅 丙 丙 两 两
liǎng　　two　　7 strokes

(5) 未　　一 二 十 丰 未
wèi　　not yet　　5 strokes

(6) 犬　　一 ナ 大 犬
quǎn　　dog　　4 strokes

(7) 云（雲）　　一 二 云 云
yún　　cloud　　4 strokes

(8) 少　　丨 丬 小 少
shǎo　　few, less　　4 strokes

(9) 士　　　一十士

shì　　　person　　　　　3 strokes

(10) 欠　　　ノ 仁 午 欠

qiàn　　　to owe　　　　　4 strokes

(11) 夕　　　ノ 夕 夕

xī　　　evening　　　　　3 strokes

(12) 卜　　　丨卜

bǔ　　　divination　　　2 strokes

(13) 百　　　一 厂 丆 万 百 百

bǎi　　　hundred　　　　6 strokes

3 认写课文中的汉字　Learn and write the Chinese characters in the texts

豕 shǐ　　　一 厂 丆 丏 豕 豕 豕　　　7 strokes

(1) 家 jiā

家 → 宀 + 豕　　　　10 strokes

(The "roof top", "宀", denotes a hut. A hut with a pig represents a house. The character "家" reflects the historical change in production mode of the ancient Chinese from hunting to animal husbandry.)

灬 (sìdiǎnr, the character "火" is written as "灬" at the bottom of a multi-component character, and is called the "four-dots" bottom.)

　　　丶 丶 灬 灬　　　4 strokes

(2) 照片 zhàopiàn

照 → 日 + 刀 + 口 + 灬　　　13 strokes

(The meaning part is "日" and the phonetic part is "召".)

(3) 和 hé

和 → 禾 + 口　　　8 strokes

丷 (dàobā, the "upside down eight" top) 、 丷 2 strokes

(4) 弟弟 dìdi

弟 → 丷 + 弔 (弔: フ ⁊ 弓 弔 弟) 7 strokes

(5) 一共 yígòng

共 → 龷 + 八 6 strokes

(6) 还 hái (還)

还 → 不 + 辶 7 strokes

(7) 妹妹 mèimei

妹 → 女 + 未 8 strokes

(The "female" side " 女 " indicates the character has a feminine connotation.)

犭 (quǎnzìpángr, the "dog" side) 丿 犭 犭 3 strokes

勹 (jùzìkuàngr, the "sentence" top) 丿 勹 2 strokes

(8) 狗 gǒu

狗 → 犭 + 勹 + 口 8 strokes

("犬" is the original character for "狗". It is written as "犭" on the left side of characters indicating animals.)

⺌ (shàngzìtóur, the "respecting" top) 丨 ⺌ ⺌ 3 strokes

彐 (xuězìdǐr, the "snow" bottom) フ ⁊ 彐 3 strokes

(9) 当然 dāngrán (當然)

当 → ⺌ + 彐 6 strokes

然 → 夕 + 犬 + 灬 12 strokes

(The combination of a "flesh" side, a "dog" side and a "fire" side, indicating "to roast dog meat over the fire", produces the character, "然", which originally meant "burning". Now this character carries different meanings.)

(10) 真 zhēn

真 → 十 + 且 + 八 10 strokes

(11) 可爱 kě'ài（可爱）

爱 → ⺤ ＋ 冖 ＋ 友　　　　10 strokes

殳 shū　丶 几 殳 殳　　　　4 strokes
(12) 没 méi

没 → 氵 ＋ 殳　　　　7 strokes

(13) 男 nán

男 → 田 ＋ 力　　　　7 strokes

(14) 做 zuò

做 → 亻 ＋ 古 ＋ 攵　　　　11 strokes

乍 zhà　丿 丿 ⺊ 乍 乍　　　　5 strokes
(15) 工作 gōngzuò

作 → 亻 ＋ 乍　　　　7 strokes

(16) 多少 duōshao

多 → 夕 ＋ 夕　　　　6 strokes

(17) 喜欢 xǐhuan（喜歡）

喜 → 士 ＋ 口 ＋ 丷 ＋ 一 ＋ 口　　　　12 strokes

欢 → 又 ＋ 欠　　　　6 strokes

(On the left side of a multi-component character, the second stroke of "又" is written as an extended dot.)

(18) 外语 wàiyǔ（外語）

外 → 夕 ＋ 卜　　　　5 strokes

Forms of Address for Family and Relatives

While the Chinese words for "mother", "father", "son", and "daughter" are used in ways similar to what we find in English, addressing siblings and relatives is fairly complex in Chinese. Two principles govern how Chinese family members are addressed: 1) relatives on the paternal side are distinguished from those on the mother's side; and 2) age relative to the speaker is taken into consideration.

The English words "grandfather" and "grandmother" can refer to grandparents on either the father's or mother's side. In Chinese, on the other hand, one has to indicate whether they are the father's or the mother's parents. The parents of one's father are *zufu* "grandfather" and *zumu* "grandmother" and are informally called *yeye* "grandpa" and *nainai* "grandma". However, the terms for one's mother's parents are *waizufu* "maternal grandfather" and *waizumu* "maternal grandmother", and in spoken Chinese, *waigong* (or *laoye*), and *waipo* (or *laolao*), meaning literally "maternal grandpa" and "maternal grandma" respectively.

In Chinese, special terms are used to indicate whether siblings are older or younger than the speaker. For instance, instead of a term equivalent to the English "brother", Chinese has *gege* "elder brother" and *didi* "younger brother". Similarly, "elder sister" is *jiejie*, and "younger sister" is *meimei*. In Chinese, one must always be sure to differentiate between elder and younger siblings and use the correct terms.

Chinese appellations for family members are highly specific. In addition to the ones introduced above, other common appellations include *bobo* (father's elder brother, uncle), *shushu* (father's younger brother, uncle), *gugu* (paternal aunt), *jiujiu* (maternal uncle), *yima* (maternal aunt), *saozi* (elder brother's wife, sister-in-law), *dimei* (younger brother's wife, sister-in-law), *jiefu* (elder sister's husband, brother-in-law), *meifu* (younger sister's husband, brother-in-law), *biaoge* (elder male cousin on mother's side), *biaojie* (elder female cousin on mother's side), *tangge* (elder male cousin on father's side), and *tangjie* (elder female cousin on father's side).

第九课

Lesson 9

Tā jīnnián èrshí suì
他 今年 二十 岁

He is 20 years old this year.

How do Chinese celebrate their birthdays?
How to ask the age and birthplace of others?
Besides, in this lesson, you will also learn the days,
weeks, months, and years in Chinese, and look at
the Chinese zodiac animals, a remarkable creation
of Chinese culture.

 一、课文 Text

🎧 37 （一）

| 王小云: | 林 娜，你 怎么样？① 忙 不 忙？ |
| Wáng Xiǎoyún： | Lín Nà, nǐ zěnmeyàng? Máng bu máng? |

| 林娜: | 我 今天 很 忙。 |
| Lín Nà： | Wǒ jīntiān hěn máng. |

| 王小云: | 明天 上午 你 有 没有 课？ |
| Wáng Xiǎoyún： | Míngtiān shàngwǔ nǐ yǒu méiyǒu kè? |

| 林娜: | 明天 是 星期 几？② |
| Lín Nà： | Míngtiān shì xīngqī jǐ? |

| 王小云: | 明天 是 星期四。 |
| Wáng Xiǎoyún： | Míngtiān shì xīngqīsì. |

| 林娜: | 我 上午、下午 都 有 课。 |
| Lín Nà： | Wǒ shàngwǔ、xiàwǔ dōu yǒu kè. |

| 王小云: | 你 星期日 有 时间 吗？ |
| Wáng Xiǎoyún： | Nǐ xīngqīrì yǒu shíjiān ma? |

约会
Making an appointment

| 林娜: | 星期日 是 几 号？ |
| Lín Nà： | Xīngqīrì shì jǐ hào? |

| 王小云: | 星期日 是 十月 二十七 号，是 宋 华 的 生日。 |
| Wáng Xiǎoyún： | Xīngqīrì shì shíyuè èrshíqī hào, shì Sòng Huá de shēngri. |

| 林娜: | 是 吗？③ 他 今年 多 大？④ |
| Lín Nà： | Shì ma? Tā jīnnián duō dà? |

| 王小云: | 宋 华 一 九 八 二 年 十月 二十七 日 出生， |
| Wáng Xiǎoyún： | Sòng Huá yī jiǔ bā èr nián shíyuè èrshíqī rì chūshēng, |

属　狗。⑤他　今年　二十　岁。
shǔ　gǒu. Tā　jīnnián　èrshí　suì.

林娜：他　是　哪儿　人？⑥
Lín Nà：Tā　shì　nǎr　rén?

王小云：他　是　北京　人。他　爸爸、妈妈　都　在　北京。星期日
Wáng Xiǎoyún：Tā　shì　Běijīng　rén. Tā　bàba、māma　dōu　zài　Běijīng. Xīngqīrì

下午　我们　有　一　个　聚会，祝贺　他　的　生日。力波、
xiàwǔ wǒmen yǒu　yí　ge　jùhuì, zhùhè　tā　de　shēngri. Lìbō、

大为　都　去，你　参加　不　参加？
Dàwéi　dōu　qù, nǐ　cānjiā　bu　cānjiā?

林娜：太　好　了！我　当然　参加。　中国　人　过　生日
Lín Nà：Tài hǎo le! Wǒ　dāngrán　cānjiā. Zhōngguó　rén guò shēngri

的　时候　吃　蛋糕　吗？
de shíhou chī dàngāo ma?

王小云：吃　蛋糕。
Wáng Xiǎoyún：Chī　dàngāo.

林娜：我　买　一　个　大　蛋糕，好　吗？
Lín Nà：Wǒ mǎi yí ge dà dàngāo, hǎo ma?

王小云：好　啊。我　买　两　瓶　红　葡萄酒。
Wáng Xiǎoyún：Hǎo a. Wǒ mǎi liǎng píng hóng pútaojiǔ.

生词 New Words

1. 今年	jīnnián	N	this year
年	nián	N	year 2010 年，1998 年，一年，两年
2. 岁	suì	M	year (of age) 五岁，十八岁，二十岁，三十六岁
*3. 怎么样	zěnmeyàng	QPr	how is... 天气怎么样，你怎么样

*4.	今天	jīntiān	N	today 今天上午，今天下午
5.	课	kè	N	class, lesson 有课，汉语课，文化课，
				第一课，两课
6.	星期	xīngqī	N	week 星期一，星期二，星期几，一个星期
7.	上午	shàngwǔ	N	morning 明天上午，一个上午
	上	shàng	N	above, last 上星期，上星期二，上个月
8.	下午	xiàwǔ	N	afternoon 明天下午，一个下午
	下	xià	N	below, next 下星期，下星期三，下个月
9.	星期日	xīngqīrì	N	Sunday 星期日上午，星期日下午
*10.	号	hào	N	day of the month 五月四号，十月一号
11.	生日	shēngri	N	birthday 他的生日，二十岁生日
	生	shēng	V	to be born
12.	多大	duō dà	IE	how old 今年多大
	多	duō	Adv	how (many/much)
	大	dà	A	big, large
13.	出生	chūshēng	V	to be born 1990年出生
	出	chū	V	to go, to come out
14.	属	shǔ	V	to be born in the year of (one of the 12 animals) 属狗
15.	聚会	jùhuì	N	get-together, party 生日聚会，有一个聚会
	会	huì	N	meeting
16.	祝贺	zhùhè	V	to congratulate 祝贺生日
	祝	zhù	V	to wish
17.	参加	cānjiā	V	to participate, to attend 参加聚会
*18.	了	le	Pt	(a modal particle, aspect particle)
19.	过	guò	V	to spend (time), to celebrate (someone's birthday, a festival, etc.)
20.	吃	chī	V	to eat

21.	蛋糕	dàngāo	N	cake 一个蛋糕，吃蛋糕
	蛋	dàn	N	egg
	糕	gāo	N	cake
22.	买	mǎi	V	to buy 买蛋糕
23.	瓶	píng	M	bottle 一瓶水
24.	红葡萄酒	hóng pútaojiǔ		red wine 一瓶红葡萄酒
	红	hóng	A	red
	葡萄	pútao	N	grape 吃葡萄，买葡萄
	酒	jiǔ	N	wine or liquor
*25.	宋华	Sòng Huá	PN	(name of a Chinese student)
26.	北京	Běijīng	PN	Beijing

注释 Notes

① 你怎么样？

   This is also a form of greeting used among acquaintances and friends, and is similar to "你好吗？".

② 明天是星期几？

   It can also be said as "明天星期几？" in spoken language, with "是" omitted.

③ 是吗？

   The phrase "是吗？" does not raise a question here, but expresses mild surprise on the part of the speaker concerning something that he / she does not know. For example:

      A：丁力波的哥哥和弟弟都在北京。

      B：是吗？

   Sometimes it expresses doubt, or modesty when receiving praise.

④ 他今年多大？

   Here "多" is an adverb, followed by an adjective. The phrase "多 + A" is used to raise a question, and in this case "大" refers to age.

   In asking about age in Chinese, one has to choose different forms for different groups of people. "你今年多大？" can only be used to ask the age of an adult, or people of the same generation as the speaker. When asking the age of a child, we usually say "你今年几岁？", and when asking the age of an elderly person or those older than the speaker, a more polite form has to be used, which will be taught in Lesson 11.

⑤ 宋华一九八二年十月二十七日出生，属狗。

It is customary for the Chinese to designate one's year of birth according to twelve animals, which are arranged in the following order: rat, ox, tiger, rabbit, dragon, snake, horse, ram, monkey, rooster, dog and pig. These form a twelve-year cycle. For example, the years 1982, 1994 and 2006 are all designated "dog" years. The people who were born in these years are said to "be born in the year of dog", which, in Chinese, is written as "属狗". The years 1988, 2000 and 2012 are dragon years. Those who were born in these years all "属龙".

⑥ 他是哪儿人？

This is an expression usually used to ask someone's place of birth. It can also be said as "他哪儿人？", with "是" omitted; and in answering "哪儿", it is usually necessary to specify a province, city or county. When asking about someone's nationality, we use the expression "哪国人？".

38 （二）

林娜：   宋　华，这是　生日　蛋糕。
Lín Nà：Sòng Huá, zhè shì shēngri dàngāo.

祝　你　生日　快乐！⑦
Zhù nǐ shēngri kuàilè!

> 祝贺生日
> **Celebrating someone's birthday**

宋华：谢谢。蛋糕　真　漂亮。你们　来，我　很　高兴。
Sòng Huá：Xièxie. Dàngāo zhēn piàoliang. Nǐmen lái, wǒ hěn gāoxìng.

马大为：今天　我们　吃　北京　烤鸭。我　很　喜欢　吃
Mǎ Dàwéi：Jīntiān wǒmen chī Běijīng kǎoyā. Wǒ hěn xǐhuan chī

烤鸭。⑧
kǎoyā.

丁力波：我们　喝　什么
Dīng Lìbō：Wǒmen hē shénme

酒？
jiǔ?

王小云：　当然　喝　红　葡萄酒，　我们　还　吃　寿面。⑨
Wáng Xiǎoyún：　Dāngrán hē hóng pútaojiǔ,　wǒmen hái chī shòumiàn.

林娜：　吃　寿面？　真　有　意思。
Lín Nà：　Chī shòumiàn? Zhēn yǒu yìsi.

宋华：　林娜，你的　生日　是哪天？
Sòng Huá：　Lín Nà, nǐ de shēngri shì nǎ tiān?

林娜：　十一月　十二　号。
Lín Nà：　Shíyīyuè shí'èr hào.

宋华：　好，　十一月　十二　号　我们　再来　吃　寿面。
Sòng Huá：　Hǎo, shíyīyuè shí'èr hào wǒmen zài lái chī shòumiàn.

生词 New Words

1.	快乐	kuàilè	A	happy　生日快乐
2.	漂亮	piàoliang	A	beautiful, nice　漂亮的小姐，漂亮的照片
3.	烤鸭	kǎoyā	N	roast duck　北京烤鸭，吃烤鸭
	鸭	yā	N	duck
*4.	喝	hē	V	to drink　喝葡萄酒，喝咖啡
*5.	再	zài	Adv	again　再来，再买，再看，再做
6.	寿面	shòumiàn	N	(birthday) longevity noodles　吃寿面
	面	miàn	N	noodles

补充生词 Supplementary Words

1.	可乐	kělè	N	coke
2.	雪碧	Xuěbì	PN	*Sprite*, name of a drink
3.	啤酒	píjiǔ	N	beer
4.	牛奶	niúnǎi	N	milk

5. 汉堡	hànbǎo	N	hamburger
6. 热狗	règǒu	N	hotdog
7. 面包	miànbāo	N	bread
8. 中餐	zhōngcān	N	Chinese food
9. 西餐	xīcān	N	Western food
10. 茶	chá	N	tea
11. 米饭	mǐfàn	N	(cooked) rice
12. 女儿	nǚ'ér	N	daughter
13. 儿子	érzi	N	son
14. 晚上	wǎnshang	N	evening
15. 店	diàn	N	store or shop

注释　Notes

⑦ 祝你生日快乐!

This is a familiar form of expression used to extend greetings to someone on his / her birthday. "祝你……" is used to express good wishes, sometimes with the implication of "congratulating sb. in advance", whereas "祝贺你……" is commonly used to congratulate someone on something that is already known or has already occurred. For example:

A：我下星期天结婚（jiéhūn，to get married）。

B：祝贺你!

⑧ 我很喜欢吃烤鸭。

A verb or a verbal phrase can funtion as the object of the predicative verb. For example:

他喜欢说汉语。

我喜欢学习。

⑨ 我们还吃寿面。

When celebrating birthdays, a traditional Chinese custom is to eat "longevity noodles". The length of noodles symbolizes "longevity".

二、练习　Exercises

练习 与运用　Drills and Practice　 39

核心句　KEY SENTENCES

1. 明天上午你有没有课?
2. 星期日是几号?
3. 他今年多大?
4. 他一九八二年十月二十七日出生。
5. 他今年二十岁。
6. 我买一个大蛋糕，好吗?
7. 祝你生日快乐!
8. 我很喜欢吃烤鸭。

---

1. 熟读下列词组　Read the following phrases until you learn them by heart

（1）今天上午　明天下午　五月八号上午　上星期　上星期三
上星期三下午　星期二上午　星期六下午　九月二十号下午
下星期　下星期日　下星期三上午

（2）一九七〇年出生　一九八五年学习汉语　一九九〇年工作
一九九九年来中国　二〇〇〇年认识张教授　二〇〇二年到北京

（3）一个蛋糕　两瓶葡萄酒　五张照片　三个朋友　一个妹妹　一个聚会

（4）宋华的生日　你的生日　他们的聚会　林娜的蛋糕　王小云的酒

（5）生日蛋糕　大蛋糕　红葡萄酒　北京烤鸭

---

2. 句型替换　Pattern drills

（1）A：今天是（几月）几号?
　　B：今天是（十一月）八号。
　　A：明天是星期几?
　　B：明天是星期二。

2010
九月小
26
星期日

2010
十月大
15
星期五

2010
十二月大
30
星期四

（2）A：六月四号是不是星期六？

　　　B：六月四号不是星期六，
　　　　　是星期五。

　　　A：星期五你有没有课？

　　　B：我上午有课，下午没有课。

星期一	星期二	星期三	星期四	星期五	星期六	星期日
1	2	3	4	5	6
7	8	9	10	11	12	13
14	15	16	17	18	19	20
21	22	23	24	25	26	27
28	29	30				

（3）A：星期一是几号？

　　　B：星期一是十二月二十号。

　　　A：星期一他做什么？

　　　B：他去朋友家。

星期五　　看京剧
星期六　　参加聚会
星期日　　吃烤鸭

（4）A：你现在忙不忙？

　　　B：我现在很忙。

　　　A：你星期几有时间？

　　　B：我星期五下午有时间。

星期日
星期四上午
星期二下午

（5）A：你几号来北京？

　　　B：我下月二号来北京。

　　　A：下月二号是星期几？

　　　B：下月二号是星期四。

去　　加拿大
来　　中国
去　　美国

（6）A：你今年多大？

　　　B：我今年21岁。

　　　A：你的生日是哪天？

　　　B：我的生日是8月21号。

19	1月6日
20	3月12日
22	4月22号

（7）A：你是哪儿人？

　　　B：我是北京人。

　　　A：北京怎么样？

　　　B：北京很漂亮。

上海（Shànghǎi　Shanghai）
莫斯科（Mòsīkē　Moscow）
多伦多（Duōlúnduō　Toronto）
纽约（Niǔyuē　New York）
伦敦（Lúndūn　London）

（8）A：你参加明天的聚会吗？

　　　B：我当然参加。

　　　A：我买两瓶红葡萄酒，
　　　　　好吗？

　　　B：好啊，我买一个大蛋糕。

两瓶可乐 (kělè)	五个汉堡 (hànbǎo)
三瓶雪碧 (Xuěbì)	八个热狗 (règǒu)
六瓶啤酒 (píjiǔ)	九个面包 (miànbāo)
八瓶牛奶 (niúnǎi)	两只烤鸭

3. 回答下列问题　Answer the following questions

（1）一年有几个月？

（2）一年有多少个星期？

（3）一个星期有几天？

（4）十一月有多少天？

（5）十一月有几个星期天？

（6）今天几月几号？星期几？

（7）星期天是几号？

（8）星期天你做什么？

（9）你喜欢吃什么？喜欢吃中餐（zhōngcān）
　　　吗？喜欢吃西餐（xīcān）吗？

（10）你喜欢喝茶（chá）吗？

（11）你喜欢吃米饭（mǐfàn）吗？

4. 会话练习　Conversation practice

【约会　Making an appointment】

（1）A：你怎么样？忙不忙？

　　　B：＿＿＿＿＿＿＿＿＿＿。

　　　A：星期五下午你有时间吗？我们去＿＿＿＿＿＿＿，好吗？

　　　B：太好了，我当然去。

（2）A：十二号你有时间吗？

　　　B：十二号是星期三吗？

　　　A：不是，十二号是星期四。我们下午有个聚会，你参加不参加？

　　　B：对不起，＿＿＿＿＿＿＿，恐怕不行。

　　　A：没关系。

【问年龄和出生地　Asking about someone's age and birthplace】

（1）A：你今年多大？

　　　B：我今年＿＿＿＿＿＿。

　　　A：你的生日是哪天？

　　　B：星期五是我的生日。

A：是吗？_____！

B：谢谢。

（2）A：您是哪儿人？

B：我是上海（Shànghǎi）人。

A：你爸爸、妈妈都在上海吗？

B：不，他们现在_____。

A：他们都好吗？

B：他们都很好，谢谢。

（3）A：你哥哥有孩子吗？

B：他有一个女儿（nǚ'ér）和一个儿子（érzi）。

A：他们今年几岁？

B：女儿_____，儿子_____。

【祝贺生日　Celebrating someone's birthday】

（1）A：下星期五是林娜的生日，我们有个聚会。你来不来？

B：我当然来。_____，好吗？

A：好啊！我买_____。

B：太好了，我们喝葡萄酒，吃蛋糕和寿面。

（2）A：今天是你的生日，祝你生日快乐！

B：谢谢。你们来，我很高兴。

5. 交际练习　Communication exercises

Your friend is going to make an appointment with you. Please reply according to your schedule for the next week:

	上午	下午	晚上（wǎnshang）
星期一	汉语课		朋友来
星期二	文化课	汉语课	
星期三	汉语课		游泳
星期四		汉语课	
星期五	汉语课	打球	
星期六	看朋友		看京剧
星期日		生日聚会	

阅读与复述 Reading Comprehension and Paraphrasing

　　宋华是经济系的学生，北京人，1982年出生。今年十月二十七日是他二十岁的生日。星期天下午，他的好朋友们有一个聚会，王小云、林娜、丁力波和马大为都来祝贺他的生日。他们在北京烤鸭店（diàn）吃烤鸭和寿面，喝红葡萄酒。朋友们祝宋华生日快乐，宋华很高兴。

　　林娜的生日是十一月十二号。宋华说那天他们再来吃寿面和烤鸭。

三、语法　Grammar

1 年、月、日和星期　Expressing the date and days of the week

　　In Chinese, the four figures making up the name of a year are read out as four separate numbers and "年" is put at the end. For example:

　　一九九八年　　yī jiǔ jiǔ bā nián
　　二〇〇〇年　　èr líng líng líng nián
　　二〇〇二年　　èr líng líng èr nián
　　二〇一〇年　　èr líng yī líng nián

　　The names of the 12 months are produced by combining the cardinal numbers 1 to 12 with "月". For example:

一月	yīyuè	January	七月	qīyuè	July
二月	èryuè	February	八月	bāyuè	August
三月	sānyuè	March	九月	jiǔyuè	September
四月	sìyuè	April	十月	shíyuè	October
五月	wǔyuè	May	十一月	shíyīyuè	November
六月	liùyuè	June	十二月	shí'èryuè	December

The names of the dates are produced by combining cardinal numbers 1 to 30 (or 31) with "号" (spoken form) or "日" (written form). For example:

（二月）六号	（èryuè）liù hào	February 6
（十月）十二号	（shíyuè）shí'èr hào	October 12
（十一月）二十二日	（shíyīyuè）èrshí'èr rì	November 22
（十二月）三十一日	（shí'èryuè）sānshíyī rì	December 31

If one mentions a date in the current month, one can omit "月" and simply say "……号".

The cardinal numbers from 1 to 6 follow "星期" are used to express Monday to Saturday. The name for Sunday is "星期天" (spoken form) or "星期日" (written form).

星期一	xīngqīyī	Monday	星期五	xīngqīwǔ	Friday
星期二	xīngqī'èr	Tuesday	星期六	xīngqīliù	Saturday
星期三	xīngqīsān	Wednesday	星期天/日	xīngqītiān/rì	Sunday
星期四	xīngqīsì	Thursday			

The word order for expressing the date and days of the week is:

年　＋　月　　＋　　日　＋　星期

二〇一〇年十二月二十五日　　　星期六

2010年 12月 　25日 　　星期六

2 表时间的词语作状语   Words expressing time as adverbials

Words expressing time, such as "现在", "今天", "下午", "二月二十号" can function as adverbials to indicate the time of occurrence of an action or a state. Adverbials of time can be placed either: (1) after the subject and before the main element of the predicate or: (2) before the subject to emphasize the time.

S + TW + VO / A

Subject	Predicate		
	Time Words	V O / A	
你	星期日	有时间	吗？
我	上午、下午	都有课。	
宋华	一九八二年十月二十七日	出生。	
我	今天	很　　　忙。	

TW ＋ S ＋ VO / A

Time Words	Subject	Predicate	
		V	O / A
明天上午	你	有没有	课？
今天	我们	吃	北京烤鸭。
十一月十二号	我们	再　来吃	寿面。
今天	我	很	忙。

Note:

(1) Adverbials of time can never be placed after the predicative verb. For example, one cannot say "我们吃烤鸭今天".

(2) If there is more than one word expressing time in one adverbial, a large unit of time should be put before a smaller one. For example: "明天上午", "星期日下午".

3 名词谓语句　Sentences with a nominal predicate

Nouns, noun phrases, and numeral-measure words can function directly as the predicate of a sentence and do not need the verb "是". This kind of sentence is especially used in spoken language to express age, price (see Lesson 10), and so on. It is also used to express time (see Lesson 11) or birthplace.

S ＋ Nu-M

Subject	Predicate
	Nu-M
宋华	今年　二十岁。
林娜	十九岁。

4 用 "……，好吗？" 提问　Questions with "……，好吗？"

Questions with "……，好吗？" are often used to give a suggestion or ask for someone's advice. The first part of such a question is a declarative sentence, and its last part can also be "可以吗？".

我们买一个大蛋糕，好吗？
我们去游泳，好吗？
现在去，可以吗？

　　Some examples of affirmative answers are: "好啊", "好", "太好了". Negative answers should be like "不用了。", "对不起，我没有时间。" or "很抱歉，我有事儿(shìr, matter)。" instead of "不好。".

四、汉字　Chinese Characters

1　汉字的结构(2)　Structure of Chinese characters (2)

The left-right structure ②

Equal left-middle-right

1	2	3

谢　娜

2　认写基本汉字　Learn and write basic Chinese characters

(1) 今　　　ノ　人　仐　今
jīn　　　today　　　　　　　　4 strokes

(2) 年　　　ノ　ト　ヒ　ヒ　丘　年
nián　　　year　　　　　　　　6 strokes

(3) 果　　　ι　冂　冂　日　旦　甲　界　果
guǒ　　　fruit　　　　　　　　8 strokes

(4) 其　　　一　十　廿　廿　甘　甘　其　其
qí　　　he(his); she(her); it(its);
they(their)　　　　　　　8 strokes

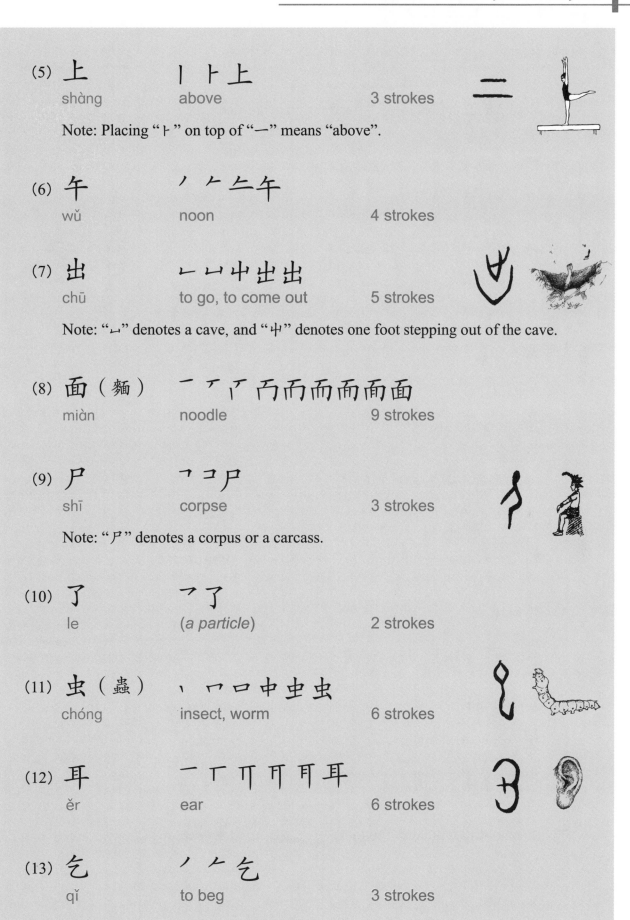

(5) 上　　ⵏ 卜 上
shàng　　above　　3 strokes

Note: Placing "卜" on top of "一" means "above".

(6) 午　　ノ 𠂉 二 午
wǔ　　noon　　4 strokes

(7) 出　　𠃊 凵 屮 出 出
chū　　to go, to come out　　5 strokes

Note: "凵" denotes a cave, and "屮" denotes one foot stepping out of the cave.

(8) 面（麵）　　一 プ プ 丙 而 而 面 面 面
miàn　　noodle　　9 strokes

(9) 尸　　𠃌 コ 尸
shī　　corpse　　3 strokes

Note: "尸" denotes a corpus or a carcass.

(10) 了　　𠃌 了
le　　(a particle)　　2 strokes

(11) 虫（蟲）　　丶 丨 口 口 中 虫 虫
chóng　　insect, worm　　6 strokes

(12) 耳　　一 丆 𠃜 𡰪 𦔮 耳
ěr　　ear　　6 strokes

(13) 乞　　ノ 𠂉 乞
qǐ　　to beg　　3 strokes

(14) 米　　　丶丶丷半米米　　　6 strokes

mǐ　　　rice

Note: The four dots in "米" stand for grains of rice.

(15) 头（頭）　丶丷二头头

tóu　　　head　　　5 strokes

(16) 瓦　　　一丆瓦瓦

wǎ　　　tile　　　4 strokes

3 认写课文中的汉字　Learn and write the Chinese characters in the texts

(1) 岁 suì（歲）

岁 → 山 + 夕　　　6 strokes

(2) 怎么样 zěnmeyàng（怎麼樣）

怎 → 乍 + 心　　　9 strokes

样 → 木 + 羊　　　10 strokes

(3) 课 kè（課）

课 → 讠 + 果　　　10 strokes

(4) 星期 xīngqī

星 → 日 + 生　　　9 strokes

期 → 其 + 月　　　12 strokes

丂 (hàozìdǐr, the "number" bottom)　一丂　2 strokes

(4) 号 hào（號）

号 → 口 + 丂　　　5 strokes

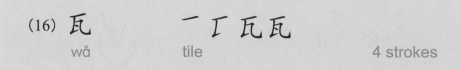

(6) 属 shǔ（屬）

属 → 尸 ＋ 一 ＋ 虫 ＋ 口　　　　　12 strokes

氺 (jùzìdǐr, the "gather" bottom)　一 丁 丁 才 氺 氺　6 strokes

(7) 聚会 jùhuì（聚會）

聚 → 耳 ＋ 又 ＋ 氺　　　　　14 strokes

会 → 人 ＋ 云　　　　　6 strokes

礻 (shìzìpángr, the "manifestation" side)　丶 亍 礻 礻　4 strokes

(8) 祝贺 zhùhè（祝賀）

祝 → 礻 ＋ 兄　　　　　9 strokes

贺 → 力 ＋ 口 ＋ 贝　　　　　9 strokes

彡 (sānpiěr, the "three-left-falling-stroke" side)　丿 彡 彡　3 strokes

(9) 参加 cānjiā（參加）

参 → 厶 ＋ 大 ＋ 彡　　　　　8 strokes

(10) 吃 chī

吃 → 口 ＋ 乞　　　　　6 strokes

(to use mouth "口" to eat "吃")

(11) 蛋糕 dàngāo

蛋 → 疋 ＋ 虫　　　　　11 strokes

糕 → 米 ＋ 羔　　　　　16 strokes

(On the left side of a character, the sixth stroke in "米" is written as a dot.)

一 (hénggōu, a horizontal stroke with a hook)   1 stroke

(12) 买 mǎi（買）

买 → 一 + 头   6 strokes

(13) 瓶 píng

瓶 → 丷 + 开 + 瓦   10 strokes

(14) 红 hóng（紅）

红 → 纟 + 工   6 strokes

艹 (cǎozìtóur, the "grass" top)   一 十 艹   3 strokes

甫 fǔ   一 丅 丆 𠬛 𡴋 甫 甫   7 strokes

缶 fǒu   丿 𠂉 𠂎 午 缶 缶   6 strokes

(15) 葡萄 pútao

葡 → 艹 + 勹 + 甫   12 strokes
萄 → 艹 + 勹 + 缶   11 strokes

酉 yǒu   一 丅 丆 丙 西 西 酉   7 strokes

(16) 酒 jiǔ

酒 → 氵 + 酉   10 strokes

(17) 宋华 Sòng Huá（宋華）

宋 → 宀 + 木   7 strokes
华 → 化 + 十   6 strokes

扌 (běizìpángr, the "north" side)   丨 十 扌   3 strokes

(18) 北京 Běijīng

北 → 扌 + 匕   5 strokes

京 → 亠 ＋ 口 ＋ 小   8 strokes

夬 (juézìpángr, the "decision" side)   一 コ ユ 夬   4 strokes

(19) 快乐 kuàilè（快樂）

快 → 忄 ＋ 夬   7 strokes

覀 (xīzìtóur, the "west" top)   一 一 冂 襾 覀 覀   6 strokes

(20) 漂亮 piàoliang

漂 → 氵 ＋ 覀 ＋ 二 ＋ 小   14 strokes

亮 → 亠 ＋ 口 ＋ 冖 ＋ 几   9 strokes

(21) 烤鸭 kǎoyā（烤鴨）

烤 → 火 ＋ 耂 ＋ 丂 （丂：一 丂）   10 strokes

鸭 → 甲 ＋ 鸟   10 strokes

     （甲：丨 冂 冃 曰 甲）

     （鸟：丿 勹 勹 鸟 鸟）

(22) 喝 hē

喝 → 口 ＋ 日 ＋ 勹 ＋ 𠆢 ＋ 乚   12 strokes

(23) 寿面 shòumiàn（壽麵）

寿 → 丰 ＋ 寸   7 strokes

     （丰：一 二 三 丰）

Chinese Styles of Cooking and Beijing Roast Duck

China is vast in territory and famous for its culture of food and drink. Influenced by factors such as geographical environment, climate, products, culture, tradition and folk customs, the food in each region has formed its own style, which is called the "style of cooking". Among these styles, Yue of Guangdong, Chuan of Sichuan, Lu of Shandong, Huaiyang of Jiangsu, Zhe of Zhejiang, Min of Fujian, Xiang of Hunan and Hui of Anhui are reputed as the "Eight Styles of Cooking". Each of them has its own distinguishing qualities: some are spicy and delicious, some are sweet and sour, while some are light and refreshing.

As the capital of China, though Beijing doesn't have its own style of cooking, it has captured the essence of the Chinese cuisine. For Beijing, the cooked food that enjoys the national fame and has the richest local flavor is Beijing Roast Duck (北京烤鸭, Běijīng Kǎoyā).

Ducks used in this cuisine are not ordinary ones, but a kind of force-fed duck which has a short growing period. Such ducks are fleshy and the meat is tender. They must be roasted with the wood of fruit trees, such as that of pears and apples, to let the tang of these trees slowly permeate the ducks. When the skin is roasted brown, the meat (with skin) can be cut into thin slices and be eaten.

The roast duck, rolled in a special thin round cake, can be eaten together with sweet bean sauce and tender onions. The crisp skin and tender meat add a special taste to it. The most famous roast duck restaurant in Beijing is the 100-year old Quanjude Roast Duck Restaurant (全聚德烤鸭店, Quánjùdé Kǎoyā Diàn).

Quanjude Roast Duck Restaurant

Beijing Roast Duck

第十课

Lesson

10

Wǒ zài   zhèr   mǎi guāngpán
我 在 这儿 买 光盘
I am here to buy a CD.

Bargaining for discounts in China can make shopping quite an experience! This lesson will show you how Chinese currency is used. Now is a chance to talk more about yourself. You will learn to describe your likes, interests, and hobbies. You will also learn what to do when you can't think of the right thing to say.

一、课文 Text

🎧 40 （一）

王小云： 大为，你 在 这儿 买 什么？
Wáng Xiǎoyún： Dàwéi, nǐ zài zhèr mǎi shénme?

马大为： 我 买 音乐 光盘。
Mǎ Dàwéi： Wǒ mǎi yīnyuè guāngpán.

王小云： 你 常常 来 这儿 吗？
Wáng Xiǎoyún： Nǐ chángcháng lái zhèr ma?

马大为： 我 不 常 来 这儿。 星期天 我 常常 跟 林
Mǎ Dàwéi： Wǒ bù cháng lái zhèr. Xīngqītiān wǒ chángcháng gēn Lín

娜 去 小 商场。 这个 商场 很 大。
Nà qù xiǎo shāngchǎng. Zhège shāngchǎng hěn dà.

王小云： 你 喜欢 什么 音乐？
Wáng Xiǎoyún： Nǐ xǐhuan shénme yīnyuè?

> 谈喜好
> **Likes and dislikes**

马大为： 我 喜欢 中国 音乐。这 张 光盘 怎么样？
Mǎ Dàwéi： Wǒ xǐhuan Zhōngguó yīnyuè.Zhè zhāng guāngpán zěnmeyàng?

王小云： 这 张 很 好，是《梁 祝》，很 有名。
Wáng Xiǎoyún： Zhè zhāng hěn hǎo, shì 《Liáng Zhù》, hěn yǒumíng.

马大为： 好，我 买 这 张。
Mǎ Dàwéi： Hǎo, wǒ mǎi zhè zhāng.

这儿 有 没有 书 和
Zhèr yǒu méiyǒu shū hé

报纸？
bàozhǐ?

王小云：这儿　没有　书，也　没有　报纸。
Wáng Xiǎoyún：Zhèr　méiyǒu　shū，yě méiyǒu　bàozhǐ.

马大为：本子　呢？
Mǎ Dàwéi：Běnzi　ne?

王小云：有，在　那儿　买。跟　我　来，我　也　买　本子。
Wáng Xiǎoyún：Yǒu，zài　nàr　mǎi. Gēn　wǒ　lái，wǒ　yě　mǎi běnzi.

生词 New Words

*1. 在	zài	Prep	at, in, on 在家，在学院，在这儿
2. 光盘	guāngpán	N	CD 一张光盘
*3. 音乐	yīnyuè	N	music 音乐光盘，中国音乐，外国音乐
4. 常常	chángcháng	Adv	often 常常来，常常去，常常看，常常做
常	cháng	Adv	often 不常
5. 跟	gēn	Prep / V	with; to follow 跟他来，跟林娜去，跟我学
6. 商场	shāngchǎng	N	market, bazaar, shopping mall 在商场，进商场
商	shāng	N	trade, commerce
7. 有名	yǒumíng	A	famous 有名的教授，有名的医生
8. 书	shū	N	book 外语书，汉语书，有名的书，看书
9. 报纸	bàozhǐ	N	newspaper 买报纸，看报纸
10. 本子	běnzi	N	exercise book, notebook 一个本子，买本子
11. 那儿	nàr	Pr	there 去那儿，在那儿
12. 梁祝	Liáng Zhù	PN	(name of a Chinese violin concerto)

注释　Notes

① 这个商场很大。

When the demonstrative pronoun "这" or "那" is used as an attributive, a measure word is generally inserted between it and the noun it modifies. For instance: "这张光盘"，"那个朋友"，"那瓶酒".

41 （二）

师傅：　先生，　　您 要 什么？②
Shīfu:　Xiānsheng, nín yào shénme?

丁力波：　您 好，师傅。③ 请问，
Dīng Lìbō:　Nín hǎo, shīfu. Qǐngwèn,

这 是 什么？
zhè shì shénme?

师傅：　您 不 认识 吗？ 这 是
Shīfu:　Nín bú rènshi ma? Zhè shì

香蕉　苹果。
xiāngjiāo píngguǒ.

解决语言困难
Solving language problems

丁力波：　对不起，我 是 问：这个 汉语 怎么 说？④
Dīng Lìbō:　Duìbuqǐ, wǒ shì wèn: Zhège Hànyǔ zěnme shuō?

师傅：　啊，您 是 外国 人！您 在 哪儿 工作？
Shīfu:　À, nín shì wàiguó rén! Nín zài nǎr gōngzuò?

丁力波：　我 在 语言 学院 学习。
Dīng Lìbō:　Wǒ zài Yǔyán Xuéyuàn xuéxí.

师傅：　您 学习 汉语，是 不 是？⑤ 您 跟 我 学，很 容易：
Shīfu:　Nín xuéxí Hànyǔ, shì bu shì? Nín gēn wǒ xué, hěn róngyì:

这 叫 香蕉，　这 叫 香蕉　苹果，　这 也 是 苹果，
Zhè jiào xiāngjiāo, zhè jiào xiāngjiāo píngguǒ, zhè yě shì píngguǒ,

那 是 葡萄……
nà shì pútao……

丁力波：　香蕉、　　苹果、　香蕉　苹果……一 斤 苹果 多少
Dīng Lìbō:　Xiāngjiāo、 píngguǒ、 xiāngjiāo píngguǒ……Yì jīn píngguǒ duōshao

钱？⑥
qián?

师傅：　一 斤 三 块 二 毛 钱。⑦
Shīfu:　Yì jīn sān kuài èr máo qián.

买东西
Shopping

丁力波：　您 的 苹果 真 贵。
Dīng Lìbō:　Nín de píngguǒ zhēn guì.

师傅：　一 斤 三 块 二 不贵。您 看，我 的 苹果 大。好，
Shīfu:　Yì jīn sān kuài èr bú guì. Nín kàn, wǒ de píngguǒ dà. Hǎo,

做 个 朋友，三 块 钱 一 斤。
zuò ge péngyou, sān kuài qián yì jīn.

丁力波：　一 斤 香蕉 多少 钱?
Dīng Lìbō:　Yì jīn xiāngjiāo duōshao qián?

师傅：　两 块 七 毛 五 分 一 斤，五 块 钱 两 斤。
Shīfu:　Liǎng kuài qī máo wǔ fēn yì jīn, wǔ kuài qián liǎng jīn.

丁力波：　我 买 三 斤 香蕉 和 两 斤 苹果。
Dīng Lìbō:　Wǒ mǎi sān jīn xiāngjiāo hé liǎng jīn píngguǒ.

师傅：　一共 十四 块 钱。我 再 送 您 一 个 苹果。 您 还
Shīfu:　Yígòng shísì kuài qián. Wǒ zài sòng nín yí ge píngguǒ. Nín hái

要 什么?
yào shénme?

丁力波：　不 要 了，谢谢。⑧ 给 您 钱。
Dīng Lìbō:　Bú yào le, xièxie. Gěi nín qián.

师傅：　好，您 给 我 二十 块 钱，我 找 您 六 块。
Shīfu:　Hǎo, nín gěi wǒ èrshí kuài qián, wǒ zhǎo nín liù kuài.

再见。
Zàijiàn.

丁力波：　再见!
Dīng Lìbō:　Zàijiàn!

生词 New Words

*1. 先生	xiānsheng	N	Mr.; sir	张先生，王先生
*2. 要	yào	V	to want	要什么，要音乐光盘
3. 师傅	shīfu	N	master	张师傅，王师傅
4. 香蕉苹果	xiāngjiāo píngguǒ		apple with the taste of a banana	一个香蕉苹果
香蕉	xiāngjiāo	N	banana	买香蕉
苹果	píngguǒ	N	apple	一个苹果
*5. 对不起	duìbuqǐ	IE	I'm sorry	
6. 怎么	zěnme	Qpr	how	怎么说，怎么做，怎么去，怎么介绍
7. 容易	róngyì	A	easy	很容易，不容易，真容易，不太容易
*8. 葡萄	pútao	N	grape	
9. 斤	jīn	M	(a measure word of weight, it is equal to 500g)	一斤苹果，两斤葡萄
10. 钱	qián	N	money	多少钱
11. 块(钱)	kuài (qián)	M	(a measure word of basic Chinese monetary unit, it is equal to 10 jiao) kuai	两块钱，十二块钱，二十块钱
12. 毛(钱)	máo (qián)	M	(a measure word of Chinese monetary unit, it is equal to 1/10 yuan) mao	两毛钱，六毛五
13. 贵	guì	A	expensive, precious	很贵，真贵，不太贵，不贵
*14. 做	zuò	V	to do, to be, to make	做个朋友，做好朋友
15. 分(钱)	fēn (qián)	M	(a measure word of Chinese monetary unit, it is equal to 1/100 yuan) fen	一分钱，八分钱
16. 送	sòng	V	to give (as a present)	送蛋糕，送葡萄酒
17. 给	gěi	V	to give	给他，给师傅，给我，给香蕉
18. 找(钱)	zhǎo (qián)	V	to give change	

补充生词 Supplementary Words

1.	售货员	shòuhuòyuán	N	shop assistant, salesperson
2.	作家	zuòjiā	N	writer
3.	书店	shūdiàn	N	bookstore
4.	体育馆	tǐyùguǎn	N	gym
5.	公园	gōngyuán	N	park
6.	便宜	piányi	A	cheap, inexpensive
7.	本	běn	M	(a measure word for books and notebooks)
8.	支	zhī	M	(a measure word for stick-like things such as pens)
9.	笔	bǐ	N	stick-like writing or drawing instruments
10.	份	fèn	M	(a measure word for publications such as newspapers)
11.	元	yuán	M	(the same as kuai, but it is used in written Chinese)
12.	卖	mài	V	to sell
13.	杯	bēi	M	(a measure word for cups or glasses)
14.	东西	dōngxi	N	thing, stuff
15.	功夫	gōngfu	N	kung fu

注释　Notes

② 先生，您要什么？

In addition to being used as a general form of address for a male adult, "先生" can be used as a title of respect to address a senior scholar or specialist, regardless of sex. Sometimes a woman also uses "我先生" to refer to her husband.

The two expressions "您要什么?", "您还要什么?", are commonly used to ask what someone wants. Shop assistants or hotel attendants often use these phrases when offering help to customers.

③ 您好，师傅。

　　"师傅" is a respectful form of address for workers and people in the service trades. It may be used to address taxi and bus drivers, ticket sellers, cooks, and hotel staff. There is a tendency now to increase the range of its usage. Sometimes the people mentioned above also use it to address people of other trades and professions.

④ 我是问：这个汉语怎么说？

　　"I am asking how to say it in Chinese. (What is this in Chinese?)"

　　"怎么 + V" is often used to ask about the ways one should act or how one should do something. "怎么" is an adverbial, modifying verbs. For example: "怎么说？", "怎么做？", "怎么去？", "怎么介绍？".

⑤ 您学习汉语，是不是？

　　"……，是不是？" (or "……，是吗？") is a sentence pattern we use to express opinion or speculation, with the expectation of a response from the listener. The affirmative answer to this question is "是啊！", and the negative answer is "不(是)". For example:

　　　　A：你喜欢中国音乐，是吗？

　　　　B：是啊。

⑥ 一斤苹果多少钱？

　　"How much is one *jin* of apples?"

　　"一斤……多少钱？" is a common sentence pattern we use to ask the price of something when shopping. This is a sentence with the noun phrase as the predicate. The predicate "多少钱" is placed immediately after the subject "一斤苹果". Note that the first part (the subject) and the second part (the predicate) can be inverted. We may also say:

　　　　A：多少钱一斤（苹果）？

　　　　B：三块五一斤。

　　Although the official Chinese system of weights and measures stipulates that "公斤(gōngjīn, kilo)" is the basic unit, people are still accustomed to using "斤", which is equivalent to half a kilogram.

　　In a supermarket or department store, people do not usually bargain over the price, but when shopping in a free market or at a stall, they frequently bargain.

⑦ 一斤三块二毛钱。

　　The various monetary units in 人民币 (Rénmínbì), the Chinese currency, are: "元 (yuán)", "角 (jiǎo)", and "分 (fēn)". In spoken Chinese, we often use "块 (kuài)" for "元", and "毛 (máo)" for "角". When "毛" or "分" is at the end, "毛钱" and "分钱" can be omitted. For example:

　　　　1.75元 —— 一块七毛五（分钱）

　　　　4.80元 —— 四块八（毛钱）

　　Note: When "2毛" is at the beginning of an amount of money, people say "两毛". When "2分" is at the end of an amount of money, the expression "二分" is often used. For example:

　　　　0.22元 —— 两毛二（分）

⑧ 不要了，谢谢。

　　"No, thanks."

二、练习　Exercises

练习与运用　**Drills and Practice**　🎧 42

核心句 KEY SENTENCES

1. 我常常跟林娜去小商场。
2. 这个商场很大。
3. 这个汉语怎么说?
4. 三块钱一斤。
5. 一斤香蕉多少钱?
6. 您在哪儿工作?
7. 再送您一个苹果。
8. 您给我二十块钱,我找您六块。

1. 熟读下列词组　Read the following phrases until you learn them by heart

（1）这张光盘　这个学生　这个人　　这个学院　这个苹果　这个蛋糕

那张名片　那个朋友　那个小姐　那个系　　那个学生　那瓶酒

哪张照片　哪个老师　哪个先生　哪个专业　哪个苹果　哪个本子

（2）买光盘　送名片　给钱　吃寿面　看书　做工作　认识你　喜欢音乐

买苹果　给照片　找钱　喝酒　看报　学专业　给他　　学习汉语

（3）在中国学习　在外国工作　在这儿买书　在那儿看报　在商场工作

跟我来　　跟他去　　跟我学　　跟老师说汉语　　跟朋友去商场

2. 句型替换　Pattern drills

（1）A: 你在哪儿学习?

B: 我在语言学院学习。

A: 你学习什么专业?

B: 我学习汉语专业。

A: 你忙不忙?

B: 我很忙。

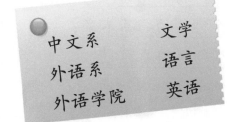

中文系　　　　文学
外语系　　　　语言
外语学院　　　英语

（2）A：你爸爸在哪儿工作？

B：他在<u>北京</u>工作。

A：他做什么工作？

B：他是<u>教授</u>。

商场	售货员 (shòuhuòyuán)
北京	作家 (zuòjiā)
学校	老师

（3）A：星期天你常常去哪儿？

B：星期天我常常去<u>商场</u>。

A：你跟谁去<u>商场</u>？

B：我跟<u>林娜</u>去<u>商场</u>。

书店 (shūdiàn)	我朋友
体育馆 (tǐyùguǎn)	马大为
公园 (gōngyuán)	我弟弟

（4）A：他送他朋友什么？

B：他送他朋友<u>一张光盘</u>。

A：这<u>张光盘</u>怎么样？

B：<u>这张光盘很好</u>。

一个大蛋糕	漂亮
一瓶葡萄酒	便宜 (piányi)
一本 (běn) 书	有意思

（5）A：他给谁二十块钱？

B：他给<u>师傅</u>二十块钱。

一张名片	力波
一张照片	老师
一本外语书	弟弟

（6）A：您买什么？

B：我买<u>两斤葡萄</u>。一共多少钱？

A：一共<u>五块钱</u>。

两瓶酒	180 元 (yuán)
三支 (zhī) 笔 (bǐ)	7.5 元
一份 (fèn) 报纸	2.6 元

（7）A：<u>这个师傅的葡萄</u> <u>贵</u>不<u>贵</u>？

B：<u>这个师傅的葡萄</u>不<u>贵</u>，
那个师傅的葡萄 <u>贵</u>。

外语系的学生	多	汉语系的学生
这一课	容易	那一课
这儿的烤鸭	贵	那儿的烤鸭
这张照片	漂亮	那张照片

3. 跟你的同学口头做下面的练习　Practice the following exercises verbally with your classmate

　　A game of giving change

E.g.　　A：一共3.24元，我给您5元。

　　　　B：我找您<u>1.76元</u>。

　→ A：一共三块两毛四，我给您五块。

　　　B：我找您<u>一块七毛六</u>。

（1）A：一共7.69元，我给您8元。

　　　B：我找您_____。

（2）A：一共13.12元，我给您15元。

　　　B：我找您_____。

（3）A：一共22.78元，我给您30元。

　　　B：我找您_____。

（4）A：一共31.49元，我给您50元。

　　　B：我找您_____。

（5）A：一共84.92元，我给您100元。

　　　B：我找您_____。

4. 根据下列陈述句用疑问代词提问题　Change the following declarative sentences into questions with interrogative pronouns

（1）这个商场很有名。　（Ask two questions）

（2）一斤葡萄两块七毛钱。　（Ask three questions）

（3）他送我三瓶酒。　（Ask four questions）

（4）我哥哥在商场卖(mài)光盘。　（Ask five questions）

（5）林娜常常跟宋华学习汉语。　（Ask six questions）

5. 会话练习　Conversation practice

【谈喜好　Likes and dislikes】

（1）A：你喜欢什么专业?

　　　B：我喜欢_____。

A：你喜欢哪国文学？

B：我喜欢＿＿＿＿＿文学。＿＿＿＿＿有很多有名的作家。

（2）A：你喜欢不喜欢哲学？

B：我＿＿＿＿＿哲学，我喜欢历史。

A：历史很有意思，我哥哥也喜欢历史。

（3）A：这本书怎么样？

B：这本书不太好，我＿＿＿＿＿。你喜欢不喜欢？

A：我也不太喜欢。

【解决语言困难　Solving language problems】

（1）A：请问，这个＿＿＿＿＿怎么说？

B：对不起，我也不知道。

C：这叫"词典"，汉语词典。

A：谢谢。

（2）A：老师，"cheap"＿＿＿＿＿？

B："便宜"。

A：谢谢。这个本子很便宜。

（3）A：今年是马年，你属什么？

B：对不起，请您再说一遍。

【买东西　Shopping】

（1）A：您买什么？

B：师傅，有好的葡萄吗？

A：有，这都是。

B：＿＿＿＿＿？

A：两块五一斤。您要多少？

B：我要四斤。

A：＿＿＿＿＿。 您给我五十，我找您＿＿＿＿＿。

（2）A：小姐，这儿有本子吗？

B：有。您看，都在这儿。

A：多少钱一个？

B：这个＿＿＿＿＿＿＿，那个＿＿＿＿＿＿＿。您要哪个？

A：哪个本子好？

B：都很好。

A：好，我都要，买两个。

B：一共＿＿＿＿＿＿＿。您给我二十，我找您两毛。

（3）A：先生，您要什么？

B：我要一杯（bēi）咖啡。

A：＿＿＿＿＿＿＿＿？

B：不要了，谢谢。

6. 看图会话　Make dialogues based on the pictures

【谈喜好　Likes and dislikes】

❶ A：我喜欢这本英文书，你呢？

B：我喜欢＿＿＿＿＿＿。

A：两本都很好。

❷ A：你喜欢喝什么？茶还是咖啡？

B：我喜欢＿＿＿＿＿＿。

＿＿＿＿＿＿也很好。

【买东西　Shopping】

❶ A：请问，这种英文报纸多少钱？

B：两块。您要吗？

A：要，那种呢？

B：那种三块。

A：好的，两种我＿＿＿＿＿。

给您＿＿＿＿钱。

❷ A：这个本子多少钱？

B：＿＿＿＿＿＿＿＿＿＿。

A：我要两个，给您钱。

7. 交际练习　Communication exercises

(1) Talk with your classmate about what you like or dislike.

(2) Suppose your classmate is a salesperson in a store and you are a customer. You are talking with each other.

阅读与复述 Reading Comprehension and Paraphrasing

　　马大为星期天常常跟林娜去小商场。今天他去一个大商场，商场里东西（dōngxi）很多。他在那儿买音乐光盘，王小云也在。马大为喜欢中国音乐。他问王小云什么音乐光盘好，王小云说《梁祝》很有名，外国朋友也喜欢。马大为很高兴，他说："好，我买这张光盘。"马大为还要买书和报纸，这个商场不卖书，也不卖报纸。他跟王小云去买本子。

　　马大为还常常去书店。那个书店也很大，书很多。他在书店买书，也看书。中国的书不贵。下月二十号是他弟弟的生日。他弟弟喜欢中国功夫（gōngfu），他要送弟弟一本《中国功夫》。

三、语法　Grammar

1 介词词组　Prepositional phrase

　　In Lesson 5, we learned the verb "在". "在" is also a preposition. When combined with words expressing location (usually a noun or a phrase indicating place), it forms a prepositional phrase. It is used before the predicative verb to indicate the location of an action.

在 + PW + V O

Subject	Predicate		
	在 + Pr / N	V	O
我	在　这儿	买	光盘。
您	在　哪儿	工作?	
他	不 在　　语言学院	学习。	

The preposition "跟……" is often combined with a noun or pronoun after it to form a prepositional phrase and used in front of the predicative verb to indicate the manner of an action.

跟 + Pr / N (person) + V O

Subject	Predicate		
	跟 + Pr / N	V	O
我	跟　　　　力波	来	这儿。
（你）	跟　我	来。	
您	跟　我	学。	

Note: The prepositional phrases "在……" and "跟……" must be placed before the verb. One cannot say: "我学习在语言学院", "你来跟我".

2 双宾语动词谓语句（1）：给、送
Sentences with double objects (1): "给" and "送"

Some verbs can take two objects. The preceding one refers to people and the following one refers to things.

给 / 送 + Pr / N (person) + NP（thing）

Subject	Predicate		
	V	Object₁	Object₂
您	给	我	二十块钱。
（我）	送	您	一个苹果。
我	找	您	十块钱。

Note: Not all Chinese verbs can take double objects.

3 形容词谓语句和副词 "很"

Sentences with an adjectival predicate and the adverb "很"

Many sentences with an adjectival predicate have been studied so far. In this kind of sentence, an adjective follows the subject directly and does not need the verb "是". If there are no other adverbs such as "真", "太" or "不" before the adjective, the adverb "很" is usually placed before it, and it is unstressed.

S＋很＋A

我很好。

我今天很忙。

这个商场很大。

In this kind of sentence, if the adjective does not have an adverb before it, the sentence indicates comparison. For example:

我忙，他不忙。

我的本子大。（他的本子小。）

The meaning of "很" here is not so obvious. "我很忙" and "我忙" are not much different in degree unless "很" is stressed. In V / A-not-V / A questions, "很" cannot be used, for example: "他高兴不高兴？" one cannot say "他很高兴不很高兴？".

四、汉字　Chinese Characters

1 汉字的结构(3)　Structure of Chinese characters (3)

The top-bottom structure

a. Equal top-bottom

1
2

男　是

b. Big top-small bottom

1
2

兴

1	2
3	

然

1	2
	3
	4

您

c. Small top-big bottom

 家　　 宿

d. Equal top-middle-bottom

 意

2 认写基本汉字　Learn and write basic Chinese characters

(1) 舟　　ノ ノ 凢 角 舟 舟
zhōu　　boat　　6 strokes

(2) 皿　　丿 冂 冂 冊 皿
mǐn　　household utensiles　　5 strokes

(3) 乐（樂）　　一 二 匚 牙 乐
yuè　　music　　5 strokes

(4) 足　　丿 冂 口 甲 甲 足 足
zú　　foot　　7 strokes

(5) 书（書）　　フ ㇅ 书 书
shū　　book　　4 strokes

(6) 本　　一 十 才 木 本
běn　　root of a tree　　5 strokes
Note: The "-" at the bottom of "本" indicates the root.

(7) 平　　一 丶 丷 亚 平
píng　　flat　　5 strokes

(8) 走　　一 十 土 キ キ 走 走
zǒu　　to walk　　7 strokes
Note: The ancient character looks like a runner.

(9) 己　　フ コ 己
jǐ　　oneself　　3 strokes

(10) 穴　　丶 丷 宀 宀 穴
xué　　cave　　5 strokes

(11) 勿　　ノ ク 勹 勿
wù　　no, not　　4 strokes

(12) 金　　ノ 人 人 今 全 全 余 金
jīn　　gold　　8 strokes

(13) 斤　　一 厂 斤 斤
jīn　　(a traditional unit of weight, 1 jin equals to 0.5 kilograms)
　　　　4 strokes

Note: The ancient character resembles an axe. It is used as a unit of weight now.

(14) 毛　　一 二 三 毛
máo　　fur; mao (a measure word of Chinese monetary unit, it is equal to 1/10 yuan)　　4 strokes

(15) 戈　　一 弋 戈 戈
gē　　an ancient weapon　　4 strokes

3 认写课文中的汉字 Learn and write the Chinese characters in the texts

(1) 光盘 guāngpán （光盤）

光 → 业 + 儿　　6 strokes

盘 → 舟 + 皿　　11 strokes

(2) 音乐 yīnyuè（音樂）

音 → 立 + 日　　　　　　　　　9 strokes

⺌ (chángzìtóur, the "constant" top)　丶 丨 丷 丷 ⺌　5 strokes

(3) 常常 chángcháng

常 → ⺌ + 口 + 巾　　　　　　　11 strokes

⻊ (zúzìpángr, on the left side of a character, the seventh stroke in "足" is written as an upward stroke.)　丶 口 口 卩 卩 卩 ⻊　7 strokes

(4) 跟 gēn

跟 → ⻊ + 艮　　　　　　　　　13 strokes

⼟ (títǔpángr, on the left side of a character, the third stroke of "土" is written as an upward stroke. It is called the "earth" side.)　一 十 ⼟　3 strokes

(5) 商场 shāngchǎng（商場）

商 → 亠 + ⸜ + 冂 + 丷 + 口　　11 strokes
场 → ⼟ + 昜　　　　　　　　　6 strokes

卩 (dān'ěrdāor, the "single-ear" side)　丨 卩　2 strokes

(6) 报纸 bàozhǐ（報紙）

报 → 扌 + 卩 + 又　　　　　　　7 strokes

(7) 梁祝 Liáng Zhù

梁 → 氵 + 刅 + 木　　　　　　　11 strokes

丱 (gàozìtóur, the "tell" top)　丿 丶 丱 生　4 strokes

(8) 先生 xiānsheng

先 → 生 + 儿　　　　　　　　　6 strokes

(9) 要 yào

要 → 西 + 女 　　　　　　　　　　9 strokes

(10) 师傅 shīfu（師傅）

傅 (fù) → 亻 + 甫 + 寸 　　　　　12 strokes

(The meaning side is "亻", and the phonetic side is "甫".)

(11) 香蕉 xiāngjiāo

香 → 禾 + 日 　　　　　　　　　　9 strokes

蕉 → 艹 + 隹 + 灬 　　　　　　　15 strokes

(12) 苹果 píngguǒ（蘋果）

苹 → 艹 + 平 　　　　　　　　　　8 strokes

(The meaning is indicated by "艹" and the pronunciation is indicated by "平".)

(13) 对不起 duìbuqǐ（對不起）

对 → 又 + 寸 　　　　　　　　　　5 strokes

起 → 走 + 己 　　　　　　　　　10 strokes

(14) 容易 róngyì

容 → 宀 + 八 + 口 　　　　　　　10 strokes

易 → 日 + 勿 　　　　　　　　　　8 strokes

钅 (jīnzìpángr, the "metal" side) (On the left side of a character, "金" is written as "钅".)　丿 𠂆 𠂤 钅　　5 strokes

(15) 钱 qián（錢）

钱 → 钅 + 一 + 戋 　　　　　　　10 strokes

(16) 块 kuài（塊）

块 → 土 ＋ 夬　　　　　　　　　　　7 strokes

(17) 分 fēn

分 → 八 ＋ 刀　　　　　　　　　　　4 strokes

(To cut things in half with a knife.)

(18) 送 sòng

送 → 丷 ＋ 天 ＋ 辶　　　　　　　　9 strokes

(19) 给 gěi（給）

给 → 纟 ＋ 合　　　　　　　　　　　9 strokes

(20) 找 zhǎo

找 → 扌 ＋ 戈　　　　　　　　　　　7 strokes

The Currency of China

The currency of China is the Renminbi, literally "people's currency", abbreviated as "RMB". The basic unit of the RMB is the *yuan* or *kuai*. One-tenth of a *yuan* is called a *jiao* or *mao*, and one one-hundredth of a *yuan* equals one *fen*. Chinese money is issued in paper notes as well as coins, in 11 different denominations:

Paper money: 100 *yuan*, 50 *yuan*, 20 *yuan*, 10 *yuan*, 5 *yuan*, 2 *yuan*, 1 *yuan*
5 *jiao*, 2 *jiao*, 1 *jiao*

Coins: 1 *yuan*, 5 *jiao*, 1 *jiao*, 5 *fen*, 2 *fen*, 1 *fen*

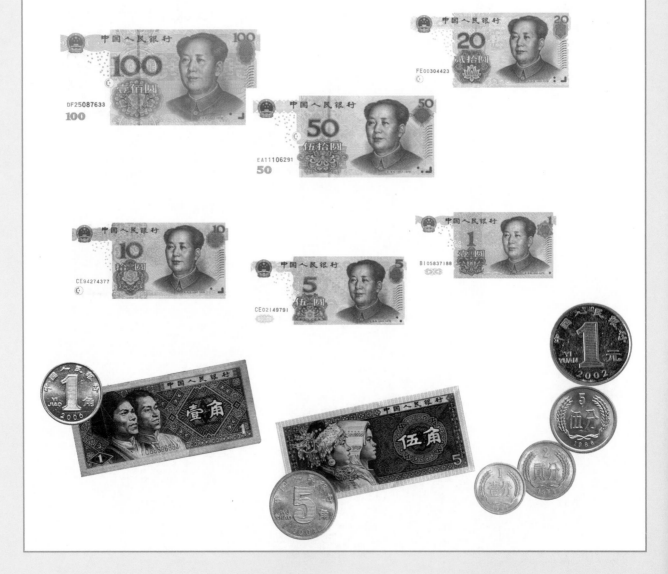

第十一课

Lesson 11

Wǒ huì shuō yìdiǎnr Hànyǔ

我 会 说 一点儿 汉语

I can speak a little Chinese.

By the end of this lesson, you will be able to ask the time, hail a taxi, ask whether something is allowed, and indicate your ability to accomplish tasks. We will pay special attention to how Chinese people respond to compliments.

一、课文 Text

🎧 43 （一）

问时间
Asking the time

林娜：师傅，我 去 语言 学院。 请问 现在 几 点？
Lín Nà：Shīfu, wǒ qù Yǔyán Xuéyuàn. Qǐngwèn xiànzài jǐ diǎn?

司机：差 一 刻 八 点。 您 会 说 汉语 啊！
Sījī：Chà yí kè bā diǎn. Nín huì shuō Hànyǔ a!

林娜：我 会 说 一点儿 汉语。① 我 是 学生， 现在 回
Lín Nà：Wǒ huì shuō yìdiǎnr Hànyǔ. Wǒ shì xuésheng, xiànzài huí

学院 上课。
xuéyuàn shàngkè.

司机：你们 几 点 上课？
Sījī：Nǐmen jǐ diǎn shàngkè?

表示能力
Expressing one's ability

林娜：八 点 上课。 师傅， 我们 八 点 能 到 吗？
Lín Nà：Bā diǎn shàngkè. Shīfu, wǒmen bā diǎn néng dào ma?

司机：能 到。 您 的 汉语 很 好。
Sījī：Néng dào. Nín de Hànyǔ hěn hǎo.

林娜：哪里，我 的 汉语 不 太 好。② 您 会 不 会 说 英语？
Lín Nà：Nǎli, wǒ de Hànyǔ bú tài hǎo. Nín huì bu huì shuō Yīngyǔ?

司机： 我 不 会 说 英语。 我 也 喜欢 外语， 常常 在家
Sījī： Wǒ bú huì shuō Yīngyǔ. Wǒ yě xǐhuan wàiyǔ, chángcháng zài jiā

学 点儿 英语。
xué diǎnr Yīngyǔ.

林娜： 谁 教 您 英语?
Lín Nà： Shéi jiāo nín Yīngyǔ?

司机： 我 孙女儿。
Sījī： Wǒ sūnnür.

林娜： 真 有 意思。 她 今年 几 岁?
Lín Nà： Zhēn yǒu yìsi. Tā jīnnián jǐ suì?

司机： 六 岁。我 的 岁数 太 大 了，学 英语 不 容易。③
Sījī： Liù suì. Wǒ de suìshu tài dà le, xué Yīngyǔ bù róngyì.

林娜： 您 今年 多 大 岁数?④
Lín Nà： Nín jīnnián duō dà suìshu?

司机： 我 今年 五十二。 语言 学院 到 了。⑤ 现在 差 五
Sījī： Wǒ jīnnián wǔshí'èr. Yǔyán Xuéyuàn dào le. Xiànzài chà wǔ

分 八 点， 您 还 有 五 分钟。⑥
fēn bā diǎn, nín hái yǒu wǔ fēnzhōng.

林娜： 谢谢， 给 您 钱。
Lín Nà： Xièxie, gěi nín qián.

司机： 您 给 我 二十， 我 找 您 五 块 四， OK?
Sījī： Nín gěi wǒ èrshí, wǒ zhǎo nín wǔ kuài sì, OK?

林娜： 您 会 说 英语!
Lín Nà： Nín huì shuō Yīngyǔ!

司机： 我 也 会 一点儿。拜拜!
Sījī： Wǒ yě huì yìdiǎnr. Báibái!

林娜： 拜拜!
Lín Nà： Báibái!

生词 New Words

1. 会	huì	OpV	to have the knowledge of, can 会说汉语
2. (一)点儿	(yì)diǎnr	Nu-M	a little bit 会说一点儿汉语，喝一点儿酒
3. 司机	sījī	N	driver
4. 点(钟)	diǎn(zhōng)	M	o'clock 两点（钟），八点（钟）
5. 差	chà	V	to be short of, to lack
6. 刻	kè	M	quarter (of an hour) 一刻（钟），差一刻八点
7. 回	huí	V	to return 回学院，回家，回中国，回北京
8. 上课	shàngkè	VO	to go to class (for both the students and teachers)
上	shàng	V	to ascend, to go to 上汉语课，上文化课
9. 能	néng	OpV	can, to be able to 能来上课
10. 到	dào	V	to arrive 到家，到学院，到商场，到北京
11. 哪里	nǎli	IE	no (an expression of mild denial)/ where
12. 教	jiāo	V	to teach, to instruct 教汉语，教文学
13. 英语	Yīngyǔ	N	English 会说一点儿英语，学习英语，上英语课
14. 孙女儿	sūnnür	N	granddaughter on son's side
女儿	nǚ'ér	N	daughter
15. 岁数	suìshu	N	years (of age) 多大岁数
数	shù	N	number
*16. 还	hái	Adv	in addition; still 还有五分钟
17. 分(钟)	fēn(zhōng)	M	minute 八点五分，差五分八点，二十分钟
18. 拜拜	báibái	IE	bye-bye (transliteration)

补充生词 Supplementary Words

1. 法语	Fǎyǔ	N	French
2. 德语	Déyǔ	N	German
3. 俄语	Éyǔ	N	Russian
4. 日语	Rìyǔ	N	Japanese

注释　Notes

① 我会说一点儿汉语。

"一点儿" is an indefinite measure word expressing the idea of a small amount, and is used to modify a noun. When the language environment is clear, the noun it modifies can be omitted. For example:

A：您会说汉语啊！

B：我会说一点儿（汉语）。

When "一点儿" is not at the beginning of a sentence, "一" may be omitted. For example: "吃（一）点儿烤鸭", "喝（一）点儿酒", "看（一）点儿书".

② 哪里，我的汉语不太好。

"哪里" is actually an interrogative pronoun with the same meaning of "哪儿", but "哪里" here has a different meaning and is often used to express modesty when responding to praise. We can also use "是吗？" to express doubt. For example: "是吗？我的汉语不太好". Whether we use a word expressing negation or doubt, the purpose is to show a person accepts other people's compliments with modesty. In Chinese culture, this is regarded as an appropriate response.

③ 学英语不容易。

"It is not easy to learn English."

④ 您今年多大岁数？

This is a courteous way of asking the age of an elderly or senior person.

⑤ 语言学院到了。

"Here we are at the Language Institute."

⑥ 您还有五分钟。

"You still have five minutes."

One of the meanings "还" already learned is to make an additional remark. Another usage of "还" is to express the continuation of a state or an action. For example:

晚上十一点他还工作。（ He is still working at eleven o'clock at night. ）

他现在还不能看中文报纸。（ He is still unable to read Chinese newspapers.)

他还没有起床（qǐchuáng）。（ He still hasn't got up. / He is still in bed. ）

🎧 44 （二）

丁力波：　陈　老师，　马　大为　今天　不　能　来　上课。
Dīng Lìbō：Chén lǎoshī，　Mǎ Dàwéi jīntiān bù néng lái shàngkè.

陈老师：他为　什么　不　能　来　上课?
Chén lǎoshī：Tā wèi shénme bù néng lái shàngkè?

丁力波：昨天　是 星期日，他　上午　去　商场　买　东西，
Dīng Lìbō：Zuótiān shì xīngqīrì， tā shàngwǔ qù shāngchǎng mǎi dōngxi，

下午　去　朋友　家玩儿。他　晚上　十一　点　半 回
xiàwǔ qù péngyou jiā wánr． Tā wǎnshang shíyī diǎn bàn huí

学院，　十二 点 写汉字，两　点钟　睡觉。 现在
xuéyuàn， shí'èr diǎn xiě Hànzì， liǎng diǎnzhōng shuìjiào． Xiànzài

他 还 没有　起床。
tā hái méiyǒu qǐchuáng．

陈老师：他 应该 来　上课。
Chén lǎoshī：Tā yīnggāi lái shàngkè．

丁力波：老师，我 能 不 能　问 您 一 个 问题？
Dīng Lìbō：Lǎoshī， wǒ néng bu néng wèn nín yí ge wèntí？

陈老师：可以。
Chén lǎoshī：Kěyǐ．

> 表示允许或禁止
> **Expressing permission or prohibition**

丁力波：我们　为 什么
Dīng Lìbō：Wǒmen wèi shénme

八 点　上课？
bā diǎn shàngkè？

生词 New Words

1. 为什么	wèi shénme	Qpr	why
为	wèi	Prep	for
*2. 昨天	zuótiān	N	yesterday 昨天上午，昨天下午
3. 东西	dōngxi	N	thing, stuff 买东西，吃东西，送东西
4. 玩儿	wánr	V	to have fun, to play 去朋友家玩儿，跟朋友 玩儿
5. 晚上	wǎnshang	N	evening, night 昨天晚上，星期六晚上， 五号晚上

	晚	wǎn	A	late 来晚了
6.	半	bàn	Nu	half 九点半，半天，半个月，半个星期，
				半年，半个苹果，半斤葡萄
7.	写	xiě	V	to write
8.	汉字	Hànzì	N	Chinese character 写汉字，一个汉字
	字	zì	N	character
9.	睡觉	shuìjiào	VO	to sleep 十一点睡觉，还没有睡觉
	睡	shuì	V	to sleep
10.	起床	qǐchuáng	VO	to get up 六点起床，还没有起床
	起	qǐ	V	to get up, to rise
	床	chuáng	N	bed 一张床
11.	应该	yīnggāi	OpV	should, ought to 应该来，应该看，应该祝贺
	该	gāi	OpV	should, ought to
12.	问题	wèntí	N	question 一个问题，问问题，有问题，
				没问题
*13.	可以	kěyǐ	OpV	may 可以进来，可以问问题，可以去
*14.	陈	Chén	PN	(a surname)

补充生词 Supplementary Words

1.	下课	xiàkè	VO	to dismiss class, to finish class
2.	吃饭	chīfàn	VO	to eat (a meal)
3.	开车	kāichē	VO	to drive a car or a train, etc.
	车	chē	N	vehicle
4.	跳舞	tiàowǔ	VO	to dance
5.	唱歌	chànggē	VO	to sing (a song)
6.	回答	huídá	V	to answer
7.	礼物	lǐwù	N	gift, present

8. 表	biǎo	N	watch
9. 快	kuài	A	fast
10. 等	děng	V	to wait
11. 吸烟	xīyān	VO	to smoke
12. 难	nán	A	difficult
13. 拍照	pāizhào	VO	to take pictures
14. 便条	biàntiáo	N	note
15. 打的	dǎdī	VO	to hail a taxi

二、练习　Exercises

练习与运用　Drills and Practice 45

核心句 KEY SENTENCES

1. 请问，现在几点？
2. 我会说一点儿汉语。
3. 你们几点上课？
4. 现在差五分八点，您还有五分钟。
5. 他为什么不能来上课？
6. 他昨天下午去朋友家玩儿。
7. 他应该来上课。
8. 我能不能问您一个问题？

1. 熟读下列词组 Read the following phrases until you learn them by heart

（1）会说汉语　会说英语　会写汉字　不会问问题　不会学习　不会工作
（2）能来学院　能到商场　能回家　不能看中文书　不能上课　不能喝酒
（3）可以进来　可以坐　可以认识一下

不可以看　　　不可以说英语　　不可以问问题

（4）应该起床　　　应该睡觉　　　　应该工作　　　　应该玩儿

　　　不应该说　　　不应该问　　　　不应该喝酒　　　不应该来

（5）还没有起床　　　　还没有睡觉　　　　还没有写汉字

　　　还不会说汉语　　　还不能看中文书　　还不认识他

（6）说点儿英语　　　吃点儿蛋糕　　　　喝点儿葡萄酒

　　　买点儿东西　　　看点儿书　　　　　有点儿时间

2. 句型替换　Pattern drills

（1）A：现在几点？

　　　B：现在<u>七点四十</u>。

　　　　　⬤　8：30　　　　9：58

　　　　　　　10：08　　　12：15

　　　　　　　3：28　　　　5：45

（2）A：你几点<u>起床</u>？

　　　B：我<u>六点十分</u> <u>起床</u>。

　　　　下课 (xiàkè)　　11：50

　　　　吃饭 (chīfàn)　　12：15

　　　　写汉字　　　　　8：20　⬤

（3）A：你现在去哪儿？

　　　B：我现在<u>回学院</u>。

　　　A：你<u>回学院</u>做什么？

　　　B：我<u>回学院</u> <u>上课</u>。

　　　　⬤

　　　　去商场　　买东西

　　　　去朋友家　玩儿

　　　　回家　　　看爸爸、妈妈

（4）A：你今天下午有没有课？

　　　B：有课。

　　　A：你有什么课？

　　　B：我有汉语课。

　　　A：谁教你们<u>汉语</u>？

　　　B：<u>陈老师</u>教我们<u>汉语</u>。

　　　　法语 (Fǎyǔ)　　　王先生 ⬤

　　　　德语 (Déyǔ)　　　宋老师

　　　　俄语 (Éyǔ)　　　　张教授

　　　　日语 (Rìyǔ)　　　　丁小姐

（5）A：你会<u>游泳</u>吗？
　　　B：我会<u>游泳</u>。
　　　A：你今天能<u>游泳</u>吗？
　　　B：我今天不能<u>游泳</u>。

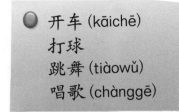

开车 (kāichē)
打球
跳舞 (tiàowǔ)
唱歌 (chànggē)

（6）A：你能不能<u>看</u> <u>中文报</u>？
　　　B：我现在还不能<u>看</u> <u>中文报</u>。
　　　A：为什么？
　　　B：我的汉语还不太好。

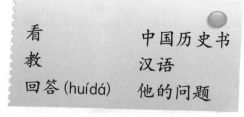

看　　　　中国历史书
教　　　　汉语
回答 (huídá)　他的问题

（7）A：现在可以<u>问</u> <u>问题</u>吗？
　　　B：可以。

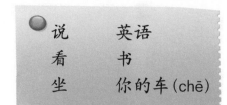

说　　　英语
看　　　书
坐　　　你的车 (chē)

（8）A：明天是不是林娜的生日？
　　　B：是她的生日。
　　　A：我们应该<u>买</u>点儿<u>苹果</u>。

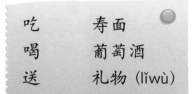

吃　　　寿面
喝　　　葡萄酒
送　　　礼物 (lǐwù)

3. 根据画线部分提出问题 Ask a question concerning the underlined words in each of the following sentences

（1）现在<u>七点三十八分</u>。
（2）他<u>五点一刻</u>回家。
（3）<u>二月二十二号</u>是他的生日。
（4）<u>明天晚上八点</u>他们有一个聚会。

4. 会话练习 Conversation practice

【问时间　Asking the time】

（1）A：请问，您的表 (biǎo) 现在几点？
　　　B：_____，我的表快 (kuài) 了一点儿。
　　　A：谢谢。

（2）A：今天晚上你有没有时间？

B：我有时间。

A：你来我家玩儿，好吗？

B：好啊。几点去？

A：＿＿＿＿＿＿＿＿＿＿，怎么样？

B：晚一点儿，＿＿＿＿＿＿＿＿，好吗？

A：好。

【表示能力　Expressing one's ability】

（1）A：你会不会＿＿＿＿＿＿＿＿？

B：我会一点儿。

A：你能教我吗？

B：没问题，有时间我们去体育馆练习。

（2）A：这个汉字怎么写？

B：对不起，我也＿＿＿＿＿＿。

（3）A：你现在能不能选修中国哲学课？

B：我现在还＿＿＿＿＿＿＿。

A：为什么？

B：我的汉语还不太好。

【表示允许或禁止　Expressing permission or prohibition】

（1）A：可以进来吗？

B：对不起，请等（děng）一下。

（2）A：可以吸烟（xīyān）吗？

B：对不起，这儿不可以＿＿＿＿＿＿＿。

（3）A：老师，今天的课很难（nán），我有问题，能不能问您？

B：＿＿＿＿＿。明天下午我有时间，你四点来，好吗？

A：好，谢谢。

5. 交际练习　Communication exercises

(1) Your classmate is a taxi driver, and you want to go to somewhere by taxi. How do you talk with the taxi driver?

(2) Your watch has stopped. How do you ask a passerby the time?

(3) You are talking about families with your friend. How do you ask him / her about the ages of his / her parents and about the children of his / her brothers and sisters?

(4) You are visiting somewhere and you want to find out whether you can take pictures (拍照, pāizhào) or smoke (吸烟, xīyān). How do you ask?

(5) You are coming to see a friend, but he / she isn't in. You can leave a note to him / her. For example:

便条(biàntiáo)

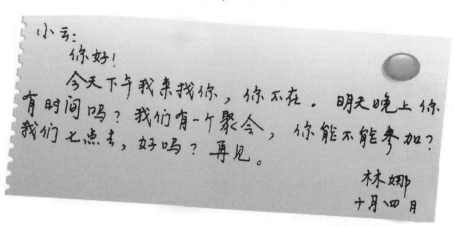

阅读与复述 Reading Comprehension and Paraphrasing

　　星期天林娜到一个英国朋友家玩儿。星期一八点她有课，七点三刻她打的 (dǎdī) 回学院上课。那个司机今年五十二岁，他有一个孙女儿，今年六岁。他说林娜的汉语很好。他也喜欢外语，现在跟他孙女儿学英语。他们差五分八点到学院。

　　马大为星期天很忙。他上午去商场买东西，下午去朋友家玩儿，晚上很晚回学院。他十二点写汉字，两点钟睡觉。星期一八点上课，他八点十分还没有起床。陈老师很不高兴，她问丁力波："马大为在哪儿？" 丁力波说马大为现在还没有起床，他不能来上课。

三、语法　Grammar

1 钟点　Telling time

These words are used to tell time in Chinese: "点（钟）", "刻" and "分". For example, "八点二十五分". In Chinese, people tell time in this way:

2:00　两点（钟）
（The "钟" in "点钟" can be omitted.）

2:05　两点（○）五分
（When "分" is a number less than ten, "○" may be added before it.）

2:10　两点十分

2:12　两点十二（分）
（When "分" is more than 10, "分" may be omitted.）

2:15　两点一刻 or 两点十五（分）

2:30　两点半 or 两点三十（分）

2:45　两点三刻 or 差一刻三点 or 两点四十五（分）

2:55　差五分三点 or 两点五十五（分）

The order of expressions of time and date is:

年 + 月 + 日 + 星期 + 上午/下午/晚上 + 钟点

| 二○一○年 | 十二月 | 一日 | 星期三 | 晚上 | 八点二十五 |
| 2010年 | 12月 | 1日 | 星期三 | 晚上 | 8:25 |

Furthermore, "分钟" can be used to indicate "minute", like "您还有五分钟 (You still have five minutes.)". However, "分钟" indicates a period of time rather than a time for something to be done or to happen.

2 能愿动词谓语句（1）：会、能、可以、应该
Sentences with the optative verbs (1): "会" "能", "可以" and "应该"

Optative verbs such as "会", "能", "可以" and "应该" are often placed before verbs to express ability, possibility, or willingness. Sometimes "要" can also be used as these meanings.

Optative verbs such as "会", "能", and "可以" indicate the ability to do something and can be translated into "can, be able to".

It should be noted, though, that "会" emphasizes skills acquired through learning, while "能" and "可以" express the possession of skills in general.

（不）OpV + VO

Subject	Predicate			
	TW	OpV	V	O
你		会不会	说	汉语？
他		不会	打	球。
我		会	写	这个汉字。
谁		会	游泳？	
他孙女儿		能	教	他英语　吗？
马大为	今天	能不能	学习？	
你朋友		能	喝	多少酒？
你		可以不可以	介绍一下	你们系？

"能" and "可以" can also be used to express permission or prohibition under specific circumstances. For example:

Subject	Predicate			
	TW	OpV	V	O
我们	八点	能不能	到	那儿？
我	明天	不能	上	课。
（我）		可以	进来	吗？
这儿		不可以	吃	东西。

Subject	Predicate		
	OpV	V	O
他	应该	来 上	课。
你	不应该	去	那儿。

Note:

❶ In a sentence with an optative verb, the affirmative-negative form (V/A-不-V/A) is formed by juxtaposing the affirmative and negative forms of the optative verb, that is OpV-不-OpV.

OpV　+　不　+　OpV　+　V　O

会　　　不　　　会　　　说　汉语

能　　　不　　　能　　　去

可以　　不　　　可以　　介绍

❷ The negative form of "能" and "可以" is usually "不能". "不可以" is only used to express prohibition. For example: "不可以吸烟". If the answer to the question "你可以不可以介绍一下你们系?" is negative, it should be "我不能介绍我们系." One cannot say "我不可以介绍我们系".

❸ To answer briefly, one may use only the optative verb. For example:

A: 你会说汉语吗?　　　　　　A: 可以进来吗?

B: 不会。　　　　　　　　　　B: 可以。

❹ Some optative verbs are also general verbs. For example:

他会英语。　　　　　　　　我要咖啡。

3 连动句(1)：表示目的

Sentences with serial verb phrases (1)：to indicate purpose

In a sentence with a verbal predicate, the subject may take two consecutive verbs or verb phrases. The order of these verb phrases is fixed. In the sentences with serial verb phrases introduced in this lesson, the second verb indicates the purpose of the action denoted by the first verb.

$$S + V_1 O + V_2 O$$

Subject	Predicate				
	TW	V_1	O	V_2	O
我	现在	回	学院	上	课。
他	下午	去不去	朋友家	玩儿?	
他	下午	不去	朋友家	玩儿。	

4 双宾语动词谓语句(2)：教、问

Sentences with double objects (2)："教" and "问"

Verbs such as "教" and "问" can take double objects, for example:

Subject	Predicate		
	V	Object₁	Object₂
他孙女儿	教	他	英语。
哪个老师	教	你们	中国文化?
他	问	我	一个问题。
他	问	你	什么?

四、汉字 Chinese Characters

1 汉字的结构(4) Structure of Chinese characters (4)

The enclosure structure ①

a. Four-side enclosure

□ 国 回

b. Left-top-right enclosure

□ 用 问

c. Top-left enclosure

□ 应 属

d. Top-left-bottom enclosure

□ 医

e. Top-right enclosure

□ 可 司

2 认写基本汉字 Learn and write basic Chinese characters

(1) 占   丨 卜 ├ 占 占

zhàn   to occupy   5 strokes

(2) 里(裏)   丨 冂 日 日 甲 甲 里

lǐ   inside   7 strokes

(3) 至   一 工 互 丢 至 至

zhì   to   6 strokes

(4) 央　丶一口央央
yāng　center　　　　　　5 strokes

(5) 东（東）　一七左东东
dōng　east　　　　　　5 strokes

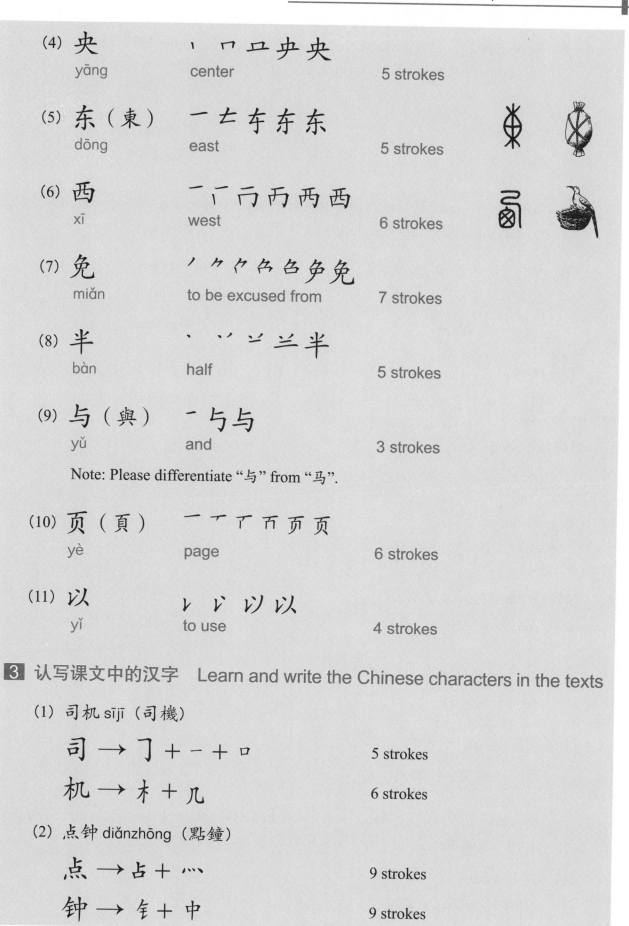

(6) 西　一一一一西西西
xī　west　　　　　　6 strokes

(7) 免　ノク午色色兔免
miǎn　to be excused from　　7 strokes

(8) 半　丶丷丷半半
bàn　half　　　　　　5 strokes

(9) 与（與）　一与与
yǔ　and　　　　　　3 strokes

Note: Please differentiate "与" from "马".

(10) 页（頁）　一一一一页页
yè　page　　　　　　6 strokes

(11) 以　乚乚以以
yǐ　to use　　　　　　4 strokes

3 认写课文中的汉字　Learn and write the Chinese characters in the texts

(1) 司机 sījī（司機）

司 → 𠃌 + 一 + 口　　　5 strokes

机 → 木 + 几　　　6 strokes

(2) 点钟 diǎnzhōng（點鐘）

点 → 占 + 灬　　　9 strokes

钟 → 钅 + 中　　　9 strokes

羊 (yángzìpángr, the "slanting-tailed-goat" side) (On the top or left side of a character, the vertical stroke in "羊" is written as a left-falling stroke "丿".)

丶 丷 丷 兰 兰 羊　　　　　　6 strokes

(3) 差 chà

差 → 羊 + 工　　　　　　9 strokes

刂 (lìdāopángr, on the right side of a multi-component character, "刀" is written as "刂". It is called the "standing knife" side.)　丨 刂　　2 strokes

亥 hài 丶 一 亠 亥 亥 亥　　　　　　6 strokes

(4) 刻 kè

刻 → 亥 + 刂　　　　　　8 strokes

(5) 回 huí

回 → 囗 + 口　　　　　　6 strokes

(6) 能 néng

能 → 厶 + 月 + 匕 + 匕　　　　　　10 strokes

(7) 到 dào

到 → 至 + 刂　　　　　　8 strokes

(8) 英语 Yīngyǔ（英語）

英 → 艹 + 央　　　　　　8 strokes

(9) 孙女儿 sūnnǚr（孫女兒）

孙 → 子 + 小　　　　　　6 strokes

(10) 岁数 suìshu（歲數）

数 → 米 + 女 + 攵　　　　　　13 strokes

手 (piěshǒu, the "slanting-hand" side) (On the left side of a character, the fourth stroke in "手" is written as "丿".)　丿 二 三 手　　4 strokes

(11) 拜拜 báibái

拜（bài）→ 手 + 一 + 丰　　　　　　9 strokes

(12) 昨天 zuótiān

昨 → 日 + 乍   9 strokes

(The "sun" side, "日", shows the character has a temporal connotation.)

(13) 玩儿 wánr（玩兒）

玩 → 王 + 元   8 strokes

(14) 晚上 wǎnshang

晚 → 日 + 免   11 strokes

(The "sun" side, "日", shows the character has a temporal connotation.)

(15) 写 xiě（寫）

写 → 冖 + 与   5 strokes

垂 chuí（千 + 艹 + 二）丿 一 二 三 三 乒 乒 垂 垂   8 strokes

(16) 睡觉 shuìjiào（睡覺）

睡 → 目 + 垂   13 strokes

(Please note the left side of the character is the "eye" side "目", not the "sun" side "日". "Sleeping" is related to the "eyes".)

觉 → 𰀀 + 见   9 strokes

(17) 起床 qǐchuáng（起牀）

床 → 广 + 木   7 strokes

(18) 应该 yīnggāi（應該）

应 → 广 + 业   7 strokes

该 → 讠 + 亥   8 strokes

(19) 问题 wèntí（問題）

题 → 是 + 页   15 strokes

(20) 陈 chén（陳）

陈 → 阝 + 东   7 strokes

Loanwords in Chinese

Like many other languages in the world, Chinese also borrows words from foreign languages. Most loanwords in Chinese come from English, French, Japanese or Russian. They generally fall into six groups:

The first are interpretative translations or semantic equivalents. Both terms refer to using Chinese words to translate imported concepts. Words of this category usually do not appear noticeably foreign. One example is the word 电视 *dianshi* "television", in which 电 *dian* (originally "lightning", later "electricity") is freely adapted to correspond to the prefix "tele" (originally from the ancient Greek word, meaning "far"), and 视 *shi* literally translates as "vision". The words 电话 *dianhua* "telephone" falls into the same category.

The second are transliterations that imitate the sound of the source word. The non-native origin stands out in this group of words, for example: 沙发 *shafa* "sofa", 咖啡 *kafei* "coffee", 可口可乐 *kekoukele* for "Coca-cola", and 夹克 *jiake* "jacket".

The third is a combination of the first and second methods described above: partly free paraphrasing / semantic matching, and partly transliteration. For example, in 浪漫主义 *langman zhuyi* (Romanticism), "浪漫" is the transliteration and "主义" is the interpretative translation.

The fourth are transliterations with annotations indicating the category. Examples include 啤酒 *pijiu* "beer", 摩托车 *motuoche* "motorcycle", and 坦克车 *tankeche* "tank". While 啤 *pi* is the transliteration for "beer", 摩托 *motuo* for "motor", and 坦克 *tanke* for "tank"; 酒 *jiu* "alcoholic drink" and 车 *che* "vehicle" indicate the categories.

The fifth are Roman letters plus Chinese characters, such as AA 制 *zhi* "go Dutch", PC 机 *ji* "personal computer", and B 超 *chao* "ultrasound". The sixth is the use of Roman letters only, in a direct borrowing of acronyms, for example: "CD", "DVD", "CPU", and "DNA".

As a rule, loanwords are added to the Chinese lexicon only in cases where available Chinese expressions are inadequate to describe new concepts, situations, or other phenomena that arise when Chinese and foreign cultures interact. However, words like 拜拜 *baibai* "bye-bye" and "OK" can be replaced by words of Chinese origin. Many people, especially the young, like using such expressions.

第十二课

Lesson

12

Wǒ quánshēn dōu bù shūfu

我 全身 都 不 舒服

I am not feeling well at all.

In China, what should you do if you don't feel well? Here you will learn to describe health problems to a doctor. You will also learn to express volition, necessity, and learn a new way of asking questions.

一、课文　Text

 46 （一）

丁力波：大为， 你 每 天 都 六 点　 起床　 去
Dīng Lìbō： Dàwéi, nǐ měi tiān dōu liù diǎn qǐchuáng qù

锻炼，① 现在 九 点 一 刻， 你 怎么 还
duànliàn, xiànzài jiǔ diǎn yí kè, nǐ zěnme hái

不 起床？②
bù qǐchuáng?

> 谈论身体状况
> **Talking about one's health**

马大为：我 头 疼。
Mǎ Dàwéi： Wǒ tóu téng.

丁力波：你 嗓子　怎么样?
Dīng Lìbō： Nǐ sǎngzi zěnmeyàng?

马大为：我 嗓子 也 疼。
Mǎ Dàwéi： Wǒ sǎngzi yě téng.

丁力波：我 想，　你 应该 去 医院　看病。③
Dīng Lìbō： Wǒ xiǎng, nǐ yīnggāi qù yīyuàn kànbìng.

马大为：我 身体 没 问题，④ 不用 去 看病。
Mǎ Dàwéi： Wǒ shēntǐ méi wèntí, búyòng qù kànbìng.

我 要　睡觉，不 想　去 医院。
Wǒ yào　shuìjiào，bù xiǎng　qù　yīyuàn.

表示意愿

Expressing one's desire

丁力波：你 不 去 看病，　明天 你 还 不 能　上课。
Dīng Lìbō：Nǐ　bú qù　kànbìng，míngtiān nǐ　hái bù néng shàngkè.

马大为：好 吧，我 去 医院。⑤ 现在　去 还是 下午 去？
Mǎ Dàwéi：Hǎo ba，wǒ qù yīyuàn.　Xiànzài qù háishi xiàwǔ qù？

丁力波：当然　现在 去，我 跟 你 一起 去。⑥ 今天 天气 很
Dīng Lìbō：Dāngrán xiànzài qù，wǒ gēn nǐ　yìqǐ qù.　Jīntiān tiānqì hěn

冷，你 要 多　穿　点儿 衣服。
lěng，nǐ yào duō chuān diǎnr　yīfu.

表示必要

Expressing need or necessity

生词 New Words

1. 全身	quánshēn	N	all over (the body)	全身疼，全身不舒服
全	quán	A	whole	
身	shēn	N	body	
2. 舒服	shūfu	A	comfortable, (to feel) well	不舒服，很舒服，舒服不舒服
3. 每	měi	Pr	every, each	每天，每年，每个学生，每瓶酒
4. 锻炼	duànliàn	V	to exercise, to work out	去锻炼
5. 头	tóu	N	head	
6. 疼	téng	A	painful, sore	头疼，手疼
7. 嗓子	sǎngzi	N	throat	嗓子疼，嗓子不舒服
8. 想	xiǎng	V/OpV	to think, to want (to do sth.)	想睡觉，想喝水
9. 医院	yīyuàn	N	hospital	去医院，有一个医院
10. 看病	kànbìng	VO	to see a doctor	去看病，去医院看病
病	bìng	N / V	illness; to get sick	看病，有病，没有病，病了

11.	身体	shēntǐ	N	body, health 身体好，锻炼身体
*12.	要	yào	OpV	must, to want (to do something) 要看病，要锻炼
13.	吧	ba	MdPt	(*a modal particle*)
14.	还是	háishi	Conj	or 早上还是晚上，睡觉还是起床
15.	一起	yìqǐ	Adv	together 跟他一起，一起去，一起锻炼
16.	冷	lěng	A	cold 天气很冷
17.	穿	chuān	V	to wear
18.	衣服	yīfu	N	clothes 穿衣服，买衣服，做衣服

注释　Notes

① 你每天都六点起床去锻炼。

　　"You get up to do morning exercises every day."

　　When the pronoun "每" modifies a noun, a measure word should be used before the noun it modifies as in the following examples: "每个学生", "每斤苹果". However, before the nouns "天" and "年", a measure word cannot be used, and measure words are optional before "月". For example, we say "每天", "每年", and say either "每月" or "每个月". "每" is often used in combination with "都". For example:

　　　　他每天都来学院。

　　　　我每月都回家。

② 你怎么还不起床？

　　"Why are you still in bed?"

　　"怎么" can also be used to ask about the cause of something, and the difference between "怎么" and "为什么" is that the former indicates a sense of surprise on the part of the speaker. For example:

　　　　八点上课，你怎么八点半才来？

　　　　今天天气很好，你怎么不去锻炼？

　　Note: "怎么" and "怎么样" are both interrogative pronouns, but "怎么" is often used as an adverbial in a sentence, whereas "怎么样" usually functions as the predicate as in "你怎么样". When asking the reason for something, "怎么样" cannot be used and so one cannot say "你怎么样还不起床？".

③ 我想，你应该去医院看病。

　　"I think you should go to the hospital to see a doctor."

　　In this sentence, "想" is a common verb.

④ 我身体没问题。

"I am fine."

"身体" means "body", but it may also mean "health". "你身体怎么样?" is also a form of greeting among friends and acquaintances. The phrase "没问题" means "no problem" and it is often used in spoken Chinese to indicate an affirmative, confident attitude. For example:

> A：明天你能来吗?
>
> B：没问题! 我能来。

⑤ 好吧，我去医院。

"OK. I'll go to hospital."

The modal particle "吧" has many usages. It is used to soften the tone of speech here and it may also be used in sentences expressing requests, commands, persuasion and consultation. For example:

> 请说吧。　　　　请坐吧。　　　　我问一下吧。

⑥ 我跟你一起去。

"I'll go with you."

When the prepositional phrase "跟 + Pr/NP" is placed before a verb as an adverbial modifier, it is generally used with the adverb "一起"; together they form the phrase "跟 + Pr/NP + 一起". For example:

> 他跟他的朋友一起做练习。
>
> 他跟宋华一起锻炼。

🎧 47 （二）

丁力波： 你 在 这儿 休息 一下，我 去 给 你 挂号。⑦
Dīng Lìbō： Nǐ zài zhèr xiūxi yíxià, wǒ qù gěi nǐ guàhào.

马大为： 好。
Mǎ Dàwéi： Hǎo.

医生： 8 号! 8 号 是 谁?
Yīshēng： Bā hào! Bā hào shì shéi?

丁力波： 我 是 8 号。
Dīng Lìbō： Wǒ shì bā hào.

医生： 你 看病 还是 他 看病?
Yīshēng： Nǐ kànbìng háishi tā kànbìng?

丁力波：他　看病。
Dīng Lìbō：Tā　kànbìng.

医生：请　坐吧。你 叫 马 大为， 是 不 是？
Yīshēng：Qǐng zuò ba. Nǐ jiào Mǎ Dàwéi, shì bu shì?

马大为：是，我 叫 马 大为。
Mǎ Dàwéi：Shì, wǒ jiào Mǎ Dàwéi.

医生：你 今年 多 大？
Yīshēng：Nǐ jīnnián duō dà?

马大为：我 今年 二十二 岁。
Mǎ Dàwéi：Wǒ jīnnián èrshí'èr suì.

医生：你 哪儿 不 舒服？⑧
Yīshēng：Nǐ nǎr bù shūfu?

看病
Seeing a doctor

马大为：我 头 疼，　全身　都 不 舒服。
Mǎ Dàwéi：Wǒ tóu téng, quánshēn dōu bù shūfu.

医生：我 看 一下。你 嗓子 有点儿　发炎，⑨ 还　有点儿
Yīshēng：Wǒ kàn yíxià. Nǐ sǎngzi yǒudiǎnr fāyán, hái yǒudiǎnr

发烧， 是　感冒。
fāshāo, shì gǎnmào.

丁力波：他 要 不要　住院？
Dīng Lìbō：Tā yào bu yào zhùyuàn?

医生：不用。 你 要 多　喝 水，还 要 吃 点儿 药。 你
Yīshēng：Búyòng. Nǐ yào duō hē shuǐ, hái yào chī diǎnr yào. Nǐ

愿意 吃 中药　还是 愿意 吃 西药？
yuànyì chī zhōngyào háishi yuànyì chī xīyào?

马大为：我 愿意 吃　中药。
Mǎ Dàwéi：Wǒ yuànyì chī zhōngyào.

医生：好， 你 吃 一点儿　中药， 下 星期一 再 来。
Yīshēng：Hǎo, nǐ chī yìdiǎnr zhōngyào, xià xīngqīyī zài lái.

生词 New Words

1. 休息	xiūxi	V	to take a break, to have a rest, to relax　休息一下，应该休息
*2. 给	gěi	Prep	to, for　给他买，给他介绍，给我们上课
3. 挂号	guàhào	V	to register (at a hospital, etc.)　给他挂号
4. 有点儿	yǒudiǎnr	Adv	somewhat, a bit　有点儿疼，有点儿不舒服
5. 发炎	fāyán	VO	to become inflamed　嗓子发炎
6. 发烧	fāshāo	VO	to have a fever　有点儿发烧
烧	shāo	V	to burn
7. 感冒	gǎnmào	V/N	to have a cold; cold　有点儿感冒
8. 住院	zhùyuàn	VO	to be in hospital, to be hospitalized
9. 水	shuǐ	N	water　喝水
10. 药	yào	N	medicine　吃药，买药
11. 愿意	yuànyì	OpV	to be willing, to be ready　愿意学习，愿意上课，不愿意
12. 中药	zhōngyào	N	traditional Chinese medicine
13. 西药	xīyào	N	Western medicine
西	xī	N	west

补充生词 Supplementary Words

1. 英文	Yīngwén	N	English
2. 开刀	kāidāo	VO	to have an operation
3. 化验	huàyàn	V	to have a medical test
4. 血	xiě	N	blood
5. 大便	dàbiàn	N	stool, faeces
6. 小便	xiǎobiàn	N	urine
7. 牙	yá	N	tooth
8. 肚子	dùzi	N	abdomen, stomach

9. 生活	shēnghuó	N	life
10. 中午	zhōngwǔ	N	noon
11. 打针	dǎzhēn	VO	to have an injection
12. 太极拳	tàijíquán	N	*taiji* boxing
13. 请假条	qǐngjiàtiáo	N	written request for leave

注释   Notes

⑦ 我去给你挂号。

"I'll register for you."

"给" is a verb (see Lesson 10), but it can also function as a preposition. When used as a preposition,"给" and the noun or noun phrase that follows it (usually the receiver of the action) form a prepositional phrase, which is placed before the predicative verb to indicate that the object of "给" is affected by the activity of the predicate.

⑧ 你哪儿不舒服？

"What's wrong with you?"

This is an everyday expression used by doctors when talking to their patients.

⑨ 你嗓子有点儿发炎。

"Your throat is inflamed."

The phrase "有（一）点儿" (with "一"often omitted) is used before certain adjectives or verbs as an adverbial modifier, indicating moderation. When used before an adjective, it often implies dissatisfaction or negation. For example:

有点儿不高兴   有点儿贵   有点儿晚   有点儿发烧

Note: There is some difference between "有一点儿" and "一点儿". "有一点儿" is used adverbially, modifying the adjective or verb that follows it, whereas "一点儿" is used as an attributive, modifying a noun. For example:

一点儿东西   一点儿钱   一点儿书

The construction "一点儿 + N" is usually placed after a verb as its object. For example:

我去买一点儿东西。

It is not right to replace "有一点儿" with "一点儿". For example:

他有点儿不高兴。（We cannot say "他一点儿不高兴。".）

我有点儿发烧。（We cannot say "我一点儿发烧。".）

二、练习　Exercises

练习与运用　**Drills and Practice** 48

核心句 KEY SENTENCES

1. 你怎么还不起床？
2. 我头疼，嗓子也疼。
3. 我身体没问题，不用去看病。
4. 我要睡觉，不想去医院。
5. 我跟你一起去。
6. 今天天气很冷，你要多穿点儿衣服。
7. 你嗓子有点儿发炎，还有点儿发烧。
8. 他要不要住院？
9. 你愿意吃中药还是愿意吃西药？

1. 熟读下列词组 Read the following phrases until you learn them by heart

（1）头疼　手疼　全身疼　学习很好　身体不太好　天气很冷

（2）下午还是晚上　　　今天还是明天　　　　两点还是三点
　　你还是我　　　　　他们还是她们　　　　老师还是学生
　　睡觉还是起床　　　工作还是休息　　　　学习还是玩儿
　　认识还是不认识　　买衣服还是买本子　　吃中药还是吃西药
　　要香蕉还是要苹果　学习语言还是学习文学　喜欢香蕉还是喜欢苹果

（3）要喝水　　　　　要回家　　　　　想认识他
　　想看京剧　　　　不想吃　　　　　不想学美术

（4）愿意参加　　　　愿意写汉字　　　愿意学习汉语
　　不愿意喝酒　　　不愿意住院　　　不愿意起床

（5）要看病　要挂号　要锻炼　要不要吃药　不用介绍　不用找钱

2. 句型替换 Pattern drills

（1）A：你想不想学习 音乐？
　　　B：我很想学习音乐。

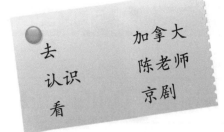

去
认识
看

加拿大
陈老师
京剧

（2）A：现在五点，你要学习还是
　　　　要锻炼？
　　　B：我要锻炼。
　　　A：我不想锻炼，我要学习。

回家　　　　去商场
看书　　　　写汉字
去买衣服　　去买苹果
看中文报　　看英文(Yīngwén)报

（3）A：你愿意吃中药还是愿意吃西药？
　　　B：我愿意吃中药。你呢？
　　　A：我愿意吃西药。

吃蛋糕　　　吃寿面
学习语言　　学习文学
去游泳　　　去打球
今天去　　　明天去
上午上课　　下午上课

（4）A：医生，他要不要住院？
　　　B：不用。

开刀 (kāidāo)　　　　　不用
化验 (huàyàn) 血 (xiě)　要
化验大便 (dàbiàn)　　　不用
化验小便 (xiǎobiàn)　　要

（5）A：现在是八点一刻，你怎么还不起床？
　　　B：我不太舒服。
　　　A：你哪儿不舒服？
　　　B：我头有点儿疼。

9:55　　　去上课　　嗓子
4:55　　　去锻炼　　牙 (yá)
11:55　　 睡觉　　　肚子 (dùzi)

（6）A：你常常去看你朋友吗?
　　B：我常常去看他。
　　A：他身体怎么样?
　　B：他身体 没问题。

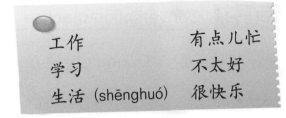

工作　　　　　有点儿忙
学习　　　　　不太好
生活 (shēnghuó)　很快乐

（7）A：他跟谁一起去?
　　B：他跟力波一起去。

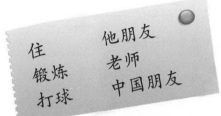

住　　　他朋友
锻炼　　老师
打球　　中国朋友

（8）A：你每天晚上都做什么?
　　B：我每天晚上都写汉字。

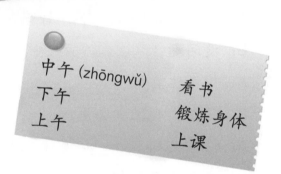

中午 (zhōngwǔ)　　看书
下午　　　　锻炼身体
上午　　　　上课

3. 看图造句 Make sentences according to the pictures

❶ A：他哪儿不舒服?
　　B：他＿＿＿＿＿＿＿＿。

❷ A：我要不要＿＿＿＿＿＿＿＿?
　　B：不用，你愿意＿＿＿＿＿＿

　　还是愿意＿＿＿＿＿＿＿?
　　（打针，dǎzhēn）

4. 会话练习　Conversation practice

【谈论身体状况　Talking about one's health】

（1）A：你怎么样？不太舒服吗？

　　　B：我_____有点儿疼。

　　　A：要不要去医院？

　　　B：不用，我想休息一下。

（2）A：我今天怎么全身不舒服？

　　　B：啊，你_____发烧。你现在不能去上课，要休息一下。

　　　A：你跟陈老师说一下，好吗？

　　　B：没问题。

（3）A：你身体真好。

　　　B：是啊，我很少去医院。

　　　A：你每天都_____身体吗？

　　　B：我每天下午都_____。

【表达意愿与必要　Expressing one's desire or need】

（1）A：明天是星期天，你想做什么？

　　　B：我_____在家休息。你_____去哪儿？

　　　A：我要去市场买点儿东西。

（2）A：你明天有时间吗？我们去打球，_____？

　　　B：对不起，我明天_____去学太极拳 (tàijíquán)。你会打太极拳吗？

　　　A：我会一点儿。

　　　B：太好了！我_____学，你能教我吗？

（3）A：你为什么_____学习汉语？

　　　B：我喜欢汉语。我_____做一个汉语老师。

　　　A：我也喜欢教孩子们汉语。

5. 交际练习 Communication exercises

(1) You feel sick while reading with your classmate in the library. How do you tell him / her?

(2) Your friend has a toothache (牙疼, yá téng). How do you help him / her tell the doctor about it?

(3) You want to go to China to study Chinese and visit Shanghai, but your friend thinks that in order to study Chinese well, you should go to Beijing. How do you talk with him / her about it?

(4) You feel sick and can't go to class. You can write a leave application letter to the teacher. For example:

请假条 (qǐngjiàtiáo)

> 陈老师：
>
> 　我今天头疼，还有点儿发烧，很不舒
> 服。医生说应该休息两天。对不起，我
> 明天不能来上课。
>
> 　　　　　　　　　　　马大为
> 　　　　　　　　　　十一月二十八日

阅读与复述 Reading Comprehension and Paraphrasing

　　大为，你怎么还不起床？什么？你头疼？你全身都不舒服？你要睡觉，不想起床？你应该去看病。你要睡觉，不愿意去医院？大为，你不能睡觉，你应该去医院看病。我跟你一起去。现在去还是下午去？当然现在去。我们应该现在去。

　　医生，他是8号，他的中文名字叫马大为，今年22岁。他头疼，全身都不舒服。您给他看一下吧。您说他发烧，嗓子还有点儿发炎，是感冒。他要不要住院？不用住院，要吃药。大为，你愿意吃中药还是愿意吃西药？你可以吃西药。你不愿意吃西药？你愿意吃中药？好吧，医生，您能不能给他开一点儿中药？

三、语法 Grammar

1 主谓谓语句(1)

Sentences with a subject-predicate phrase as predicate (1)

The main element of the predicate in this kind of sentence is a subject-predicate phrase. In many cases, the person or thing that the subject of the subject-predicate phrase (subject$_2$) denotes is a part of the person or thing denoted by the subject of the whole sentence (subject$_1$).

Subject$_1$	Predicate$_1$	
	Subject$_2$	Predicate$_2$
马大为	头	疼。
他	全身	都 不 舒服。
你	身体	好 吗?
宋华	学习	怎么样?
今天	天气	冷不冷?

The negative adverb "不" is usually placed before the predicate of the subject-predicate phrase (predicate$_2$). Its A / V-not-A / V form is produced by juxtaposing the affirmative and negative forms of predicate$_2$.

2 选择疑问句 Alternative questions

An alternative question is created when two possible situations, A and B, are connected by the conjunction "还是". The person to whom the question is addressed is expected to choose one of the alternatives.

Question			Answer
Alternative A	还是	Alternative B	
现在去	还是	下午去?	现在去。(Alternative A)
你看病	还是	他看病?	他看病。(Alternative B)
你愿意吃中药	还是	愿意吃西药?	我愿意吃中药。(Alternative A)
你是老师	还是	学生?	我是学生。(Alternative B)

3 能愿动词谓语句(2)：要、想、愿意
Sentences with the optative verbs (2): "要", "想" and "愿意"

Both the optative verbs "要" and "想" express subjective intention and demand. They are basically the same in meaning. Sometimes "要" emphasizes the intention or demand, while "想" places more emphasis on the intention or hope. For example:

> 我要吃烤鸭。
>
> 我想去北京吃烤鸭。

The negative form for both "想" and "要" (denoting a demand) is "不想".

"愿意" is also used to express one's wishes. It means a willingness to do something or a hope that something will occur according to the wishes of the person denoted by the subject.

Subject	Predicate		
	OpV	V	O
马大为	要	睡觉。	
丁力波	想	学习	美术。
他	不想	去	医院。
她	愿意不愿意	参加	聚会？

The optative verb "要" is also used to express the actual need. Its negative form is "不用". For example:

> 他要不要住院？
>
> 明天天气怎么样？要多穿衣服吗？
>
> 明天不用多穿衣服。

四、汉字　Chinese Characters

1 汉字的结构(5)　Structure of Chinese characters (5)

The enclosure structure ②

a. Left-bottom-right enclosure

　画

b. Left-bottom enclosure

　这　起　题

2 认写基本汉字 Learn and write basic Chinese characters

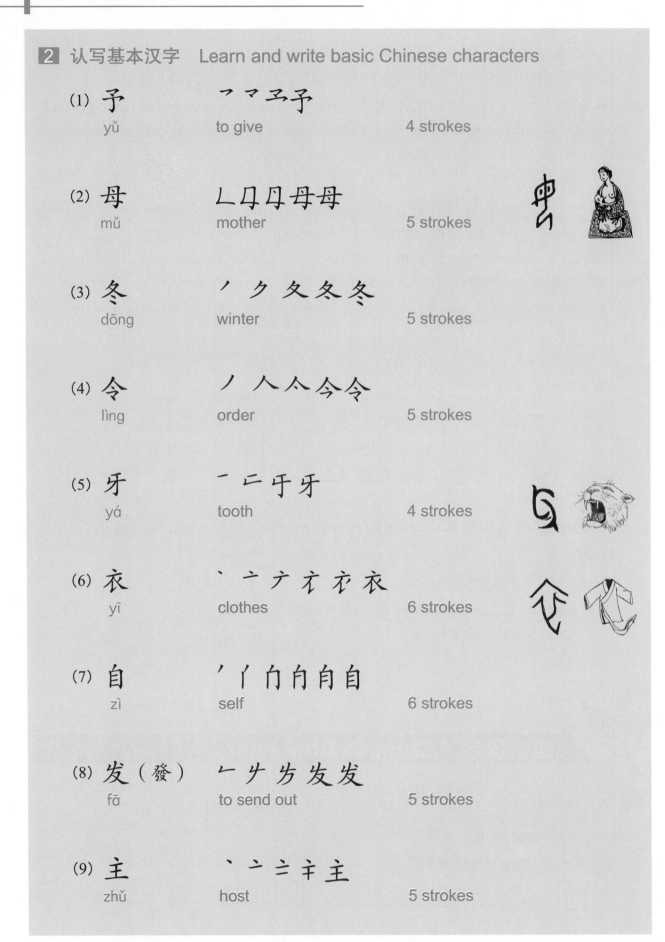

(1) 予 フ マ 孑 予
yǔ to give 4 strokes

(2) 母 乚 丹 丹 母 母
mǔ mother 5 strokes

(3) 冬 ノ ク 夂 冬 冬
dōng winter 5 strokes

(4) 令 ノ 人 △ 今 令
lìng order 5 strokes

(5) 牙 一 二 于 牙
yá tooth 4 strokes

(6) 衣 丶 一 宀 宀 ㆆ 衣
yī clothes 6 strokes

(7) 自 ノ 亻 自 自 自 自
zì self 6 strokes

(8) 发 (發) 乚 屮 步 发 发
fā to send out 5 strokes

(9) 主 丶 一 亠 宇 主
zhǔ host 5 strokes

(10) 厂（廠）　　　一 厂
chǎng　　　　　　factory　　　　　　2 strokes

3　认写课文中的汉字　Learn and write the Chinese characters in the texts

(1) 全身 quánshēn

全 → 人 + 王　　　　　　6 strokes

(2) 舒服 shūfu

舒 → 𠆢 + 舌 + 予　　　12 strokes

服 → 月 + 卩 + 又　　　8 strokes

𠆢 (wòrénpángr, the "sleeping person" side)　ノ 𠆢　2 strokes

(3) 每 měi

每 → 𠂉 + 母　　　　　7 strokes

火 (huǒzìpángr, on the left side of a multi-component character, the fourth stroke in "火" is written as a dot. It is called the " fire" side.)

、 ゛ 少 火　　　　　　4 strokes

(4) 锻炼 duànliàn（鍛煉）

锻 → 钅 + 段　　　　　14 strokes
(The meaning side is "钅" and the phonetic side is "段".)

炼 → 火 + 东　　　　　9 strokes

疒 (bìngzìpángr, the "illness" side, denoting disease or ailment.)

、 一 广 疒 疒　　　　5 strokes

(5) 疼 téng

疼 → 疒 + 冬　　　　　10 strokes
(The "illness" side denotes the meaning and "冬" indicates the pronunciation.)

(6) 嗓子 sǎngzi

嗓 → 口 + 又 + 又 + 又 + 木 13 strokes

(7) 想 xiǎng

想 → 木 + 目 + 心 13 strokes

(The meaning part is "心" and the phonetic part is "相".)

(8) 看病 kànbìng

病 → 疒 + 丙 10 strokes

(The meaning side is "疒" and the phonetic side is "丙".)

(9) 身体 shēntǐ（身體）

体 → 亻+ 本 7 strokes

(10) 吧 ba

吧 → 口 + 巴 7 strokes

(The meaning side is "口" and the phonetic side is "巴".)

冫 (liǎngdiǎnshuǐr, the "two-drops-of-water" side) 丶 冫 2 strokes

(11) 冷 lěng

冷 → 冫 + 令 7 strokes

(12) 穿 chuān

穿 → 穴 + 牙 9 strokes

(13) 休息 xiūxi

休 → 亻 + 木 6 strokes

息 → 自 ＋ 心 10 strokes

(14) 挂号 guàhào（掛號）

挂 → 扌 ＋ 土 ＋ 土 9 strokes

(15) 发炎 fāyán（發炎）

炎 → 火 ＋ 火 8 strokes

尧 (yáozìtóur, the "eminent" top) (Please differentiate it from "戈".)

一 弋 尧 3 strokes

(16) 发烧 fāshāo（發燒）

烧 → 火 ＋ 尧 ＋ 兀 10 strokes

(17) 感冒 gǎnmào

感 → 戊 ＋ 一 ＋ 口 ＋ 心 13 strokes

冒 → 曰 ＋ 目 9 strokes

(18) 住院 zhùyuàn

住 → 亻 ＋ 主 7 strokes

(The meaning side is "亻" and the phonetic side is "主".)

(19) 中药 zhōngyào（中藥）

药 → 艹 ＋ 纟 ＋ 勺 9 strokes

(20) 愿意 yuànyì（願意）

愿 → 厂 ＋ 白 ＋ 小 ＋ 心 14 strokes

Traditional Chinese Medicine and Chinese Herbal Medicine

China has its own traditional medical science, that is, Chinese medicine. With a long history and different from Western medicine, it is based on the traditional Chinese philosophy. Its major diagnosis methods are watching, hearing, asking and touching. Chinese herbal medicine is used and acupuncture and moxibustion are operated to cure diseases.

Chinese herbal medicine is used in traditional Chinese medical practice, which has a history of thousands of years. According to legend, an emperor of remote antiquity called Shennong ("Holy Farmer") experimented with many types of herbs in order to find cures for the people. Traditional Chinese herbal medicine differs from modern Western medicine in that it basically does not use artificially created chemicals but is directly extracted from natural substances. Traditional Chinese remedies can be divided into three categories, according to their sources. The first are the medicines from vegetables. The second are the medicines from animals, including their organs and secretions. The third are the medicines from mineral sources. Traditional Chinese medicine can be effective to prevent and cure many diseases. With the advancement of modernization of Chinese herbal medicine, this common wealth of mankind will be used by more people in the world.

第十三课

Lesson 13

Wǒ rènshile yí ge piàoliang de gūniang
我 认识了 一 个 漂亮 的 姑娘
I knew a beautiful girl.

Ma Dawei recently met a beautiful girl. In this lesson, he will show us how to make phone calls, rent a house, ask for help, and make an invitation in Chinese.

一、课文 Text

 49 （一）

宋华：　　大为，　　听说　你　得了　感冒，　现在　你　身体
Sòng Huá：Dàwéi，　tīngshuō　nǐ　déle gǎnmào，　xiànzài nǐ　shēntǐ

怎么样？
zěnmeyàng？

马大为：　我　去了　医院，　吃了　很　多　中药。① 　现在　我
Mǎ Dàwéi：Wǒ qùle　yīyuàn，　chīle　hěn　duō　zhōngyào．　Xiànzài wǒ

头　还　有点儿　疼。
tóu　hái　yǒudiǎnr　téng．

> 谈已经发生的事
> **Talking about something**
> **that has happened**

宋华：　你　还　应该　多　休息。
Sòng Huá：Nǐ　hái　yīnggāi duō　xiūxi．

马大为：　宋　华，我　想　告诉 你 一 件 事儿。
Mǎ Dàwéi：Sòng Huá，　wǒ xiǎng gàosu nǐ yí jiàn shìr．

宋华：　什么　事儿？
Sòng Huá：Shénme shìr？

马大为：　我　认识 了 一 个 漂亮　的 姑娘，　她 愿意 做 我
Mǎ Dàwéi：Wǒ rènshi le yí ge piàoliang de gūniang，　tā yuànyì zuò wǒ

女　朋友。我们
nǚ　péngyou．Wǒmen

常常　　一起 散步，
chángcháng yìqǐ sànbù，

一起 看　电影、喝
yìqǐ　kàn diànyǐng、hē

咖啡，一起 听 音乐。
kāfēi，yìqǐ tīng yīnyuè．

宋华：祝贺 你！ 这 是 好 事 啊。
Sòng Huá: Zhùhè nǐ! Zhè shì hǎo shì a.

马大为：谢谢。 是 好 事，可是 我 的 宿舍 太 小，她 不 能
Mǎ Dàwéi: Xièxie. Shì hǎo shì, kěshì wǒ de sùshè tài xiǎo, tā bù néng

常　来 我 这儿。② 我 想　找 一 套 房子。
cháng lái wǒ zhèr.　Wǒ xiǎng zhǎo yí tào fángzi.

宋华：你 想　租 房子？③
Sòng Huá: Nǐ xiǎng zū fángzi?

租房
Renting a house

马大为：是 啊，我 想　租 一 套 有　厨房 和 厕所 的 房子，④
Mǎ Dàwéi: Shì a, wǒ xiǎng zū yí tào yǒu chúfáng hé cèsuǒ de fángzi,

房租 不 能 太 贵。
fángzū bù néng tài guì.

宋华：星期六 我 跟 你 一起 去 租 房 公司，好　吗?
Sòng Huá: Xīngqīliù wǒ gēn nǐ yìqǐ qù zū fáng gōngsī, hǎo ma?

马大为：太 好 了。
Mǎ Dàwéi: Tài hǎo le.

生词 New Words

1. 姑娘	gūniang	N	girl 漂亮的姑娘，小姑娘
2. 听说	tīngshuō	V	to be told
听	tīng	V	to listen
3. 得	dé	V	to have, to get 得感冒，得病
4. 告诉	gàosu	V	to tell
5. 件	jiàn	M	(*a measure word*) piece 一件事儿，一件衣服
6. 事儿	shìr	N	matter, affair, thing 好事儿，什么事儿
7. 散步	sànbù	VO	to take a walk, to walk 一起散步
步	bù	N	step
8. 电影	diànyǐng	N	movie 看电影，中国电影

	电	diàn	N	electricity
	影	yǐng	N	shadow
*9.	咖啡	kāfēi	N	coffee
10.	可是	kěshì	Conj	but
*11.	宿舍	sùshè	N	dormitory 学生宿舍，回宿舍
*12.	找	zhǎo	V	to look for 找房子，找人，找东西
13.	房子	fángzi	N	house 没有房子，买房子
14.	租	zū	V	to rent 租房子，租车
15.	套	tào	M	(a measure word for houses) 一套房子
16.	厨房	chúfáng	N	kitchen 一间厨房
17.	厕所	cèsuǒ	N	toilet 一间厕所，男厕所，女厕所
18.	房租	fángzū	N	rent (for a house, flat, etc.)
19.	公司	gōngsī	N	company 小公司，大公司，租房公司

注释　Notes

① 我吃了很多中药。

"I have taken many doses of traditional Chinese medicine."

When the adjectives "多" and "少" are used as attributive modifiers, we must put adverbs such as "很" before them. For example: "很多中药" or "很多学生", and not "多中药", "多学生". "的" may be left out after "很多".

② 她不能常来我这儿。

"She cannot often come to my place."

The objects of the verbs "来、去、到、在" and the preposition "在" are generally words of place or location; if they are not, then "这儿" and "那儿" must be added. For example: "来我这儿", "去力波那儿", "到我朋友那儿", "在老师这儿".

We cannot say "来我" or "在老师".

Generally, "常常" and "常" are used interchangeably.

③ 你想租房子？

"Do you want to rent a house?"

A declarative sentence can be turned into a question by reading it with the same intonation as an interrogative sentence.

④ 我想租一套有厨房和厕所的房子。

"I want to rent a house with a kitchen and a bathroom."

We must add "的" to a verb or verbal phrase to turn it into an adjective modifier. For example:

有厨房的房子

给她的蛋糕 (the cake for her)

今天来的人 (the people who came today)

🎧50　（二）

（宋华与马大为在家美租房公司）

马大为：那 套 房子 房租 太贵，你 说，我 应该 怎么 办？⑤
Mǎ Dàwéi：Nà tào fángzi fángzū tài guì, nǐ shuō, wǒ yīnggāi zěnme bàn?

宋华：你 想 租 还是 不 想 租？
Sòng Huá：Nǐ xiǎng zū háishi bù xiǎng zū?

征求建议
Asking for suggestions

马大为：当然 想 租。
Mǎ Dàwéi：Dāngrán xiǎng zū.

宋华：我 给 陆 雨平 打 个 电话，让 他 来 帮助 我们。
Sòng Huá：Wǒ gěi Lù Yǔpíng dǎ ge diànhuà, ràng tā lái bāngzhù wǒmen.

马大为：他 很 忙，会 来 吗？
Mǎ Dàwéi：Tā hěn máng, huì lái ma?

宋华：他 会 来。
Sòng Huá：Tā huì lái.

（宋华给陆雨平打电话）

陆雨平：喂，哪 一 位 啊？⑥
Lù Yǔpíng：Wèi, nǎ yí wèi a?

打电话
Making a phone call

宋华：我 是 宋 华，我 和 大为 现在 在 家美
Sòng Huá：Wǒ shì Sòng Huá, wǒ hé Dàwéi xiànzài zài Jiāměi

租 房 公司。
Zū Fáng Gōngsī.

陆雨平：你们 怎么 在 那儿？
Lù Yǔpíng：Nǐmen zěnme zài nàr?

宋华：大为 要 租 房子。
Sòng Huá：Dàwéi yào zū fángzi.

陆雨平: 你们 看 没 看 房子?
Lù Yǔpíng: Nǐmen kàn méi kàn fángzi?

宋华: 我们 看了一 套 房子。那 套 房子 很 好, 有 一
Sòng Huá: Wǒmen kànle yí tào fángzi. Nà tào fángzi hěn hǎo, yǒu yì

间 卧室 和 一 间 客厅, 可是 房租 有点儿 贵。
jiān wòshì hé yì jiān kètīng, kěshì fángzū yǒudiǎnr guì.

陆雨平: 你们 找了 经理 没有?⑦
Lù Yǔpíng: Nǐmen zhǎole jīnglǐ méiyǒu?

宋华: 我们 没有 找 经理。
Sòng Huá: Wǒmen méiyǒu zhǎo jīnglǐ.

陆雨平: 宋 华, 这个 公司 的 经理 是 我 朋友, 我 跟
Lù Yǔpíng: Sòng Huá, zhège gōngsī de jīnglǐ shì wǒ péngyou, wǒ gēn

他 说 一下, 请 他 帮助 你们, 我 想 可能
tā shuō yíxià, qǐng tā bāngzhù nǐmen, wǒ xiǎng kěnéng

没有 问题。
méiyǒu wèntí.

邀请
Making an invitations

宋华: 好 啊。 晚上 我们 请 你 和 你 朋友 吃饭。⑧
Sòng Huá: Hǎo a. Wǎnshang wǒmen qǐng nǐ hé nǐ péngyou chīfàn.

陆雨平: 好, 你们 在 公司 等 我, 再见。
Lù Yǔpíng: Hǎo, nǐmen zài gōngsī děng wǒ, zàijiàn.

宋华: 再见。
Sòng Huá: Zàijiàn.

生词 New Words

1. 办	bàn	V	to do 怎么办
2. 打电话	dǎ diànhuà	VO	to make a phone call 给她打电话
电话	diànhuà	N	telephone, phone call 你的电话

3.	让	ràng	V	to let, to allow, to make
4.	帮助	bāngzhù	V	to help
5.	喂	wèi	Int	hello, hey
6.	位	wèi	M	(*a polite measure word for persons*)
				一位小姐，一位老师，一位医生，哪一位
7.	间	jiān	M	(*a measure word for rooms, houses, etc*)
				一间厨房
8.	卧室	wòshì	N	bedroom
9.	客厅	kètīng	N	living room
10.	经理	jīnglǐ	N	manager
11.	可能	kěnéng	OpV	maybe　可能来，可能感冒，可能住院
12.	吃饭	chīfàn	VO	to eat (a meal)
	饭	fàn	N	meal　饭店，米饭
13.	等	děng	V	to wait　等人，等他们，等一下
14.	家美	Jiāměi	PN	(name of a house rental agency)

补充生词 Supplementary Words

1.	包括	bāokuò	V	to include
2.	水电费	shuǐdiànfèi	N	charges for water and electricity
3.	亲爱	qīn'ài	A	dear
4.	想	xiǎng	V	to miss
5.	方便	fāngbiàn	A	convenient
6.	巧	qiǎo	A	coincidental
7.	热心	rèxīn	A	warm-hearted
8.	合适	héshì	A	suitable
9.	新	xīn	A	new
10.	回信	huíxìn	N/VO	reply; to reply to a letter
11.	过去	guòqù	N	in the past
12.	去年	qùnián	N	last year

注释　Notes

⑤ 你说，我应该怎么办?

"What do you think I should do?"

"你说" (or "你看") is used here to solicit the listener's opinion.

⑥ 喂，哪一位啊?

"Hello, who is speaking?"

"喂" is an interjection often used in phone calls as a form of greeting or response. For example:

喂，是丁力波吗?

喂，我是马大为，请问您找谁?

喂，您好，我想找一下王小云。

The measure word "位" only applies to people and is a more polite and respectful form than the measure word "个". For example:

这位先生　二十位老师　两位教授

⑦ 你们找了经理没有?

"Have you (found and) talked to the manager?"

"找经理" here means "to talk to the manager".

⑧ 晚上我们请你和你朋友吃饭。

"We would like to invite you and your friend to dinner this evening."

"吃饭" means "to eat (a meal)". "请……吃饭" means "to invite someone to dinner".

二、练习　Exercises

练习与运用　Drills and Practice

 51

核心句　KEY SENTENCES

1. 她不能常来我这儿。
2. 我想租一套有厨房和厕所的房子。
3. 我给陆雨平打个电话，让他来帮助我们。
4. 他会来吗?
5. 你们看没看房子?
6. 我们看了一套房子。
7. 你们找了经理没有?
8. 我们没有找经理。
9. 晚上我们请你和你朋友吃饭。

1. 熟读下列词组 Read the following phrases until you learn them by heart

（1）看了一套房子　认识了一位教授　买了两斤香蕉　　找了两块钱
　　　说了一件事　　送了一张光盘　　参加了一个聚会　喝了红葡萄酒
（2）找没找　租没租　等没等　买没买　看没看　问没问　来没来
　　　上课没上课　休息没休息　起床没起床　锻炼没锻炼　帮助没帮助
（3）这儿　他那儿　老师那儿　我朋友那儿　我哥哥这儿　王经理那儿
（4）可能来　可能去　可能做　不可能等　不可能租　可能不可能得
（5）一件事儿　　一件工作　　这件衣服　　那间厨房　　这间宿舍
　　　这位小姐　　那位医生　　一位朋友　　一位经理　　一位记者
（6）让他帮助你　　让他去那儿　　　让他写汉字
　　　请他们吃饭　　请小姐喝咖啡　　请我朋友教我

2. 句型替换 Pattern drills

（1）A：我想告诉你一件事儿。
　　　B：什么事儿？
　　　A：我认识了 一个姑娘。
　　　B：好啊。

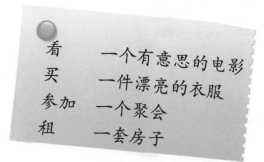

看　　一个有意思的电影
买　　一件漂亮的衣服
参加　一个聚会
租　　一套房子

（2）A：他们看没看 房子？
　　　B：他们看了一套房子。
　　　A：你呢？
　　　B：我没有看。

买　苹果　　五斤
吃　蛋糕　　很多
喝　葡萄酒　一瓶

（3）A：你去了租房公司没有？
　　　B：我去了租房公司。
　　　A：租房公司怎么样？
　　　B：租房公司很好。

吃　生日蛋糕
买　那本中文书
听　那张光盘
租　那套房子

（4）A：你给大为打个电话，好吗？

　　　B：什么事儿？

　　　A：让他<u>去</u> <u>租房公司</u>。

　　　B：没（有）问题。

来	我这儿
找	张教授
等	他女朋友
去	老师那儿

（5）A：你请他做什么？

　　　B：我请他<u>吃饭</u>。

　　　A：他会<u>来</u>吗？

　　　B：他会<u>来</u>。

看电影	去
散步	来去
喝咖啡	去
介绍中国文化	来

（6）A：喂，哪一位啊？

　　　B：我是<u>马大为</u>。我现在在<u>租房公司</u>。

　　　A：你怎么在那儿？

　　　B：我要<u>租房子</u>。

丁力波	医院	看病
宋华	汉语系	找陈老师
陆雨平	宋华家	祝贺他的生日
王小云	丁力波宿舍	帮助他学汉语

3. 看图造句　Make sentences according to the pictures

❶ A：他想买什么？

　　B：他＿＿＿＿＿＿＿＿。

❷ A：她买了什么？

　　B：她＿＿＿＿＿＿＿＿。

③ A：他要什么？

　　B：他＿＿＿＿＿＿＿＿。

④ A：她要了咖啡还是要了酒？

　　B：她＿＿＿＿＿＿＿＿。

4. 会话练习　Conversation practice

【租房　Renting a house】

（1）A：我想租一间房子。

　　　B：你的宿舍不好吗？

　　　A：我的宿舍＿＿＿＿＿＿，想＿＿＿＿＿＿。

　　　B：好，我跟你一起去租房公司。

（2）A：您想租房子吗？

　　　B：是，我想租一套有＿＿＿＿＿＿、＿＿＿＿＿＿的房子。

　　　A：我们家美租房公司有很多好房子。

　　　B：房租贵不贵？

　　　A：不贵，每月＿＿＿＿＿＿元。

　　　B：包括（bāokuò）水电费（shuǐdiànfèi）吗？

　　　A：不包括。

　　　B：可以看一下吗？

　　　A：当然可以。

【征求建议　Asking for suggestions】

（1）A：明天是我姐姐的生日。你说，我应该给她买什么？

　　　B：你可以买＿＿＿＿＿＿。

A：我应该在哪儿买＿＿＿＿＿＿＿＿？

B：＿＿＿＿＿＿＿＿＿。

（2）A：我想跟你说一件事儿。

B：什么事儿？

A：星期日是我女朋友的生日，可是宋华让我参加一个聚会。你说，我应该怎么办？

B：＿＿＿＿＿＿＿＿＿＿＿＿＿＿＿＿。

【打电话　Making a phone call】

（1）A：喂，哪一位啊？

B：我是＿＿＿＿＿＿＿＿＿。

A：是你啊。你怎么样？有什么事儿？

B：＿＿＿＿＿＿＿＿＿＿＿＿＿。

（2）A：喂，你好，请问您找谁？

B：我找丁力波，我是他朋友。

A：好，请等一下。

C：喂，我是＿＿＿＿＿。

B：你好，力波，我想告诉你一件事儿。

（3）A：喂，是403号宿舍吗？

B：是啊，您找谁？

A：王小云在吗？

B：＿＿＿＿＿。

A：请问，她家的电话号码是多少？

B：82305647。

A：谢谢。

【邀请 Making an invitation】

（1）A：星期天你有时间吗？

B：我＿＿＿＿＿＿＿＿。

A：我想请你＿＿＿＿＿＿＿＿。

B：＿＿＿＿＿＿＿＿＿。

（2）A：白小姐，晚上我请你＿＿＿＿＿＿＿，好吗？

　　B：对不起，我＿＿＿＿＿＿＿＿。

　　A：你什么时候有时间？

　　B：＿＿＿＿＿＿＿＿。

5. 交际练习　Communication exercises

（1）Make a phone call from the university dormitory to one of your friends to tell him / her something that has happened recently in your life or studies.

（2）Your mother and father are coming to China to see you, and you want to rent a house for them. You asked the rental company to find a large house with a kitchen and a bathroom for you. Your parents will live in it for half a month.

（3）Thanksgiving Day (感恩节, Gǎn'ēn jié) is coming and you are inviting a few good friends to dinner. Some of them can come and some cannot.

（4）You are buying things in a supermarket to make a Thanksgiving dinner. How will you ask for help from the salesperson?

阅读与复述 Reading Comprehension and Paraphrasing

马大为给女朋友小燕子 (Xiǎoyànzi) 的一封信

亲爱(qīn'ài)的小燕子：

　　你好吗？我很想(xiǎng)你。

　　星期三我得了感冒，头疼，嗓子有点儿发炎，还有点儿发烧。可是现在我好了。

　　我想跟你说一件事儿。小燕子，我很喜欢你。我想让你常常来看我，跟我一起听音乐，喝咖啡。可是我住的宿舍太小，也不方便(fāngbiàn)。我想租一套房子，有厨房，有厕所。我请宋华帮助我找房子。

　　星期六我和宋华一起去了家美租房公司，我们看了一套房子，房子很好，很大，有厨房、厕所。宋华给陆雨平打了一个电话，问他我们应该怎么办。真巧(qiǎo)，家美租房公司的经理是陆雨平的朋友，陆雨平请他帮助我们。这位经理很热心 (rèxīn)，他让我们看了很多房子。我租了一套很合适 (héshì) 的房子，房租不太贵。晚上我们请陆雨平和经理去吃了北京烤鸭。我真高兴。

　　小燕子，我想请你来看一下我的新 (xīn) 房子。你说，什么时候合适？

　　我等你的回信 (huíxìn)。

你的大为
12月10日

三、语法　Grammar

1 助词 "了" (1)　　The particle "了" (1)

The particle "了" can be used after a verb to indicate somebody has done something. For example:

你买了几个苹果？　　　　Compare:　你买几个苹果？
(How many apples have you 　　　　　　(How many apples are you going to buy?/
bought?)　　　　　　　　　　　　　　 How many apples will you buy?)

我买了五个苹果。　　　　　　　　　我买五个苹果。
(I have bought five apples.)　　　　　(I'm going to buy five apples./ I will buy
　　　　　　　　　　　　　　　　　　 five apples.)

If the verb with a "了" takes an bject, this object usually has an attributive, which is a numeral-measure word, an adjective or a pronoun in many cases.

V ＋ 了 ＋ Nu–M / Pr / A ＋ O

Subject	Predicate			
	Verb	了	Nu-M / Pr / A	Object
我们	看	了	一套	房子。
王小云	买	了	两瓶	酒。
马大为	认识	了	一个　　　漂亮的	姑娘。
大为	吃	了	很多	中药。
我	介绍	了	那位	教授。
他	看	了	有名的	京剧。
她朋友	租	了	她的	房子。

If the object does not have an attributive（eg:"他买了苹果"or"大为得了感冒"）, other elements are needed in the predicate to form a complete sentence. For example:

听说你得了感冒，现在你身体怎么样？

我去了医院，也吃了很多中药。

The negative form of this kind of sentence is made by placing "没", or "没有", before the verb and omitting "了" after the verb.

没(有) ＋ V ＋ O

我们没有找经理。

他没买酒。

Note: One can never use"不"to negate this kind of sentence.
The V/A-not-V/A form is: "V ＋ 没 ＋ V（＋ O）" or "V ＋ 了（＋ O）＋ 没有".

V ＋ 没 ＋ V(＋ O)

你们看没看房子？

你们找没找经理？

V ＋ 了 (＋ O) ＋ 没有

你们看了房子没有？

你们找了经理没有？

Note："了" only indicates the realization or completion of an action, but not the time at which this action occurs (which may be in the past, present, or future). In this kind of sentence, the action, in many cases, has already happened. It is also possible, though, that the completion of the action will occur in the future. For example:

明天下午我买了本子去吃饭。

（Tomorrow afternoon I'll have supper after I buy the notebooks.）

Not all the past actions need the particle "了". If an action occurs frequently or a sentence describes an action in the past but does not emphasize the completion of the action, "了" is not used. For example:

过去（guòqù）他常常来看我，现在他不常来看我。

去年（qùnián）我在美术学院学习美术。

2 兼语句　Pivotal sentences

The pivotal sentence is also a sentence with a verbal predicate. Its predicate is composed of two verbal phrases. The object of the first verb is also the subject of the second verb. The first verb in a pivotal sentence should be a verb with the meaning of "making" or "ordering" somebody to do something, such as "请" or "让".

Both "请" and "让" have the meaning of "asking someone to do something". "请" is used in a formal situation and sounds polite. "请" also has the meaning of "to invite". For example:

晚上我们请你和你朋友吃饭。

Subject₁	Predicate₁			
	Verb₁	Object₁ (Subject₂)	Verb₂	Object₂
宋华	让	陆雨平	来帮助	他们。
陆雨平	请	经理	帮助	马大为。
妈妈	不让	她	喝	咖啡。

3 能愿动词谓语句(3)：可能、会

Sentences with the optative verbs (3): "可能" and "会"

The optative verb "可能" expresses possibility. Besides expressing ability, "会" is also used to express possibility. For example:

今年八月他可能去上海。

现在八点，他不可能睡觉。

明天他会不会来上课？

他得了感冒，明天不会来上课。

四、汉字　Chinese Characters

1 部首查字法　Consulting a Chinese dictionary based on radicals

Many Chinese character dictionaries are compiled according to the order of the characters' "radicals". Radicals are common components, located on the top, bottom, left, right, or outer part of characters, which usually indicate the category of meaning to which a character belongs. For example, "好", "她", "妈", "姐", "妹", "姓", and "娜" are grouped under the radical "女", which is the common component on the left side of these characters. However, "意", "思", "想", "您", and "愿" are grouped under the radical "心", which is the common component at the bottom of these characters.

In the radical index of a dictionary, radicals are listed in order according to the number of their strokes. In the index of entries, characters of the same radical are arranged in groups according to the number of their strokes excluding those of the radical.

Therefore, after determining the radical of a character, you should count the number of strokes in the radical and consult the radical index to obtain the page number where the radical entry can be found in the index of entries. Then, count the number of strokes in the character excluding the radical and consult the corresponding group to find the character and its page number in the dictionary. For example, the character "锻" will be found under the "钅" radical and in the section containing characters with 9 strokes apart from those of the radical.

2 认写基本汉字　Learn and write basic Chinese characters

(1) 古　一 十 古 古 古
gǔ　ancient　5 strokes

(2) 良　` ㄱ ㄱ ㄢ 白 良 良
liáng　good　7 strokes

(3) 斥　一 厂 斤 斥 斥
chì　to scold　5 strokes

(4) 事　　　　　一 一 一 一 一 一 事

shì　　　　　matter　　　　　　　　　8 strokes

(5) 步　　　　　丶 卜 止 止 止 步 步

bù　　　　　step　　　　　　　　　7 strokes

Note: The ancient character depicts two feet walking.

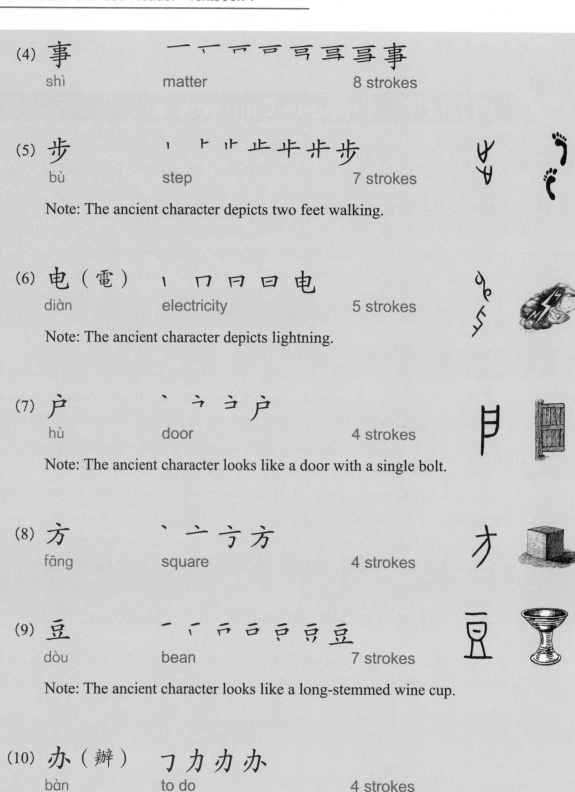

(6) 电（電）　　丨 冂 冂 日 电

diàn　　　　electricity　　　　　　5 strokes

Note: The ancient character depicts lightning.

(7) 户　　　　　丶 ㇇ 二 户

hù　　　　　door　　　　　　　　　4 strokes

Note: The ancient character looks like a door with a single bolt.

(8) 方　　　　　丶 一 亠 方

fāng　　　　square　　　　　　　4 strokes

(9) 豆　　　　　一 一 亡 戸 戸 豆 豆

dòu　　　　　bean　　　　　　　　7 strokes

Note: The ancient character looks like a long-stemmed wine cup.

(10) 办（辦）　　乛 力 力 办

bàn　　　　　to do　　　　　　　4 strokes

(11) 竹　　　　　丿 𠂉 𠂉 𠂉 竹 竹

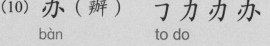

zhú　　　　　bamboo　　　　　　6 strokes

Note: The ancient character resembles bamboo leaves.

(12)　反　　　　一 厂 厂 反
　　　fǎn　　　　reverse　　　　4 strokes

3 认写课文中的汉字　Learn and write the Chinese characters in the texts

(1) 姑娘 gūniang

姑 → 女 ＋ 古　　　　8 strokes

(The meaning side is "女" and the phonetic side is "古".)

娘 → 女 ＋ 良　　　　10 strokes

("女" suggests that the character is associated with female in meaning.)

(2) 听说 tīngshuō（聽说）

听 → 口 ＋ 斤　　　　7 strokes

(3) 得 dé

得 → 彳 ＋ 日 ＋ 一 ＋ 寸　　　　11 strokes

(4) 告诉 gàosu（告訴）

告 → 生 ＋ 口　　　　7 strokes

(The meaning side is "口".)

诉 → 讠 ＋ 斥　　　　7 strokes

(The meaning side is "讠". Note how it differs from "斤".)

(5) 件 jiàn

件 → 亻 ＋ 牛　　　　6 strokes

(6) 散步 sànbù

散 → 艹 ＋ 月 ＋ 攵　　　　12 strokes

(7) 电影 diànyǐng（電影）

影 → 日 ＋ 京 ＋ 彡   15 strokes

(8) 咖啡 kāfēi

咖 → 口 ＋ 力 ＋ 口   8 strokes

啡 → 口 ＋ 非   11 strokes

(The meaning side is "口" and the phonetic side is "非".)

(9) 宿舍 sùshè

宿 → 宀 ＋ 亻 ＋ 百   11 strokes

("宀" denotes a house, "百" shows a mat, and "亻" suggests a person.)

舍 → 人 ＋ 舌   8 strokes

("人" denotes a shelter and "舌" indicates the pronunciation.)

(10) 房子 fángzi

房 → 户 ＋ 方   8 strokes

(The meaning is suggested by "户" and the pronunciation is shown by "方".)

(11) 租 zū

租 → 禾 ＋ 且   10 strokes

(12) 厨房 chúfáng（廚房）

厨 → 厂 ＋ 豆 ＋ 寸   12 strokes

(13) 厕所 cèsuǒ（廁所）

厕 → 厂 ＋ 贝 ＋ 刂   8 strokes

所 → 戶 ＋ 斤   8 strokes

(14) 公司 gōngsī

公 → 八 + 厶　　　　　　　　　　　4 strokes

(15) 打 dǎ

打 → 扌 + 丁　　　　　　　　　　　5 strokes

(16) 电话 diànhuà（電話）

话 → 讠 + 舌　　　　　　　　　　　8 strokes

(Speaking is related to the tongue.)

(17) 让 ràng（讓）

让 → 讠 + 上　　　　　　　　　　　5 strokes

(18) 帮助 bāngzhù（幫助）

帮 → 邦 + 巾　　　　　　　　　　　9 strokes

（"邦" denotes the pronunciation.)

助 → 且 + 力　　　　　　　　　　　7 strokes

(19) 喂 wèi

喂 → 口 + 田 + 氏（氏：一 丆 亇 氏）　12 strokes

(20) 位 wèi

位 → 亻 + 立　　　　　　　　　　　7 strokes

圣 (qīngzìbiānr, the "light" side)　　フ ス ヱ 圣 圣　5 strokes

(21) 经理 jīnglǐ（經理）

经 → 纟 + 圣　　　　　　　　　　　8 strokes

理 → 王 + 里　　　　　　　　　　　11 strokes

（"里" indicates the pronunciation.)

饣 (shízìpángr, the "food" side)　丿 𠂉 饣　　　　3 strokes

(22) 吃饭 chīfàn（吃飯）

饭 → 饣 + 反　　　　7 strokes

⺮ (zhúzìtóur, the vertical stroke and the vertical stroke with a hook in "竹" are both written as a dot, when this character is on the top of a multi-component character.)

　丿 𠂉 𠂉 𠂉 ⺮ ⺮　　　　6 strokes

(23) 等 děng

等 → ⺮ + 土 + 寸　　　　12 strokes

学唱中文歌
Sing a song

稍慢 饱满地

四川民歌

Students' Dormitory

Unlike most Western universities, in China, there is usually a residential area on the university's campus, where all the students live. Many students find living in the dormitory convenient. Since the buildings on campus are close to classrooms and research facilities, students may go to class and libraries on foot and thus save time. Moreover, living in the dormitory is convenient for students to help each other, exchange ideas, and gain interpersonal skills. However, some students feel sharing a room with others inconvenient at times. At universities nowadays, there are usually four to six students sharing a room. Sometimes, there are eight people living in a much bigger room. When there are more students in a room, they may interfere with each other. For instance, a dormitory cannot possibly provide the privacy needed for a date. In this lesson, Ma Dawei is eager to move out of the dormitory in order to gain some private space.

If you're studying in China but don't want to live in a dormitory, you may also consider renting an off-campus apartment. If you decide to rent an apartment, you can ask for help from a professional rental agency, or simply go online to get the latest information on rental housing.

第十四课
Lesson
14

● 复习 Review

Zhù nǐ Shèngdàn kuàilè
祝 你 圣诞 快乐
Merry Christmas to you!

It's time for you to learn the last lesson of this volume! By the end of the lesson, you will know how to: 1) make a complaint or an apology; 2) send regards on someone else's behalf; 3) ask how a friend is getting along and 4) express greetings at festival times. This lesson also includes a summary and review of the major grammatical points covered in the previous lessons. With this review you will find that you have learned so many Chinese sentence patterns. Please keep working hard!

一、课文　Text

🎧 53

马大为：力波，　上午　十点半，　你妈妈给你打了一个
Mǎ Dàwéi：Lìbō,　shàngwǔ shí diǎn bàn,　nǐ māma gěi nǐ dǎle　yí ge

电话。我告诉她你不在。我让她中午再
diànhuà. Wǒ gàosu tā　nǐ bú zài. Wǒ ràng tā zhōngwǔ zài

给你打。
gěi nǐ　dǎ.

丁力波：谢谢。我刚才去邮局给我妈妈寄了点儿
Dīng Lìbō：Xièxie. Wǒ gāngcái qù yóujú gěi wǒ māma jìle diǎnr

东西。大为，我今天打扫了宿舍，你的脏
dōngxi. Dàwéi, wǒ jīntiān dǎsǎole sùshè,　nǐ de zāng

衣服太多了。
yīfu　tài duō le.

> 抱怨与致歉
> **Making a complaint or an apology**

马大为：不好意思。[1] 这两天我太忙了，我想星
Mǎ Dàwéi：Bù hǎoyìsi. Zhè liǎng tiān wǒ tài máng le,　wǒ xiǎng xīng-

期六一起洗。[2]
qīliù　yìqǐ xǐ.

（力波的妈妈给他打电话）

马大为：喂，你好，你找谁？啊，丁力波在，请等
Mǎ Dàwéi：Wèi, nǐ hǎo, nǐ zhǎo shéi? À, Dīng Lìbō zài, qǐng děng

一下。力波，你妈妈的电话。
yíxià. Lìbō, nǐ māma de diànhuà.

丁力波：谢谢。妈妈，你好！
Dīng Lìbō：Xièxie. Māma,　nǐ hǎo!

丁云： 力波，你 好 吗?
Dīng Yún： Lìbō， nǐ hǎo ma?

丁力波： 我 很 好。你 和 爸爸 身体 怎么样?
Dīng Lìbō： Wǒ hěn hǎo. Nǐ hé bàba shēntǐ zěnmeyàng?

丁云： 我 身体 很 好，你 爸爸 也 很 好。 我们 工作
Dīng Yún： Wǒ shēntǐ hěn hǎo， nǐ bàba yě hěn hǎo. Wǒmen gōngzuò

都 很 忙。 你 外婆
dōu hěn máng. Nǐ wàipó

身体 好 吗?
shēntǐ hǎo ma?

转达问候
Passing on someone's regards

丁力波： 她 身体 很 好。 她 让 我 问 你们 好。③
Dīng Lìbō： Tā shēntǐ hěn hǎo. Tā ràng wǒ wèn nǐmen hǎo.

丁云： 我们 也 问 她 好。 你 哥哥、弟弟 怎么样?
Dīng Yún： Wǒmen yě wèn tā hǎo. Nǐ gēge、 dìdi zěnmeyàng?

丁力波： 他们 也 都 很 好。 哥哥 现在 在 一 个 中学
Dīng Lìbō： Tāmen yě dōu hěn hǎo. Gēge xiànzài zài yí ge zhōngxué

打工，弟弟 在 南方 旅行。 我们 都 很 想 你们。
dǎgōng， dìdi zài nánfāng lǚxíng. Wǒmen dōu hěn xiǎng nǐmen.

丁云： 我们 也 想 你们。你 现在 怎么样? 你 住 的
Dīng Yún： Wǒmen yě xiǎng nǐmen. Nǐ xiànzài zěnmeyàng? Nǐ zhù de

宿舍 大 不 大?④ 住 几 个 人?
sùshè dà bu dà? Zhù jǐ ge rén?

丁力波： 我们 留学生 楼 两 个 人 住 一 间。⑤我 跟 一
Dīng Lìbō： Wǒmen liúxuéshēng lóu liǎng ge rén zhù yì jiān. Wǒ gēn yí

个 美国 人 住，他 的 中文 名字 叫 马 大为。
ge Měiguó rén zhù, tā de Zhōngwén míngzi jiào Mǎ Dàwéi.

丁云： 他 也 学习 汉语 吗?
Dīng Yún： Tā yě xuéxí Hànyǔ ma?

丁力波： 对，他 也 学习 汉语。 我 还 有 很 多 中国
Dīng Lìbō： Duì, tā yě xuéxí Hànyǔ. Wǒ hái yǒu hěn duō Zhōngguó

朋友， 他们 常常 帮助 我 念 生词、复习
péngyou, tāmen chángcháng bāngzhù wǒ niàn shēngcí、 fùxí

课文、 练习 口语。我 还 常常 问 他们 语法
kèwén、 liànxí kǒuyǔ. Wǒ hái chángcháng wèn tāmen yǔfǎ

问题，他们 都 是 我 的 好 朋友。
wèntí, tāmen dōu shì wǒ de hǎo péngyou.

丁云： 这 很 好。力波，今年 你 要 在 中国 过
Dīng Yún： Zhè hěn hǎo. Lìbō, jīnnián nǐ yào zài Zhōngguó guò

圣诞 节，不 能 回家，我 和 你 爸爸 要 送
Shèngdàn Jié, bù néng huí jiā, wǒ hé nǐ bàba yào sòng

你 一件 圣诞 礼物。
nǐ yí jiàn Shèngdàn lǐwù.

丁力波： 谢谢 你们。我 也 给 你们 寄了 圣诞 礼物。
Dīng Lìbō： Xièxie nǐmen. Wǒ yě gěi nǐmen jìle Shèngdàn lǐwù.

丁云： 是 吗？ 圣诞 节我 和 你 爸爸 想 去 欧洲
Dīng Yún： Shì ma? Shèngdàn Jié wǒ hé nǐ bàba xiǎng qù Ōuzhōu

旅行。 你 呢？ 你 去 不 去 旅行？
lǚxíng. Nǐ ne? Nǐ qù bu qù lǚxíng?

丁力波： 我 要 去 上海 旅行。
Dīng Lìbō： Wǒ yào qù Shànghǎi lǚxíng.

丁云： 上海 很 漂亮。 祝 你 旅行 快乐！
Dīng Yún： Shànghǎi hěn piàoliang. Zhù nǐ lǚxíng kuàilè!

丁力波： 谢谢。 我 也 祝 你 和 爸爸 圣诞 快乐！
Dīng Lìbō： Xièxie. Wǒ yě zhù nǐ hé bàba Shèngdàn kuàilè!

节日祝愿
Extending holiday greetings

生词 New Words

1. 中午	zhōngwǔ	N	noon 今天中午，明天中午，星期一中午
2. 刚才	gāngcái	Adv	just now
3. 邮局	yóujú	N	post office
邮	yóu	V	to post, to mail
局	jú	N	office, bureau
4. 寄	jì	V	to post, to mail 寄书，寄光盘，寄东西
5. 打扫	dǎsǎo	V	to clean 打扫房子，打扫宿舍
扫	sǎo	V	to sweep
6. 脏	zāng	A	dirty 脏衣服
7. 不好意思	bù hǎoyìsi	IE	sorry 不好意思说，不好意思去
8. 洗	xǐ	V	to wash 洗衣服，洗手，洗苹果
*9. 外婆	wàipó	N	(maternal) grandmother
10. 中学	zhōngxué	N	middle school 中学老师，中学生

11.	打工	dǎgōng	VO	to have a part-time job 在中学打工，在哪儿打工
12.	南方	nánfāng	N	south 中国南方，去南方
13.	旅行	lǚxíng	V	to travel 去旅行，去北京旅行
*14.	想	xiǎng	V	to miss with longing 想妈妈，想家
15.	留学生	liúxuéshēng	N	student studying abroad, international student 外国留学生，留学生宿舍
16.	住	zhù	V	to live, to stay
17.	楼	lóu	N	building, floor, level 八号楼，四楼，留学生楼
18.	对	duì	A	right, correct 不对
19.	念	niàn	V	to read
20.	生词	shēngcí	N	new word 念生词，写生词，教生词
	生	shēng	A	new
	词	cí	N	word
21.	复习	fùxí	V	to review 复习生词，复习外语
22.	课文	kèwén	N	text 念课文，学习课文，复习课文，教课文
23.	练习	liànxí	V/N	to practice; exercise 练习生词，做练习
	练	liàn	V	to practice
24.	口语	kǒuyǔ	N	spoken language 练习口语，教口语
25.	语法	yǔfǎ	N	grammar 学习语法，教语法
*26.	过	guò	V	to spend (time), to celebrate (a birthday, a festival)
27.	节	jié	N	festival
*28.	礼物	lǐwù	N	gift, present 一件礼物，圣诞礼物，送他礼物
29.	圣诞	Shèngdàn	PN	Christmas 圣诞快乐
30.	欧洲	Ōuzhōu	PN	Europe
31.	上海	Shànghǎi	PN	Shanghai

补充生词 Supplementary Words

1.	乱	luàn	A	disordered, messy
2.	整理	zhěnglǐ	V	to put in order, to arrange, to sort out
3.	电视	diànshì	N	TV
4.	元旦	Yuándàn	PN	New Year's Day
5.	春节	Chūn Jié	PN	the Spring Festival
6.	复活节	Fùhuó Jié	PN	Easter
7.	日记	rìjì	N	diary
8.	晴	qíng	A	sunny
9.	第一次	dì yī cì		the first time
10.	年轻	niánqīng	A	young
11.	包裹	bāoguǒ	N	parcel
12.	惊喜	jīngxǐ	N	pleasant surprise
13.	接到	jiēdào	VC	to receive

注释 Notes

① 不好意思。

　　"不好意思" originally meant "to feel shy", or "to find it embarrassing to do something". For example:

　　　　不好意思说　　不好意思问　　不好意思吃

　　At present, this phrase is often used to make an apology. For example:

　　　　不好意思，我的宿舍很脏。

　　　　让你们等我，真不好意思。

② 这两天我太忙了，我想星期六一起洗。

　　"I've been very busy during the last few days. I want to wash them all on Saturday."

　　"这两天" means "during the last few days".

③ 她让我问你们好。

　　"She asks me to send her greetings to you."

　　"问 + Pr / NP + 好" is a construction used to extend greetings. For example:

　　　　他问你好。（He asked me to send you his greetings.）

　　　　（我请你）问他好。（I would like to ask you to send him my greetings.）

④ 你住的宿舍大不大?

"Is the dormitory you live in big?"

When the subject-verb phrase is used as an attributive, "的" must be placed between the attributive and the head word it modifies. For example:

他租的房子怎么样?

这是谁给你的书?

他常去买东西的商场很大。

⑤ 我们留学生楼两个人住一间。

"Two students share a room in our International Students' Dormitory Building."

二、练习　Exercises

练习与运用　**Drills and Practice** 54

核心句 KEY SENTENCES

1. 你不在，我让她中午再给你打。

2. 我刚才去邮局给我妈妈寄了点儿东西。

3. 她让我问你们好。

4. 我们也问她好。

5. 你住的宿舍大不大?

6. 祝你和爸爸圣诞快乐!

1. 熟读下列词组　Read the following phrases until you learn them by heart

（1）给你　给爸爸　给田医生　给司机钱　给他香蕉　给大为中药
给他打了一个电话　给妈妈寄了一件礼物　给他做了一件事儿
给宋华买了一个生日蛋糕　给陆雨平打了一个电话
给马大为租了一套房子

（2）再打一个电话　再吃一个苹果　再洗一件衣服　再说一遍

（3）刚才在餐厅　　刚才在汉语系　刚才在留学生楼　刚才在陆雨平家
　　刚才去了邮局　刚才看了电影　刚才看了外婆　　刚才打扫了宿舍

（4）他问你好　　　杨老师问白小姐好　　外婆问丁云和古波好
　　（我）请你问林娜好

（5）常常去锻炼　　常常回家　　常常去旅行　　常常在家喝咖啡
　　常常在一起说汉语

（6）祝你生日快乐　祝你旅行快乐　祝你圣诞快乐　祝你工作快乐

2. 句型替换　Pattern drills

（1）A：刚才丁力波给你来了一个电话。
　　B：他说什么？
　　A：他下午再给你打。

你哥哥　　让你去邮局
陆雨平　　给你租了一套大房子
张教授　　请你明天去一下学院

（2）A：你的宿舍太脏了。
　　B：不好意思。这两天太忙
　　　了，我想明天打扫。

衣服　　脏　　　　洗
书　　　乱 (luàn)　整理 (zhěnglǐ)
厨房　　脏　　　　打扫

（3）A：爸爸，您身体好吗？
　　B：我身体很好。你妈妈问你好。
　　A：我也问她好。

王医生　　　陈老师
外婆　　　　你姐姐
张教授　　　林娜

（4）A：你每天下午做什么？
　　B：我每天下午锻炼。
　　A：晚上呢？
　　B：晚上复习课文。

上课　　　　做练习
复习语法　　写汉字
练习口语　　看电视 (diànshì)

（5）A：他住的宿舍怎么样？

　　　B：他住的宿舍很大。

租	房子	舒服
买	礼物	漂亮
寄	东西	贵

（6）A：今年你在哪儿过圣诞节？

　　　B：我在北京过圣诞节。

　　　A：我要送你一件圣诞礼物。
　　　　祝你圣诞快乐！

元旦 (Yuándàn)	元旦快乐
春节 (Chūn Jié)	春节快乐
复活节 (Fùhuó Jié)	复活节快乐
生日	生日快乐

3. 完成对话　Complete the following conversation

A：刚才你男朋友来了。你不在，我让他_____。

B：谢谢。我刚才去学院_____。

A：你男朋友今年多大？

B：_____。

A：他在哪儿工作？

B：_____。

A：他家有几口人？

B：_____。

4. 会话练习　Conversation practice

【抱怨与致歉　Making a complaint or an apology】

（1）A：你看一下你的表，现在几点了？

　　　B：_____，我刚才有点儿事儿，来晚了。

（2）A：今天星期天，我要休息一下。

　　　B：你能不能整理一下你的书？你的东西太多了。

　　　A：不好意思。我现在_____，我不想今天整理。

B：你想什么时候整理呢？

A：_____。

【转达问候　Passing on someone's regards】

（1）A：张先生，你好吗？

　　B：我_____。你爸爸、妈妈身体怎么样？

　　A：他们_____。

　　B：你爸爸、妈妈今年多大岁数？

　　A：我爸爸今年_____，妈妈_____。

　　B：请你问他们好。

　　A：谢谢。

（2）A：雨平，你怎么样？工作忙不忙？

　　B：我_____，你呢？

　　A：我现在在_____学习法语，也很忙。

　　B：你女朋友好吗？

　　A：她很好。她让我问你好。

　　B：谢谢。请你也_____。

【节日祝愿　Extending holiday greetings】

（1）A：今天是元旦，祝你_____。

　　B：我也_____。

　　A：我有一件礼物给你。

　　B：谢谢你。啊，是_____！我很喜欢。

（2）A：喂，哪一位啊？

　　B：我是_____。

　　A：是_____啊！你好吗？

　　B：_____。今天是你的_____生日，我要祝你_____！

　　A：谢谢。你的生日是哪天？

　　B：明天是我的生日。

　　A：是吗？我也祝你生日快乐！

【建议与邀请　Making a suggestion or an invitation】

（1）A：明天你有时间吗？

B：明天我有时间。什么事儿？

A：我们去游泳，好吗？

B：太好了！几点去？

A：_____。

（2）A：星期五你忙不忙？

B：不太忙。什么事儿？

A：我们有个聚会，你能不能参加？

B：很抱歉，_____。

5. 交际练习　Communication exercises

（1）Your new roommate moved in yesterday. Today you returned to the dormitory and found everything in a mess, including the kitchen and the bathroom. When you are complaining, your roommate apologizes over and over.

（2）You come across an old classmate whom you haven't seen for a long time. You ask how he / she is doing, and then ask him / her to send your regards to his / her family.

（3）On Christmas Eve, you and your friends are extending holiday greetings to each another. One of them mentions that it is his / her eighteenth birthday, so everyone wishes him / her a happy birthday.

阅读与复述 Reading Comprehension and Paraphrasing

丁力波的日记 (rìjì)

12月20日　星期一　天气　晴 (qíng)

这个星期六是圣诞节。这是我第一次 (dì yī cì) 在中国过圣诞节。我要跟小云一起去上海旅行。现在中国年轻 (niánqīng) 人也很喜欢过圣诞节。很多商场都有圣诞老人 (Santa Claus)。商场东西很多，买东西的人也很多。

上午十点，我去邮局给爸爸、妈妈寄了一个包裹 (bāoguǒ)，是十张京剧光盘。爸爸很喜欢京剧，妈妈也喜欢，我想给他们一个惊喜 (jīngxǐ)。我很想家，也想加拿大。

上午十点半，妈妈给我打了一个电话。我不在，大为让妈妈中午再给我打。

中午我接到（jiēdào）了妈妈的电话。我真高兴。爸爸、妈妈身体都很好，他们工作都很忙。妈妈让我问外婆好。我告诉她哥哥、弟弟也都很好，哥哥在中学打工，教英语；弟弟在南方旅行。我还给她介绍了我的好朋友马大为。爸爸、妈妈圣诞节要去欧洲旅行，我祝他们旅行快乐。

爸爸、妈妈也给我寄了一件圣诞礼物，我还不知道那是什么礼物。

三、语法　Grammar

1 四种汉语句子　Four kinds of Chinese sentences

Simple Chinese sentences can be divided into four kinds according to the elements, which comprise the main part of their predicates.

❶ 动词谓语句　Sentences with a verbal predicate

The majority of Chinese sentences have a verbal predicate and are relatively complex. Several types have already been learned and more examples will be given in the following lessons. For example:

林娜的男朋友是医生。

他有一个姐姐。

我们学习汉语。

她回学院上课。

我们请他吃饭。

❷ 形容词谓语句　Sentences with an adjectival predicate

In a sentence with an adjectival predicate, "是" is not needed. For example:

我很好。

他这两天太忙。

❸ 名词谓语句　Sentences with a nominal predicate

In a sentence with a nominal predicate, nouns, noun phrases, or numeral-measure words function directly as the main elements of the predicate, which especially describe age or price. In spoken Chinese, it is also used to express time, birthplace, and so on. For example:

马大为二十二岁。

一斤苹果两块五。

现在八点半。

今天星期天。

宋华北京人。

❹ 主谓谓语句　Sentences with a subject-predicate phrase as the predicate

In a sentence with a subject-predicate phrase as the predicate, the thing denoted by the subject of the subject-predicate phrase is usually a part of the thing denoted by the subject of the whole sentence. The subject-predicate phrase describes or explains the subject of the whole sentence. For example:

你身体怎么样?

我头疼。

他学习很好。

2 常用的六种提问方法　Six common question types

❶ 用“吗”提问　Questions with “吗”

This is the most commonly used type of question. The person who asks this kind of question has some idea concerning the answer. For example:

您是张教授吗?

你现在很忙吗?

明天你不来学院吗?

❷ 正反疑问句　V/A-not-V/A question

This type of question is also frequently used. The person who asks this kind of question doesn't know how to answer it. For example:

你朋友认识不认识他?

你们学院大不大?

你有没有弟弟？

他去没去那个公司？

❸ 用疑问代词的问句　Questions with an interrogative pronoun

By using "谁", "什么", "哪", "哪儿", "怎么", "怎么样", "多少" or "几", this type of question specifically asks who, what, which, where, how, how about, or how many. For example:

今天几号？

他是哪国人？

他的房子怎么样？

❹ 用"还是"的选择问句　Alternative questions with "还是"

There are two (or more) possibilities in this type of question for the person addressed to choose from. For example:

他是英国人还是美国人？

我们上午去还是下午去？

你喜欢香蕉还是喜欢苹果？

❺ 用"好吗？"（或"是不是？""是吗？""可以吗？"）的问句

Tag questions with "好吗？", "是不是？", "是吗？" or "可以吗？"

Questions with "好吗？" or "可以吗？" are usually used to ask someone's opinion concerning the suggestion put forward in the first part of the sentence. Questions with "是不是？" or "是吗？" are usually used to confirm the judgement made in the first part of the sentence. For example:

我们去锻炼，好吗？

您学习汉语，是不是？

❻ 用"呢"的省略式问句　Elliptical questions with the question particle "呢"

The meaning of this type of question is usually illustrated clearly by the previous sentence. For example:

我很好，你呢？

他上午没有课，你呢？

四、汉字 Chinese Characters

1 音序查字法
Consulting a Chinese dictionary based on *pinyin*

    In many Chinese dictionaries, the entries are arranged alphabetically according to Chinese phonetics (*Hanyu pinyin*). Characters with the same *pinyin* spelling are put under the same entry and then sub-divided according to their tones. Characters in the same tone group are arranged in order, according to their number of strokes. When the pronunciation of a character is known, it is easy to find a character in this type of dictionary.

2 认写基本汉字 Learn and write basic Chinese characters

(1) 才   一 十 才
    cái   just   3 strokes

(2) 由   丨 冂 日 由 由
    yóu   by   5 strokes

(3) 州   丶 丿 丷 州 州 州
    zhōu   state   6 strokes

Note: "川" is the drawing of a river and the three dots "丶" show its islets.

3 认写课文中的汉字 Learn and write the Chinese characters in the texts

廴 (jiànzhīpángr, the "construction" side)   乛 廴   2 strokes

(1) 圣诞 Shèngdàn (聖誕)

圣 → 又 + 土   5 strokes

诞 → 讠 + 正 + 廴   8 strokes

(2) 刚才 gāngcái（剛才）

刚 → 冈 + 刂   6 strokes

(The pronunciation is indicated by "冈".)

(3) 邮局 yóujú（郵局）

邮 → 由 + 阝   7 strokes

(The pronunciation is shown by "由".)

局 → 尸 + 句   7 strokes

(4) 寄 jì

寄 → 宀 + 大 + 可   11 strokes

(5) 打扫 dǎsǎo（打掃）

扫 → 扌 + ヨ   6 strokes

(The meaning is indicated by "扌".)

(6) 脏 zāng（髒）

脏 → 月 + 广 + 土   10 strokes

(7) 洗 xǐ

洗 → 氵 + 先   9 strokes

(8) 外婆 wàipó

婆 → 波 + 女   11 strokes

(The meaning is suggested by "女".)

(9) 南方 nánfāng

南 → 十 + 冂 + 羊（ : 丶 丷 丷 兰 半 ）   9 strokes

氏 (lǚzìbiānr, the "travel" side)　´ ㇐ ㇇ 氏　　　　4 strokes

丁 chù　´ 二 丁　　　　3 strokes

(10) 旅行 lǚxíng

旅 → 方 + ㇠ + 氏　　　　10 strokes

行 → 彳 + 丁　　　　6 strokes

(11) 留学生 liúxuéshēng（留學生）

留 → ㇈ + 刀 + 田　　　　10 strokes
　　（㇈：´ ㇇ ㇈）

(12) 念 niàn（唸）

念 → 今 + 心　　　　8 strokes

(13) 生词 shēngcí（生詞）

词 → 讠 + 司　　　　7 strokes

(The meaning side is "讠".)

(14) 复习 fùxí（複習）

复 → ㇒ + 日 + 夂　　　　9 strokes

(15) 练习 liànxí（練習）

练 → 纟 + 东　　　　8 strokes

(16) 语法 yǔfǎ（語法）

法 → 氵 + 去　　　　8 strokes

(17) 节 jié（節）

节 → 艹 + 卩　　　　5 strokes

牛 (niúzìpángr, the "ox" side) (On the left side of a multi-component character, "牛" is written as "牜".) ノ ㇒ 牛 牛　　　4 strokes

(18) 礼物 lǐwù（禮物）

礼 → 礻 + 乚　　　　　　　5 strokes

物 → 牛 + 勿　　　　　　　8 strokes

(The pronunciation is indicated by "勿".)

(19) 欧洲 Ōuzhōu（歐洲）

欧 → 区 + 欠　　　　　　　8 strokes

洲 → 氵 + 州　　　　　　　9 strokes

(The meaning side is "氵" and the phonetic side is "州". The character "洲" means an islet in a river or a continent in an ocean.)

(20) 上海 Shànghǎi

海 → 氵 + 每　　　　　　　10 strokes

(The meaning side is "氵".)

文化知识 Cultural Note

Beijing, Shanghai, the Changjiang River, the Huanghe River, and the Great Wall

The two largest cities in China are Beijing (北京) and Shanghai (上海). Beijing is the capital of the People's Republic of China as well as its political, diplomatic and cultural center. Beijing was the capital for Liao, Jin, Yuan, Ming and Qing dynasties and it is rich in historic sites, including the Great Wall, the Forbidden City (the Imperial Palace) (故宫, Gùgōng), the Summer Palace (颐和园, Yíhé Yuán), and the Temple of Heaven (天坛, Tiān Tán), etc. With the latest economic development, Beijing has become one of the most cosmopolitan cities in the world. Shanghai is China's biggest city as well as its largest industrial and economic center.

There are many rivers in China, the largest ones of which are the Changjiang River (长江, Cháng Jiāng) and the Huanghe River (黄河, Huáng Hé). Changjiang, literally, the "Long River", is commonly known as the Yangtze River in English. It is the longest river in China and one of the longest in the world. It stretches more than 6,000 kilometers. Huanghe, or literally the "Yellow River", is the second longest river in China, flowing a total of more than 5,000 kilometers. The Huanghe River Valley is considered as the cradle of Chinese civilization.

The Great Wall (长城, Chángchéng) is one of the most well-known anthropological spectacles in China. Construction of the Great Wall began more than 2,200 years ago. It is one of the architectural wonders of the ancient world. There are numerous stretches where several walls run parallel to each other. It is more than 6,000 kilometers or more than 12,000 *li* long, so the Great Wall is often referred to as the *Wan Li Changcheng* or the "Long Wall of Ten Thousand *Li*".

北京：天坛

北京：长城

上海

北京：鸟巢(Niǎocháo)

黄河

长江三峡

附录 Appendices

中 华 人 民 共 和 国 地 图
Map of China

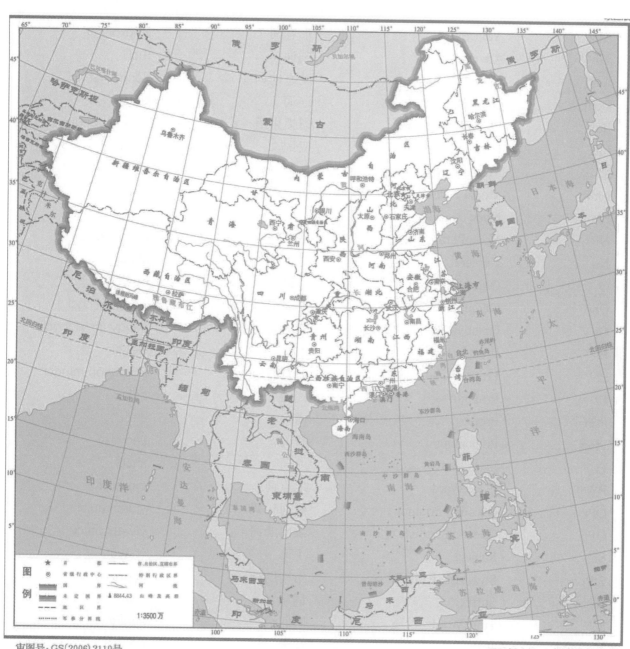

审图号：GS(2006) 2110号

2006年 3月　国家测绘局制

语法术语缩略形式一览表
Abbreviations for Grammar Terms

Abbreviation	Grammar Terms in English	Grammar Terms in Chinese	Grammar Terms in *pinyin*
A	Adjective	形容词	xíngróngcí
Adv	Adverb	副词	fùcí
AsPt	Aspect Particle	动态助词	dòngtài zhùcí
Conj	Conjunction	连词	liáncí
IE	Idiom Expression	习惯用语	xíguàn yòngyǔ
Int	Interjection	叹词	tàncí
M	Measure Word	量词	liàngcí
MdPt	Modal Particle	语气助词	yǔqì zhùcí
N	Noun	名词	míngcí
NP	Noun Phrase	名词词组	míngcí cízǔ
Nu	Numeral	数词	shùcí
O	Object	宾语	bīnyǔ
Ono	Onomatopoeia	象声词	xiàngshēngcí
OpV	Optative Verb	能愿动词	néngyuàn dòngcí
P	Predicate	谓语	wèiyǔ
PN	Proper Noun	专有名词	zhuānyǒu míngcí
Pr	Pronoun	代词	dàicí
Pref	Prefix	词头	cítóu
Prep	Preposition	介词	jiècí
Pt	Particle	助词	zhùcí
PW	Place Word	地点词	dìdiǎncí
QPr	Question Pronoun	疑问代词	yíwèn dàicí
QPt	Question Particle	疑问助词	yíwèn zhùcí
S	Subject	主语	zhǔyǔ
StPt	Structural Particle	结构助词	jiégòu zhùcí
Suf	Suffix	词尾	cíwěi
TW	Time Word	时间词	shíjiāncí
V	Verb	动词	dòngcí
VC	Verb plus Complement	动补式动词	dòngbǔshì dòngcí
VO	Verb plus Object	动宾式动词	dòngbīnshì dòngcí
VP	Verbal Phrase	动词词组	dòngcí cízǔ

生词索引（简繁对照）
Vocabulary Index

(Simplified Chinese vs Traditional Chinese)

词条	繁体	拼音	词性	英译	课号
A					
啊	啊	à	Int	ah, oh	7
爱	愛	ài	V	to love	8
B					
吧	吧	ba	MdPt	(a modal particle)	12
爸爸	爸爸	bàba	N	dad	2, 7
拜拜	拜拜	báibái	IE	bye-bye (transliteration)	11
百	百	bǎi	Nu	hundred	8
办	辦	bàn	V	to do	13
半	半	bàn	Nu	half	11
帮助	幫助	bāngzhù	V	to help	13
报纸	報紙	bàozhǐ	N	newspaper	10
抱歉	抱歉	bàoqiàn	A	sorry	6
北京	北京	Běijīng	PN	Beijing	9
贝贝	貝貝	Bèibei	PN	(name of a dog)	8
本子	本子	běnzi	N	exercise book, notebook	10
遍	遍	biàn	M	(for action) a time	6
病	病	bìng	N/V	illness; to get sick	12
不	不	bù	Adv	not, no	2
不好意思	不好意思	bù hǎoyìsi	IE	sorry	14
不用	不用	búyòng	Adv	need not	5
步	步	bù	N	step	13

C

参加	參加	cānjiā	V	to participate, to attend	9
餐厅	餐廳	cāntīng	N	dining hall	5
厕所	廁所	cèsuǒ	N	toilet	13
层	層	céng	M	story, floor	5
差	差	chà	V	to be short of, to lack	11
常	常	cháng	Adv	often	10
常常	常常	chángcháng	Adv	often	10
陈	陳	Chén	PN	(a surname)	3, 11
吃	吃	chī	V	to eat	9
吃饭	吃飯	chīfàn	VO	to eat (a meal)	13
出	出	chū	V	to go, to come out	9
出生	出生	chūshēng	V	to be born	9
厨房	廚房	chúfáng	N	kitchen	13
穿	穿	chuān	V	to wear	12
床	牀	chuáng	N	bed	11
词	詞	cí	V	word	14

D

打	打	dǎ	V	to play	6
打电话	打電話	dǎ diànhuà	V O	to make a phone call	13
打工	打工	dǎgōng	VO	to have a part-time job	14
打球	打球	dǎ qiú	V O	to play ball games	6
打扫	打掃	dǎsǎo	V	to clean	14
大	大	dà	A	big, large	8, 9
蛋	蛋	dàn	N	egg	9
蛋糕	蛋糕	dàngāo	N	cake	9
当然	當然	dāngrán	Adv	of course	8
到	到	dào	V	to arrive	11
得	得	dé	V	to have, to get	13
的	的	de	StPt	(*a possessive or modifying particle*)	4

等	等	děng	V	to wait	13
弟弟	弟弟	dìdi	N	younger brother	2, 8
点(钟)	點(鐘)	diǎn (zhōng)	M	o'clock	11
电	電	diàn	N	electricity	13
电话	電話	diànhuà	N	telephone, phone call	13
电影	電影	diànyǐng	N	movie	13
丁	丁	Dīng	PN	(a surname)	2
丁力波	丁力波	Dīng Lìbō	PN	(name of a Canadian student)	7
东西	東西	dōngxi	N	thing, stuff	11
都	都	dōu	Adv	both, all	2, 3
锻炼	鍛煉	duànliàn	V	to exercise, to work out	12
对	對	duì	A	right, correct	14
对不起	對不起	duìbuqǐ	IE	I'm sorry	5, 10
多	多	duō	A	many, much	8
			Adv	how (many/much)	9
多大	多大	duō dà	IE	how old	9
多少	多少	duōshao	QPr	how many, how much	8

E

二	二	èr	Nu	two	5

F

发烧	發燒	fāshāo	VO	to have a fever	12
发炎	發炎	fāyán	VO	to become inflamed	12
饭	飯	fàn	N	meal	13
房子	房子	fángzi	N	house	13
房租	房租	fángzū	N	rent (for a house, flat, etc.)	13
分(钱)	分(錢)	fēn (qián)	M	*(a measure word of Chinese monetary unit, it is equal to 1/100 yuan) fen*	10
分(钟)	分(鐘)	fēn (zhōng)	M	minute	11
复习	復习	fùxí	V	to review	14

G

该	該	gāi	OpV	should, ought to	11
感冒	感冒	gǎnmào	V/N	to have a cold, cold	12
刚才	剛才	gāngcái	Adv	just now	14
高	高	gāo	A	tall	4, 7
高兴	高興	gāoxìng	A	happy, pleased	4, 7
糕	糕	gāo	N	cake	9
告诉	告訴	gàosu	V	to tell	13
哥哥	哥哥	gēge	N	elder brother	2
个	個	gè	M	(a measure word for general use)	8
给	給	gěi	V	to give	10
			Prep	to, for	12
跟	跟	gēn	Prep/V	with; to follow	10
工作	工作	gōngzuò	V/N	to work; work, job	8
公司	公司	gōngsī	N	company	13
狗	狗	gǒu	N	dog	8
姑娘	姑娘	gūniang	N	girl	13
挂号	掛號	guàhào	V	to register (at a hospital, etc.)	12
光盘	光盤	guāngpán	N	CD	10
贵	貴	guì	A	expensive, precious	10
贵姓	貴姓	guìxìng	IE	your surname (polite form)	4
国	國	guó	N	country, nation	3
过	過	guò	V	to spend (time), to celebrate (someone's birthday, a festival, etc.)	9, 14

H

还	還	hái	Adv	in addition; still	8, 11
还是	還是	háishi	Conj	or	12
汉语	漢語	Hànyǔ	N	Chinese (language)	4
汉字	漢字	Hànzì	N	Chinese character	11
好	好	hǎo	A	good, well, fine, OK	1, 5
号	號	hào	N	ordinal number	5
			N	day of the month	9

喝	喝	hē	V	to drink	2, 9
和	和	hé	Conj	and	8
很	很	hěn	Adv	very	1, 7
红	红	hóng	A	red	9
红葡萄酒	红葡萄酒	hóng pútaojiǔ		red wine	9
回	回	huí	V	to return	11
会	會	huì	N	meeting	9
			OpV	to have the knowledge of, can	11

J

几	幾	jǐ	QPr	how many, how much	8
记者	記者	jìzhě	N	reporter	4
寄	寄	jì	V	to post, to mail	14
加拿大	加拿大	Jiānádà	PN	Canada	4, 7
家	家	jiā	N	family, home	8
家美	家美	Jiāměi	PN	(name of a house rental agency)	13
间	間	jiān	M	(a measure word for rooms, houses, etc.)	13
件	件	jiàn	M	(a measure word) piece	13
教	教	jiāo	V	to teach, to instruct	11
叫	叫	jiào	V	to be called	4
教	教	jiào	V	to teach, to instruct	7
教授	教授	jiàoshòu	N	professor	7
节	節	jié	N	festival	14
姐姐	姐姐	jiějie	N	elder sister	8
介绍	介绍	jièshào	V	to introduce	7
斤	斤	jīn	M	(a measure word of weight, it is equal to 500g)	10
今年	今年	jīnnián	N	this year	9
今天	今天	jīntiān	N	today	6, 9
进	進	jìn	V	to enter	4, 5
进来	進來	jìnlai	VC	to come in	4
京剧	京劇	jīngjù	N	Beijing opera	6
经理	經理	jīnglǐ	N	manager	13

酒	酒	jiǔ	N	wine or liquor	9
局	局	jú	N	office, bureau	14
聚会	聚會	jùhuì	N	get-together, party	9

K

咖啡	咖啡	kāfēi	N	coffee	2, 13
开	開	kāi	V	to open, to start	7
开学	開學	kāixué	VO	school opens, term begins	7
看	看	kàn	V	to watch, to look at	7
看病	看病	kànbìng	VO	to see a doctor	12
烤鸭	烤鴨	kǎoyā	N	roast duck	9
可爱	可愛	kě'ài	A	lovely, cute	8
可能	可能	kěnéng	OpV	maybe	13
可是	可是	kěshì	Conj	but	13
可以	可以	kěyǐ	OpV	may	4, 11
刻	刻	kè	M	quarter (of an hour)	11
客厅	客廳	kètīng	N	living room	13
课	課	kè	N	class, lesson	9
课文	課文	kèwén	N	text	14
恐怕	恐怕	kǒngpà	Adv	afraid that...	6
口	口	kǒu	M	*(a measure word mainly for the number of people in a family)*	8
口语	口語	kǒuyǔ	N	spoken language	14
块(钱)	塊(錢)	kuài (qián)	M	*(a measure word of basic Chinese monetary unit, it is equal to 10 jiao) kuai*	10
快乐	快樂	kuàilè	A	happy	9

L

来	來	lái	V	to come	4, 7
老师	老師	lǎoshī	N	teacher	3
了	了	le	Pt	*(a modal particle, aspect particle)*	5, 9
冷	冷	lěng	A	cold	12

礼物	禮物	lǐwù	N	gift, present	11, 14
力波	力波	Lìbō	PN	(name of a Canadian student)	1
练	練	liàn	V	to practice	14
练习	練習	liànxí	V/N	to practice; exercise	14
梁祝	梁祝	Liáng Zhù	PN	(name of a Chinese violin concerto)	10
两	兩	liǎng	Nu	two	8
林娜	林娜	Lín Nà	PN	(name of a British student)	1
○/零	○/零	líng	Nu	zero	5
留学生	留學生	liúxuéshēng	N	student studying abroad, international student	14
楼	樓	lóu	N	building, floor, level	14
陆雨平	陸雨平	Lù Yǔpíng	PN	(name of a Chinese reporter)	1
旅行	旅行	lǚxíng	V	to travel	14

M

妈妈	媽媽	māma	N	mom	2
马大为	馬大爲	Mǎ Dàwéi	PN	(name of an American student)	4, 7
吗	嗎	ma	QPt	(a particle used for a question expecting a yes-no answer)	1, 2
买	買	mǎi	V	to buy	9
忙	忙	máng	A	busy	2, 6
毛(钱)	毛(錢)	máo (qián)	M	(a measure word of Chinese monetary unit, it is equal to 1/10 yuan) mao	10
没	沒	méi	Adv	not	8
没关系	沒關係	méi guānxi	IE	never mind, it doesn't matter	5
每	每	měi	Pr	every, each	12
美	美	měi	A	beautiful	7
美国	美國	Měiguó	PN	the United States of America	4, 7
美术	美術	měishù	N	fine arts	7
妹妹	妹妹	mèimei	N	younger sister	8
们	們	men	Suf	(used after pronouns 我, 你, 他, 它 or certain nouns to denote plurality)	2
面	麵	miàn	N	noodles	9

名片	名片	míngpiàn	N	business card	7
名字	名字	míngzi	N	name	7
明天	明天	míngtiān	N	tomorrow	6

N

哪	哪	nǎ	QPr	which	3
哪儿	哪兒	nǎr	QPr	where	5
哪里	哪裏	nǎli	IE	no (an expression of mild denial)	11
那	那	nà	Pr	that	3
那儿	那兒	nàr	Pr	there	10
奶奶	奶奶	nǎinai	N	(paternal) grandmother	3
男	男	nán	A	male	2, 8
南方	南方	nánfāng	N	south	14
呢	呢	ne	QPt	(*a modal particle used for elliptical questions*)	1, 2
能	能	néng	OpV	can, to be able to	11
你	你	nǐ	Pr	you	1, 3
你们	你們	nǐmen	Pr	you (pl.)	6
年	年	nián	N	year	9
念	唸	niàn	V	to read	14
您	您	nín	Pr	you (polite form)	3, 4
女	女	nǚ	A	female	5
女儿	女兒	nǚ'ér	N	daughter	11

O

| 欧洲 | 歐洲 | Ōuzhōu | PN | Europe | 14 |

P

朋友	朋友	péngyou	N	friend	2, 4
漂亮	漂亮	piàoliang	A	beautiful, nice	9
苹果	蘋果	píngguǒ	N	apple	10

瓶	瓶	píng	M	bottle	9
葡萄	葡萄	pútao	N	grape	9, 10

Q

起	起	qǐ	V	to get up, to rise	11
起床	起牀	qǐchuáng	VO	to get up	11
钱	錢	qián	N	money	10
请	請	qǐng	V	please	4
请问	請問	qǐngwèn	V	May I ask...?	4, 5
球	球	qiú	N	ball	6
去	去	qù	V	to go	6
全	全	quán	A	whole	12
全身	全身	quánshēn	N	all over (the body)	12

R

让	讓	ràng	V	to let, to allow, to make	13
人	人	rén	N	people, person	3
认识	認識	rènshi	V	to know (somebody)	4
容易	容易	róngyì	A	easy	10

S

散步	散步	sànbù	VO	to take a walk, to walk	13
嗓子	嗓子	sǎngzi	N	throat	12
扫	掃	sǎo	V	to sweep	14
商	商	shāng	N	trade, commerce	10
商场	商場	shāngchǎng	N	market, bazaar, shopping mall	10
上	上	shàng	N	above, last	9
			V	to ascend, to go to	11
上海	上海	Shànghǎi	PN	Shanghai	14
上课	上課	shàngkè	VO	to go to class (for both students and teachers)	11

上午	上午	shàngwǔ	N	morning	9
烧	燒	shāo	V	to burn	12
少	少	shǎo	A	few, less	8
谁	誰	shéi	QPr	who, whom	3, 7
身	身	shēn	N	body	12
身体	身體	shēntǐ	N	body, health	12
什么	甚麼	shénme	QPr	what	4,6
生	生	shēng	A	to be born	9
			A	new	14
生词	生詞	shēngcí	N	new word	14
生日	生日	shēngri	N	birthday	9
圣诞	聖誕	Shèngdàn	PN	Christmas	14
师傅	師傅	shīfu	N	master	10
时候	時候	shíhou	N	time, moment	6
时间	時間	shíjiān	N	time	6
事儿	事兒	shìr	N	matter, affair, thing	13
是	是	shì	V	to be	3
寿面	壽麵	shòumiàn	N	(birthday) longevity noodles	9
书	書	shū	N	book	10
舒服	舒服	shūfu	A	comfortable, (to feel) well	12
属	屬	shǔ	V	to be born in the year of (one of the 12 animals)	9
数	數	shù	N	number	11
水	水	shuǐ	N	water	12
睡	睡	shuì	V	to sleep	11
睡觉	睡覺	shuìjiào	VO	to sleep	11
说	說	shuō	V	to say, to speak	6
司机	司機	sījī	N	driver	11
四	四	sì	Nu	four	5
宋华	宋華	Sòng Huá	PN	(name of a Chinese student)	5, 9
送	送	sòng	N	to give (as a present)	10
宿舍	宿舍	sùshè	N	dormitory	5, 13
岁	歲	suì	M	year (of age)	9
岁数	歲數	suìshu	N	years (of age)	11

| 孙女儿 | 孫女兒 | sūnnür | N | granddaughter on son's side | 11 |

T

他	他	tā	Pr	he, him	2, 3
他们	他們	tāmen	Pr	they, them	2, 3
她	她	tā	Pr	she, her	3
太	太	tài	Adv	too, extremely	6
套	套	tào	M	(a measue word for houses)	13
疼	疼	téng	A	painful	12
天	天	tiān	N	day	6
天气	天氣	tiānqì	N	weather	6
听	聽	tīng	V	to listen	13
听说	聽説	tīngshuō	V	to be told	13
头	頭	tóu	N	head	12

W

外	外	wài	N	foreign, outside	8
外国	外國	wàiguó	N	foreign country	8
外婆	外婆	wàipó	N	(maternal) grandmother	3, 14
外语	外語	wàiyǔ	N	foreign language	3, 8
玩儿	玩兒	wánr	V	to have fun, to play	11
晚	晚	wǎn	A	late	5, 11
晚上	晚上	wǎnshang	N	evening, night	11
王小云	王小雲	Wáng Xiǎoyún	PN	(name of a Chinese student)	5, 8
为	爲	wèi	Prep	for	11
为什么	爲甚麼	wèi shénme	QPr	why	11
位	位	wèi	M	(a polite measure word for persons)	13
喂	喂	wèi	Int	hello, hey	13
文学	文學	wénxué	N	literature	7
问	問	wèn	V	to ask	4, 5, 7
问题	問題	wèntí	N	question	11
我	我	wǒ	Pr	I, me	1, 5

| 我们 | 我們 | wǒmen | Pr | we, us | 2 |
| 卧室 | 卧室 | wòshì | N | bedroom | 13 |

X

西	西	xī	N	west	12
西药	西藥	xīyào	N	Western medicine	12
洗	洗	xǐ	V	to wash	14
喜欢	喜歡	xǐhuan	V	to like	8
系	系	xì	N	faculty, department	7
下	下	xià	N	below, next	9
下午	下午	xiàwǔ	N	afternoon	9
先生	先生	xiānsheng	N	Mr.; sir	4, 10
现在	现在	xiànzài	N	now	6
香蕉	香蕉	xiāngjiāo	N	banana	10
香蕉苹果	香蕉蘋果	xiāngjiāo píngguǒ		apple with the taste of a banana	10
想	想	xiǎng	V/OpV	to think, to want (to do sth.)	12
			V	to miss with longing	14
小	小	xiǎo	A	little, small	8
小姐	小姐	xiǎojie	N	Miss, young lady	5
写	寫	xiě	V	to write	11
谢谢	謝謝	xièxie	V	to thank	5, 6
星期	星期	xīngqī	N	week	9
星期日	星期日	xīngqīrì	N	Sunday	9
行	行	xíng	V	to take a break, to have a rest, to relax	6
姓	姓	xìng	V/N	one's surname is.../surname	4
休息	休息	xiūxi	V	to take a rest	12
学	學	xué	V	to learn, to study	4, 7
学生	學生	xuésheng	N	student	4, 5
学习	學習	xuéxí	V	to learn, to study	4, 7
学院	學院	xuéyuàn	N	institute, college	4, 7

Y

鸭	鴨	Yā	N	duck	9
杨	楊	Yáng	PN	(a surname)	4
药	藥	yào	N	medicine	12
要	要	yào	V	to want	2, 10
			OpV	must, to want to do something	12
也	也	yě	Adv	too, also	1
(一)点儿	(一)點兒	(yì) diǎnr	Nu-M	a little bit	11
一共	一共	yígòng	Adv	altogether	8
一起	一起	yìqǐ	Adv	together	12
一下	一下	yíxià	Nu-M	(*used after a verb to indicate a short, quick, random, informal action*)	7
衣服	衣服	yīfu	N	clothes	12
医生	醫生	yīshēng	N	doctor, physician	3
医院	醫院	yīyuàn	N	hospital	12
音乐	音樂	yīnyuè	N	music	10
应该	應該	yīnggāi	OpV	should, ought to	11
英国	英國	Yīngguó	PN	Great Britain, England	4
英语	英語	Yīngyǔ	N	English	11
影	影	yǐng	N	shadow	13
邮	郵	yóu	V	to post, to mail	14
邮局	郵局	yóujú	N	post office	14
游泳	游泳	yóuyǒng	VO	to swim	6
有	有	yǒu	V	to have	6
有点儿	有點兒	yǒudiǎnr	Adv	somewhat, a bit	12
有名	有名	yǒumíng	A	famous	10
有意思	有意思	yǒu yìsi	IE	interesting	6
语	語	yǔ	N	language	8
语法	語法	yǔfǎ	N	grammar	14
语言	語言	yǔyán	N	language	4
愿意	願意	yuànyì	OpV	to be willing, to be ready	12

Z

再	再	zài	Adv	again	5, 9
再见	再見	zàijiàn	IE	goodbye	5
在	在	zài	V	to be (here, there), to be (in, on, at)	5
			Prep	at, in, on	10
脏	髒	zāng	A	dirty	14
怎么	怎麼	zěnme	QPr	how	10
怎么样	怎麼樣	zěnmeyàng	QPr	how is ...	6, 9
张	張	Zhāng	PN	(a surname)	7
		zhāng	M	(*a measure word for flat objects*)	8
找	找	zhǎo	V	to look for	13
找(钱)	找(錢)	zhǎo (qián)	V	to give change	10
照片	照片	zhàopiàn	N	picture, photo	8
这	這	zhè	Pr	this	3, 5
这儿	這兒	zhèr	Pr	here	5
真	真	zhēn	A/Adv	real; really	8
知道	知道	zhīdao	V	to know	5
中国	中國	Zhōngguó	PN	China	3
中文	中文	Zhōngwén	N	Chinese	7
中午	中午	zhōngwǔ	N	noon	14
中学	中學	zhōngxué	N	middle school	14
中药	中藥	zhōngyào	N	traditional Chinese medicine	12
住	住	zhù	V	to live, to stay	14
住院	住院	zhùyuàn	VO	to be in hospital, to be hospitalized	12
祝	祝	zhù	V	to wish	9
祝贺	祝賀	zhùhè	V	to congratulate	9
专业	專業	zhuānyè	N	major, speciality	7
字	字	zì	N	character	11
租	租	zū	V	to rent	13
昨天	昨天	zuótiān	N	yesterday	6, 11
坐	坐	zuò	V	to sit	5
做	做	zuò	V	to do, to be, to make	8, 10

补充生词

Supplementary Words

词条	繁体	拼音	词性	英译	课号
B					
包裹	包裹	bāoguǒ	N	parcel	14
包括	包括	bāokuò	V	to include	13
杯	杯	bēi	M	(*a measure wold for cups or glasses*)	10
本	本	běn	M	(*a measure word for books and notebooks*)	10
笔	筆	bǐ	N	stick-like writing or drawing instruments	10
便条	便條	biàntiáo	N	note	11
表	錶	biǎo	N	watch	11
C					
茶	茶	chá	N	tea	9
常常	常常	chángcháng	Adv	often	8
唱歌	唱歌	chànggē	VO	to sing (a song)	11
车	車	chē	N	vehicle	8, 11
吃饭	吃飯	chīfàn	VO	to eat (a meal)	11
春节	春節	Chūn Jié	PN	the Spring Festival	14
词典	詞典	cídiǎn	N	dictionary	8
D					
打的	打的	dǎdī	VO	to hail a taxi	11
打针	打針	dǎzhēn	VO	to have an injection	12

大便	大便	dàbiàn	N	stool, faeces	12
德国	德國	Déguó	PN	Germany	4
德语	德語	Déyǔ	N	German	11
等	等	děng	V	to wait	11
第一次	第一次	dì yī cì		the first time	14
电脑	電腦	diànnǎo	N	computer	8
电视	電視	diànshì	N	TV	14
店	店	diàn	N	store or shop	9
东西	東西	dōngxi	N	thing, stuff	10
肚子	肚子	dùzi	N	abdomen, stomach	12

F

法国	法國	Fǎguó	PN	France	4
法语	法語	Fǎyǔ	N	French	11
方便	方便	fāngbiàn	A	convenient	13
份	份	fèn	M	(*a measure word for publications such as newspapers*)	10
复活节	復活節	Fùhuó Jié	PN	Easter	14

E

俄罗斯	俄羅斯	Éluósī	PN	Russia	4
俄语	俄語	Éyǔ	N	Russian	11
儿子	兒子	érzi	N	son	9

G

工程师	工程師	gōngchéngshī	N	engineer	8
公园	公園	gōngyuán	N	park	10
功夫	功夫	gōngfu	N	kung fu	10
过去	過去	guòqù	N	in the past	13

H

孩子	孩子	háizi	N	child	8
汉堡	漢堡	hànbǎo	N	hamburger	9
合适	合適	héshì	A	suitable	13
化学	化學	huàxué	N	chemistry	7
化验	化驗	huàyàn	V	to have a medical test	12
回答	回答	huídá	V	to answer	11
回信	回信	huíxìn	N/VO	reply; to reply	13

J

教育	教育	jiàoyù	N	education	7
接到	接到	jiēdào	VC	to receive	14
经济	經濟	jīngjì	N	economics	7
惊喜	驚喜	jīngxǐ	N	pleasant surprise	14

K

开车	開車	kāichē	VO	to drive a car or a train, etc.	11
开刀	開刀	kāidāo	VO	to have an operation	12
可乐	可樂	kělè	N	coke	9
快	快	kuài	A	fast	11

L

礼物	禮物	lǐwù	N	gift, present	11
历史	歷史	lìshǐ	N	history	7
律师	律師	lùshī	N	lawyer	8
乱	亂	luàn	A	disordered, messy	14

M

| 卖 | 賣 | mài | V | to sell | 10 |

| 米饭 | 米飯 | mǐfàn | N | (cooked) rice | 9 |
| 面包 | 麵包 | miànbāo | N | bread | 9 |

N

难	難	nán	A	difficult	11
年	年	nián	N	year	8
年轻	年輕	niánqīng	A	young	14
牛奶	牛奶	niúnǎi	N	milk	9
女儿	女兒	nǚ'ér	N	daughter	9

P

拍照	拍照	pāizhào	VO	to take pictures	11
啤酒	啤酒	píjiǔ	N	beer	9
便宜	便宜	piányi	A	cheap, inexpensive	10

Q

前	前	qián	N	ago	8
巧	巧	qiǎo	A	coincidental	13
亲爱	親愛	qīn'ài	A	dear	13
晴	晴	qíng	A	sunny	14
请假条	請假條	qǐngjiàtiáo	N	written request for leave	12
去年	去年	qùnián	N	last year	13

R

热狗	熱狗	règǒu	N	hotdog	9
热心	熱心	rèxīn	A	warm-hearted	13
日本	日本	Rìběn	PN	Japan	4
日记	日記	rìjì	N	diary	14
日语	日語	Rìyǔ	N	Japanese	11

S

生活	生活	shēnghuó	N	life	12
售货员	售貨員	shòuhuòyuán	N	shop assistant, salesperson	10
书店	書店	shūdiàn	N	bookstore	10
数学	數學	shùxué	N	mathematics	7
水电费	水電費	shuǐdiànfèi	N	charges for water and electricity	13

T

太极拳	太極拳	tàijíquán	N	*taiji* boxing	12
体育馆	體育館	tǐyùguǎn	N	gym	10
跳舞	跳舞	tiàowǔ	VO	to dance	11

W

外公	外公	wàigōng	N	(maternal) grandfather	8
晚上	晚上	wǎnshang	N	evening	9
位	位	wèi	M	*(a polite measure word for persons)*	8
文化	文化	wénhuà	N	culture	7
物理	物理	wùlǐ	N	physics	7

X

西餐	西餐	xīcān	N	Western food	9
吸烟	吸煙	xīyān	VO	to smoke	11
系主任	系主任	xìzhǔrèn	N	director of the department	8
下课	下課	xiàkè	VO	to dismiss class, to finish class	11
想	想	xiǎng	V	to miss	13
小便	小便	xiǎobiàn	N	urine	12
血	血	xiě	N	blood	12
新	新	xīn	A	new	13
选修	選修	xuǎnxiū	V	to take an elective course	7

| 雪碧 | 雪碧 | Xuěbì | PN | *Sprite*, name of a drink | 9 |

Y

牙	牙	yá	N	tooth	12
爷爷	爺爺	yéye	N	(paternal) grandfather	8
音乐	音樂	yīnyuè	N	music	7
英文	英文	Yīngwén	N	English	12
英语	英語	Yīngyǔ	N	English	8
元	元	yuán	M	(the same as *kuai*, but it is used in written Chinese)	10
元旦	元旦	Yuándàn	PN	New Year's Day	14

Z

哲学	哲學	zhéxué	N	philosophy	7
整理	整理	zhěnglǐ	V	to put in order, to arrange, to sort out	14
支	支	zhī	M	(*a measure word for stick-like things such as pens*)	10
中餐	中餐	zhōngcān	N	Chinese food	9
中午	中午	zhōngwǔ	N	noon	12
助教	助教	zhùjiào	N	teaching assistant	8
作家	作家	zuòjiā	N	writer	10

汉字索引
Character Index

作者简介

Introduction to the Authors

刘珣 Liú Xún 北京语言大学教授，北京语言大学出版社汉语教材总编审，国家汉语水平考试委员会顾问委员会委员。历任国家汉办对外汉语教学学术研究专家咨询小组成员，北京市高等教师职务系列评审委员会对外汉语学科组组长，美国纽约州教育厅中文教学顾问，世界汉语教学学会理事。主要研究方向为对外汉语教育学科理论、第二语言教学理论和教材编写理论及师资培养问题。主要论著有《对外汉语教育学科初探》、《对外汉语教育学引论》、《汉语作为第二语言教学简论》、《对外汉语教学概论》；主持编写《实用汉语课本》、《儿童汉语》、《交际汉语一百课》等对外汉语教材；负责研制我国第一套汉语水平考试试题。获国务院颁发的政府特殊津贴。

张凯 Zhāng Kǎi 北京语言大学教授、研究员。1989年起在北京语言大学汉语水平考试中心工作至今。主要研究方向为语言和语言测验理论。主要论文有"语言测验和乔姆斯基理论"、"汉语水平考试的描述性参数及其他"、"对外汉语教学学科的基本问题和基本方法"、"能力问题在语言测验中的变迁"等。专著有《标准参照测验理论研究》、《语言测验的理论与实践》等，并有译著《行为互动：小范围相遇中的行为模式》（亚当•肯顿）。参加编写的教材有：《标准汉语教程》（黄政澄主编）、《新实用汉语课本》（刘珣主编）。

刘社会 Liú Shèhuì 北京语言大学副教授。曾在法国巴黎第七大学和突尼斯布尔吉巴语言学院任教。参加编写对外汉语教材《基础汉语课本》和《实用汉语课本》。参与策划和编写《中国古代文学作品选》、《中国现代文学作品选》和《中国当代文学作品选》，并主持编写《世界汉语教学概况》和《世界汉语教学书目概览》，发表过多篇有关现代汉语句型研究和对外汉语汉字教学的论文。

陈曦 Chén Xī 北京语言大学教授。曾任比利时国立根特大学汉语教师，在国家对外汉语教学领导小组工作多年；著有《汉字发展说略》、《西周铜器铭文内容考察》等学术专著，在各类核心期刊发表学术论文数篇；承担和参与国家"十五"社会科学规划项目"汉字认知与应用"、"中文应用能力测评"，国家青年社科基金项目"宋明文字学研究"；参与北京语言大学"留学生学习水平测试与成绩测验"、"欧美留学生汉字系统认知研究"等专项课题。

左珊丹 Zuǒ Shāndān 北京语言大学讲师。曾在日本东京大学、东洋大学和荷兰莱顿大学任教。主编基础汉语教材《轻轻松松学汉语》（韩国出版），主编中国大百科版《小学生易错易混字辨析手册》，参与编写对外汉语教材《桥梁——实用汉语中级教程》及大型工具书《中日辞典》（日本讲谈社出版）。发表论文"论对外汉语中级阶段的教学原则与方法"、"汉语的活性与文学语言实验"、"文学语言的日常化"等，出版有文化随笔《可以风车，也可以荷兰》，短篇小说集《水下有座城》。

施家炜 Shī Jiāwěi 北京语言大学副教授。曾赴北京大学、南开大学、香港中文大学、新疆等地的高校及美国讲学或培训汉语教师。主要研究方向为第二语言习得与语言教学，发表《外国留学生22类现代汉语句式的习得顺序研究》等20余篇学术论文，主持或参与多项国家级或部委级科研项目，出版译著《跨文化交际：话语分析法》，合作主编《对外汉语教学论文选评（第二集）》。2006年获霍英东教育基金会第十届高等院校青年教师奖（研究类），2009年获"北京市优秀教师"称号。